"Fenella Eason's investigation of how the chronically ill engage with medical alert assistance dogs in their daily lives serves as an example of how research can be both empirically rigorous and compassionate. It is timely, top-notch scholarship. It will inspire research in multispecies ethnography, the sociology of health and illness, anthrozoology, and anthropology."

Leslie Irvine, *Professor of Sociology,*
University of Colorado Boulder, USA

"A novel and moving account of multi-species relationships where health and wellbeing is becoming a more-than-human accomplishment. It sets the standard for future work on animal-assisted care of chronic illness."

Hannah Brown, *Associate Professor of Anthropology,*
University of Durham, UK

Human–Canine Collaboration in Care

Adopting an anthrozoological perspective to study the participation of non-human animals in regimes of care, this book examines the use of canine scent detection to alert 'hypo-unaware' individuals to symptoms of human chronic illness. Based on ethnographic research and interviews, it focuses on the manner in which trained assistance dogs are able to use their sense of smell to alert human companions with Type 1 diabetes to imminent hypoglycaemic episodes, thus reducing the risk of collapse into unconsciousness, coma, or, at worst, death. Through analyses of participant narrations of the everyday complexities of 'doing' diabetes with the assistance of medical alert dogs, the author sheds light on the way in which each human–canine dyad becomes acknowledged as a team of 'one' in society. Based on the concept of dogs as friends and work colleagues, as animate instruments and biomedical resources, the book raises conceptual questions surrounding the acceptable use of animals and their role within society. As such, this volume will appeal to scholars across the social sciences with interests in human–animal interactions and intersections. It may also appeal to healthcare practitioners and individuals interested in innovative multispecies methods of managing chronic illness.

Fenella Eason is a Postdoctoral Research Associate in the Exeter Anthrozoology as Symbiotic Ethics (EASE) Working Group at the University of Exeter, UK.

Multispecies Encounters
Series editors:

Samantha Hurn is Associate Professor in Anthropology, Director of the Exeter Anthrozoology as Symbiotic Ethics (EASE) working group and Programme Director for the MA and PhD programmes in Anthrozoology at the University of Exeter, UK. She is the author of Human-Animal Farm: A Multi-Sited, Multi-Species Ethnography of Rural Social Networks in a Globalised World, Humans and Other Animals: Human-Animal Interactions in Cross-Cultural Perspective and editor of Modern Myths, Unusual Heritage, and Anthropology and Cryptozoology: Researching Encounters with Mysterious Creatures.

Chris Wilbert is Senior Lecturer in Tourism & Geography at the Lord Ashcroft International Business School at Anglia Ruskin University, UK. He is the co-editor of Autonomy, Solidarity, Possibility: The Colin Ward Reader, and Technonatures: Environments, Technologies, Spaces and Places in the Twenty-first Century.

Multispecies Encounters provides an interdisciplinary forum for the discussion, development and dissemination of research focused on encounters between members of different species. Re-evaluating our human relationships with other-than-human beings through an interrogation of the 'myth of human exceptionalism' which has structured (and limited) social thought for so long, the series presents work including multi-species ethnography, animal geographies and more-than-human approaches to research, in order not only better to understand the human condition, but also to situate us holistically, as human animals, within the global ecosystems we share with countless other living beings.

As such, the series expresses a commitment to the importance of giving balanced consideration to the experiences of all social actors involved in any given social interaction, with work advancing our theoretical knowledge and understanding of multi-species encounters and, where possible, exploring analytical frameworks which include ways or kinds of 'being' other than the human.

The full list of titles for this series can be found here: https://www.routledge.com/Multispecies-Encounters/book-series/ASHSER1436

Published

Humans, Animals and Biopolitics: The more-than-human condition
Edited by Kristin Asdal, Tone Druglitrø, Steve Hinchliffe

Anthropology and Cryptozoology: Researching Encounters with Mysterious Creatures
Edited by Samantha Hurn

Animal Places: Lively Cartographies of Human-Animal Relations
Jacob Bull, Tora Holmberg and Cecilia Åsberg

Human-Canine Collaboration in Care: Doing Diabetes
Fenella Eason

Human–Canine Collaboration in Care
Doing Diabetes

Fenella Eason

LONDON AND NEW YORK

First published 2020
by Routledge
2 Park Square, Milton Park, Abingdon, Oxon OX14 4RN

and by Routledge
52 Vanderbilt Avenue, New York, NY 10017

Routledge is an imprint of the Taylor & Francis Group, an informa business

First issued in paperback 2021

© 2020 Fenella Eason

The right of Fenella Eason to be identified as author of this work has been asserted by her in accordance with sections 77 and 78 of the Copyright, Designs and Patents Act 1988.

All rights reserved. No part of this book may be reprinted or reproduced or utilised in any form or by any electronic, mechanical, or other means, now known or hereafter invented, including photocopying and recording, or in any information storage or retrieval system, without permission in writing from the publishers.

Trademark notice: Product or corporate names may be trademarks or registered trademarks, and are used only for identification and explanation without intent to infringe.

British Library Cataloguing-in-Publication Data
A catalogue record for this book is available from the British Library

Library of Congress Cataloging-in-Publication Data
A catalog record for this book has been requested

ISBN: 978-0-367-22777-7 (hbk)
ISBN: 978-1-03-208768-9 (pbk)
ISBN: 978-0-429-27678-1 (ebk)

Typeset in Times New Roman
by Apex CoVantage, LLC

**For Douglas
and in memory of Michael**

Contents

Preface		x
Series Editor's Foreword		xii
Acknowledgements		xiii
1	Multispecies care in chronic illness	1
2	Anthrozoological and sociological perspectives	28
3	The canine sense of smell and olfactory acuity	63
4	'Doing' diabetes Type 1	71
5	Dogs as biomedical resources and health technologies	97
6	Symbiotic practices of care	135
7	Endings and 'ethical' decision-making	163
	References	172
	Index	188

Preface

TINA (*her voice drops as she speaks*): I just thought they're going to come and find me dead.

I: That must be frightening.

TINA: Well, you'd go to bed of a night and sleep straight out so if they come, they haven't got much to do . . . (*she demonstrates as if lying on her back, legs together, arms close to her body, resembling an alabaster effigy of a medieval knight on a church tomb chest*).

I: So you were preparing?

TINA: Yes, have I got everything clean and I'd get into my new pyjamas. . .

Complacency, likely created by ignorance, laziness, or disinterest, allows all manner of negligence, unkindness, and condescension to occur in everyday life. For example, an overheard coffee-shop conversation might reveal: 'Oh, Jenny told me she's got diabetes . . .' Response: 'Poor thing, no more cream teas for her. Did you see that film on . . .?' Instantly the unfortunate Jenny is disenfranchised, boxed into the category of invisibly unwell individuals who probably could do something to improve their health if they made an effort. There is no endeavour by her friends to discover which type of diabetes was diagnosed or whether she might need to increase rather than decrease carbohydrate ingestion; it is as if Jenny has 'a bit of a headache'. Complacency enables disparaging sympathy – even vague condemnation – and an avoidance of the need to care, to 'do something about it', or to question the significance of such a diagnosis.

When Tina, a participant in this research who has Type 1 diabetes, describes her long-term fight to live on her own and 'survive' frequent and lengthy hypoglycaemic collapses, any trace of complacency in my attitude to this illness is given a trenchant shake-up. Her consideration of the feelings of others, such as care-workers and undertakers, in the situation above is mind-blowing and in total contrast to the attitude of my imagined café conversationalists. She adds: 'You get to the point in your life where you think, am I going to wake up? Or you spend all night up. . .'.

Preface xi

Tina could remain unconscious for four to five hours after a hypoglycaemic collapse at home. She recalls that, if she were to collapse in the street:

> People would just walk past. They'd think 'you're drunk', and really it's no different to what I'd do, but I was in desperate need, you know, for someone to know that I'm not right.

Series Editor's Foreword

Much has been written about the use of animals as service providers or as interventions to improve human physical and mental health. Considerably less academic attention has been paid, however, to the experiences and perspectives of the nonhuman assistants or therapists themselves or to the ethical dimensions of these trans-species relationships. The research presented in the current volume addresses both of these lacunae. Through her sensitive exploration of the intersubjective bonds which develop between humans who are chronically ill with Type 1 diabetes, and the medical detection dogs with whom they are paired, Fenella Eason acknowledges and celebrates the complexity of the relationships which form and can flourish under the ever present threat of hyper or hypoglycaemic collapse.

As an anthrozoologist, an academic student of human and canine psychologies and of human and nonhuman animal bereavements, and as someone who has first-hand experience of the emotional and physical turbulence of living with and caring for someone with chronic illness, Fenella is ideally placed to narrate the individual and collective struggles and triumphs of these trans-species dyads from a truly trans-species perspective. Her sensitivity to the predicaments of her human and canine interlocuters, and the deeply empathetic and engaging way in which she writes about their experiences, results in a rich exemplar of trans-species ethnography. I use the term trans-species in place of multi-species here because in the specific examples of the chronically ill humans and their canine partners Fenella discusses, a blurring occurs which complicates clearly delineated boundaries between bodies and between species. Through their sophisticated sense of smell, the dogs are able to access chemical changes within their human companions that are associated with potentially fatal medical episodes; and through their embodied experiences, learning to live together and flourish despite the physical and emotional compromises wrought by disease, the humans come to depend on their canine partners as extensions or replacements of their own sensory and perceptive abilities.

Samantha Hurn
Associate Professor in Anthropology, Director of the
Exeter Anthrozoology as Symbiotic Ethics (EASE)
Working Group and Programme Director for the
MA and PhD programmes in Anthrozoology
at the University of Exeter, UK.

Acknowledgements

What I have gained from the generosity of the dogs and humans in this research cannot be sufficiently acknowledged, but I wish to thank, as best I can, Claire, 'Val', and the multispecies members of Medical Detection Dogs who enabled me to explore the workings of their charity. Above all, the families and partnerships whose lives are embedded in chronic illness deserve full appreciation for volunteering information that will benefit others by making the complex and lesser-known facets of Type 1 diabetes more familiar and for sharing their improved ways of living chronic illness when assisted by diabetes alert dogs. I thank them sincerely for their patience with my questions and for the time that both species donated to communicating and demonstrating their 'doing' of diabetes so I, and others, might better understand what living chronic illness might be like.

1 Multispecies care in chronic illness

Mentally ripped out of their comfort zone by the unexpected tearing of their corporeal mantle, people often are forced to discover alternative modes of social existence and other resources that enable coping with newly shaped ways of being. One method of locating these is to talk of upsetting events and experiences with psychologists and physicians and with those who have had similar disruptions in their lives. Gradually and often uneasily, the altered selves are enabled to release stories of their embodied corruption and its forceful entourage of side effects. Sarah Nettleton exemplifies the significance of personal narrative: 'When people have the opportunity to give voice to their experiences of illness, it becomes evident that their accounts are woven into their biographies' (2013: 73).

The voluntary participants in this study, who are accustomed through necessity to communicate personal illness and well-being issues to their family, work colleagues, and members of healthcare professions, are therefore enabled to narrate tales of medical and social upheaval in their own lives as a result of a Type 1 diabetes diagnosis. They relate personal stories of internal and external bodily damage and repair, they laugh when they might weep over the obstacles that beset them in society and at home, and they become grave when contemplating the life-changing experiences of others faced with unpredictable hurdles in similar minority groupings.

They are expert but vulnerable witnesses to the inconsistencies and uncertainties of their lives and are conscious of the need for ongoing medical and social practices. They recognise when things are 'out of synch' within their embodied worlds and, often, how to get the external world to intervene so they may adapt and achieve safe passage onwards. They are explorers and adventurers, consultants and chemists, who traverse the world of chronic illness and, in so doing, reveal to others their best practices of self- and other-care.

But they are also conscious of their inability to recognise when their own fluctuating blood glucose levels are rising or falling to extremes. This loss of hyper- (too high) or hypoglycaemic (too low) awareness constantly endangers their lives.

Sources of increased self-confidence and of companionship in social reintegration are the diabetes alert assistance dogs who share the human home and give advance warning when blood sugar levels enter 'danger' zones. Their keen sense of smell, combined with training by the charity Medical Detection Dogs

2   *Multispecies care in chronic illness*

(MDD) to perform active alarm signals, ensures the dogs retain a much-vaunted significance in the lives of their human partners. These are dogs (*Canis familiaris*) of diverse breeds and backgrounds credited by those with Type 1 diabetes with being lifesavers and confidence-boosters and as having full membership of their families and of the society in which their close interspecies relationships are situated. Adrian Franklin (2006: 142) relates this new concept, of companion animals viewed as 'belonging' to and becoming family, to a 'hybridization of the family' and not to imagined anthropomorphism whereby a dog's qualities and characteristics are observed as 'human-like' (see also Milton, 2005). Importantly, the diabetes alert dogs are considered to be fully deserving of respect, recognition, and gratitude for their incomparable prowess in scent detection for human benefit. And the good-natured dogs seemingly acknowledge praise and reward, as is their wont, and accept the need to collaborate, tolerate, and enact the requisite behaviours as worthwhile and customary practices.

As Franklin contends:

> Unproblematic similarities might include co-residence, enduring ties, emotional inter-dependence, friendship, company and shared activities. When this happens, it is important to realize that it is not a one-way, human-orchestrated attribution, but one built of close feelings and emotions self-evidently expressed also by the animals themselves.
>
> (2006: 142)

'Shared activities' and hybridized practices are prominent in the daily routines of the species under focus here. These interactive human and nonhuman animal partners are the central figures performing on the ethnographic stage of this research into trans-species coexistences and the practices of normalising lives unsettled by chronic illness – lives in bodies that fail to function as expected and desired in a human, but also lives that enable bodily adaptation, alteration, survival, and the creation of new identities through the exceptional sensory perception of a nonhuman animal. These closely united companions are actors whose 'lines', spoken and unspoken, and vivid images of life in chronic illness, animate and illuminate their interconnecting biographies. Following Irvine (2013: 5), their narrations become 'resources, helping us understand and share what we find meaningful and what gives us purpose'.

The perspective of symbolic interactionism (Irvine, for example, 2004, 2007, 2012) is employed to disentangle the shared meanings from the symbiotic practices of care inherent in the coexisting partnerships that work within the bounds of chronic illness. The ecofeminist-derived ethics of care theory (Hamington, 2008; Adams and Gruen, 2014) supports exploration of interdependency and what it might be like to care and be cared for (Taylor, 2014: 109) in a symbiotic human–nonhuman coexistence.

Ethics of care theory also enables questioning of the elastic moral boundaries that humans construct to differentiate between the use and the exploitation of others. A firm moral stance needs to be considered and activated to avoid abuse and cruelty in human–nonhuman animal interactions. Symbiosis enables the pairing of unlike couples so that at least one member of the partnership gains benefit, be it improved self-worth, nutrition, or increased ability to achieve goals and rewards. Under the symbiosis umbrella huddle parasitism, commensalism, and mutualism (refer Leung and Poulin, 2008), and it is mutualism in this canine–human coexistence that motivates and leads towards acceptance of certain morally justifiable interspecies usages. A respectful mutualistic form of usage can impel development of credible and ethical multispecies collaboration, even unification, when compared with the unethical exploitation of commodified nonhuman animal masses.

The importance of animal 'mattering' (Irvine, 2013; Law, 2004; Rollin, 2011) is investigated to explore the question: 'how do chronically ill people engage with medical alert assistance dogs in their self- and other- care behaviours and in their lives?' The responses offered by clients of MDD record and explore action and performance, the doings and reshapings of life with chronic illness, by themselves and their MDD-trained working canine companions as they together effect and experience best practices that maintain lives worth living, lives that matter to more than one lone being.

The complexities examined and resolved by these multispecies practitioners in their everyday lives enable a visible becoming of an emotional, familiar, and self- and other-respecting amalgamation – a dyad identifiable as 'one-self'. Gazing into, and reflecting on, these harmonising coexistences enables an ethnographic contribution to the social sciences, drawing attention to innovative multispecies health care practices and raising awareness of the multidisciplinary science of anthrozoology. Anthrozoology is a recent but significant addition to the social sciences, as John Bradshaw (2017) affirms in the title of his most recent volume: *The animals among us: the new science of anthrozoology*. It emphasises a present and future need for an ethics that is involved in, allows for, and advocates multispecies independencies and interdependencies.

Students in this fast-developing field explore the relationships and interactions – whether collaborating or conflicting, whether bringing risk or gain to either or both – that are shared by human and nonhuman animals. An attempt is made to avoid, as far as is possible, an anthropocentric bent and an ontological assumption that the 'other' is an already fully known and understood being; further, there is effort to engage in self-reflection to encourage challenges to human interpretations and analyses of nonhuman animals.

Embedded in and emanating from this 'new science', this project studies domesticated healthy members of the canine species, who are educated to use their olfactory sensitivity in working for unwell members of the human species, and examines their situatedness, attempting also to comprehend their perspectives. Unlike anthropology, which investigates humans and their cultures and for the most part ignores nonhuman animal participants' impact in such cultures, and sociology, which has refused acknowledgement of the nonhuman animal's position in our society until very recently (Irvine, 2012), anthrozoology borrows evidence from many disciplines, including the aforementioned and, for example,

4   *Multispecies care in chronic illness*

from those of philosophy, geography, biology, and psychology to accentuate the significance of 'other' animal species in our evolutionary coexistences.

Research literature already published on multispecies entanglements within the field of health and illness is examined to provide a broad backdrop to the innovative influence of working scent-detecting dogs on chronic illness. This research is based on the anthropological and sociological intention to make the familiar strange and the strange familiar. In the words of Raymond Madden (2014: 281), 'we all know that a close and knowing experience with some "other" (regardless of their relative strangeness or familiarity) can be a transforming experience'. So this study aims to make a space for anthrozoological research on the shelves of social science by sourcing meanings and extending knowledge of the efforts by both dogs and humans to 'do' daily life better together; indeed, to do a life of vibrancy that leads to an improved method of survival in chronic illness and engenders increased enthusiasm for the possibilities of ethical transformation in those multispecies lives.

Humans and other animals: the familiar and the foreign

Humans and other animals, or human and nonhuman animals, are newly talked of as a single collective, one that enables us to imagine we are of the same ilk and of similar classification, one that enables us anthropocentrically to feel more comfortable about be(com)ing with (Maurstad, Davis and Cowles, 2013) or being alongside (Latimer, 2013) those whose discourse and gait are commonly at variance with human modes of communication and mobility.

However, there remains a pronounced divide between human and nonhuman animals encouraged by the frequent use of 'non'; such wording segregates one species from the other just as effectively as 'more-than-human' or 'other-than-human' succeed in distancing those with whom we might want to live more closely. Hurn (2012) notes the terms nonhuman or other-than-human animal may be used to show that humans are also animals, but the good intentions also highlight an opportunity to emphasise human anthropocentricity. Talking about human exceptionalism, Hurn reminds that 'the humanist approach has been guilty of taking humans out of context and putting them on a pedestal' (2012: 205). However, to mitigate for such human error, she draws attention to the greater opportunity for choice and 'liking' among friends than our already-selected family members; thus, 'when humans choose to take responsibility for the welfare of another animal, one of the reasons for doing so is because of some spark of mutual attraction, or a recognition of personhood across the species barrier' (Hurn, 2012: 109).

Would we therefore perhaps be better off by talking of humans and animals as (potential) allies, colleagues and friends, and retreating from what may sometimes seem an overly fastidious attempt to make ourselves into a more-than-similar species when we anyway majorly belong to the taxonomic 'kingdom' of *Animalia?*

The use of 'other' can also distance humans from those creatures with whom we wish to communicate, collaborate, and coexist. 'Othering' produces disenfranchisement, no matter how it is induced; it highlights mental and physical differences that can lead to alienation, isolation, and discrediting of that other's identity. It is an encouragement or stimulus of alterity that intentionally conjures more than difference – it may create distance and provoke ageism, racism, sexism, or speciesism, inviting objectification of nonhuman animals to the 'status of lesser beings' (Hurn, 2012: 25) and the oppression of minority groupings (also Nibert, 2002). Yet, in the perhaps comforting words of Rosa Braidotti (2009: 526), 'a bioegalitarian turn is encouraging us to relate to animals as animals ourselves'. Such movement denounces 'modes of embodiment, in the sense of both dialectical otherness (nonwhite, nonmasculine, nonnormal, nonyoung, nonhealthy) and categorical otherness (zoomorphic, disabled, or malformed)' and enables 'rich new alliances' (2009: 529).

Involving images of the domesticated animal 'other', rather than the still-wild nonhuman animal, this research highlights a microcosm of society in which both human and nonhuman animals succeed in cooperating and communicating to achieve a 'rich new alliance', an interspecies mutualistic coexistence – a form of functioning, mostly stable homeostasis that is not only physiologically but also socially successful. This coembodied way of living negates the anthropocentric historical drive for dominance and control over domesticated companion animals explored by Ingold (2000) and Palmer (1997) and further contemplated by Tuan (2007: 148):

> Power over another being is demonstrably firm and perversely delicious when it is exercised for no particular purpose and when submission to it goes against the victim's own strong desires and nature.

Instead, the shared way of life and the inter-subjective appreciation of each other's capabilities under discussion in these pages, also frame inter-dependency – a need by each for the other – and mutuality – an avoidance of intentional harm by one to the other. A trans-species coexistence is activated in which interconnectedness is paramount and alterity takes a more positive turn in reducing the significance of differences in appearance, linguistic skill and degrees of sentience and in illuminating the similarities and capacities for mutual understanding. The alien 'other' animal visage that has been expected and accepted by society instead becomes a familiar one and no longer accentuates Cartesian distinctions between human and nonhuman animals.

As postscript to this section, I draw attention to Kendra Coulter's (2016b: 201) consideration of her readers and of the nonhuman animals of whom she speaks: 'For linguistic efficiency, . . . and to avoid continuously identifying others in relation to but one of the species they are not, I use terms like people, humans, women, men, and so forth for *homo sapiens*, and refer to nonhuman animals as animals, or by their species or common name'. However, in this writing, as will become obvious, I have intentionally maintained the use of 'human' and 'nonhuman', or 'more-than-human' and 'other-than-human' animals, as terms to illustrate how language does differentiate categories and to emphasise – irritatingly drawn-out as these identifiers may be to the reader – how such differentiation may further divide rather than meld multispecies existences.

6 *Multispecies care in chronic illness*

One method of ensuring that trans-species communication is consistently shared between, for example, a horse, acting as a nonhuman animal, and an equestrienne, as a human rider, is the coembodiment of mobility and emotion in their working recognition of 'feel'.

Becoming 'one-self'

Global scrutiny and knowledge of other-than-human animals becomes meaningful only when there is human recognition and engagement with these 'animate objects' (Czerny, 2012: 8) in interpersonal relationships. Such engagement and performance, acted out between the medical alert assistance dog and the human with Type 1 diabetes, endow significance that affects both species beyond the visible partnership. Identity becomes a shared image not only in the eyes of the human partner but also under the searching gaze of society.

This study involves dogs and humans 'doing' diabetes (Mol and Law, 2004; Mol, 2008) and reflects Ingold and Palsson (2013) research in which he encourages demolition of Agamben's (2004: 33–38) 'anthropological machine' that separates humans from 'the continuum of organic life' (Ingold and Palsson, 2013: 8). He suggests action begins by thinking of humans and all other beings 'in terms not of what they *are*, but of what they *do*' (Ingold and Palsson, 2013: 8, italics in text). And further, 'to think of ourselves not as *beings* but as *becomings* – that is, not as discrete and pre-formed entities but as trajectories of movement and growth' (Ingold and Palsson, 2013: 8): *becomings* who work to 'forge' ways forward and 'guide the ways of consociates' (2013: 8).

In the world of assistance dogs too, there are those who 'forge ways forward and guide the ways of consociates' (Ingold and Palsson, 2013: 8), be they diabetes alert dogs or the service dogs who 'guide' their sight-impaired human partners. There is a becoming of a unique entity, a becoming of 'one-self' that involves a mutual understanding gained through effort and practice, discovered by Rod Michalko (1999) in the always-developing symbiotic relationship conducted between himself and his assistance dog, Smokie. Perhaps this is more a 'co-becoming' concept that is also gaining prominence in natural horsemanship where 'embodied collaboration' is felt within some, although not all, human–equine partnerships (Birke and Hockenhull, 2015: 82). The coembodiment of 'feel' provides an important human means of gauging equine temperament and movement, the horse's most apposite 'way of going'. 'Feel' allows the nonhuman to respond to questions asked of him or her, and the human to comprehend that response so that a communication channel becomes open to an unspoken two-way flow of information.

'Feel' may be considered instinctive and derived through emotion, but it is also sourced through vision, from seeing and reading 'a different look in a horse's eyes, ear positioning and tail swishing' (Coulter, 2016a: 35) as well as from the physically tactile, minute muscle movements continuously communicated between horse and rider, or between horse and human guardian, as perceived in the tale of Clever Hans, the horse first thought able to count by tapping his hoof on the ground, until psychologist Oskar Pfungst (1998) reported that the horse reacted

Multispecies care in chronic illness 7

to cues from his questioners' minute muscle movements. Vinciane Despret notes that Pfungst considered horses were well able to comprehend their riders' minds 'through the pressure of the bit' (2004: 114). Good riders today might prefer the horse read their minds through the 'minute muscle movements' learned from intuition and feeling than from the controlling influence effected by a human's sometimes severe pressure on the metal bit in the horse's mouth. A thinking rider produces a coembodied 'feel' that enables the horse to 'reproduce' (Despret, 2004: 115) the rider's thoughts in actively performing a wanted movement.

Lynda Birke (2008: 113) highlights an increasing recognition of equine signs of comfort and discomfort in horse–human partnerships. 'Touch', a more obviously tactile version of the coembodied 'feel', may elicit an unspoken, comfortable, and comforting comprehension of the equine partner – although not, of course, when produced by Ingold's (2000: 307) 'tools of coercion', the whip or spur, that touch a horse's flanks as 'aids' to encourage performance.

However, touch may fittingly contribute to interspecies communication and so succeed in explicating the need for, and the production of, empathy and compassion and the importance of these emotional attributes in the lives of intermingling species. A clear example appears in Donna Haraway's 'touching comfort' (2008: 202–204), in which an interspecies tactile closeness between dog and human results in the assuaging of reciprocal need. A similar 'touching comfort' was observed at a country hospital, where a cat lay draped over the lap of an elderly, bedridden female patient who never appeared to have contact with human visitors beyond the nursing staff. Repetitively, she stroked the cat, the cat purred soothingly and settled closer to her; both gave and received mutual care, increasing each other's levels of oxytocin, known variously as the 'love' or 'hug' hormone. Odendaal and Meintjes (2003) found that oxytocin levels almost doubled in 18 participants and in their dogs when the humans touched and stroked their nonhuman companions. Fine and Beck (2010: 11) suggest that their study 'highlights the enormous physiological impact that animals have or could have on our lives', impact that is slowly being recognised in human-animal studies and animal-assisted interventions.

Facilitators of human-human relationships

A stranger's conversational gambit may be addressed to the canine as often as to the human when the interspecies dyad walks down a street or through a public park – and an ensuing presumptive dialogue may be expressed by the human or humans on behalf of the dog. Hurn (2012: 102) suggests that dogs can be 'effective "ice-breakers"' when it comes to forming new social relationships.

Participant Terry achieves mobility with the aid of a wheelchair but says he is 'below most people's eyeline'. However, he continues:

> It's a case that people see the wheelchair and they don't want to know; people see the dog and they come and talk to you, so the dog is a bit of an ice-breaker, they talk to disabled people *because* they've got a dog; they want to know what he does and about the charity.

8 *Multispecies care in chronic illness*

Sanders (1990: 662–668) claims that, in general, 'companion animals act as facilitators of human-to-human interactions', suggesting that human animal–companion animal social exchanges acknowledge 'coparticipation in the encounter, mutual definition of the perspective of the other, imaginative estimation of the other's intentional definition of the situation, and mutual adjustment of behaviour'.

How guide dogs impact the identity of people with visual impairments is the focus of Sanders' research (1990) and his words retrieve memories of a conversation held with a bereaved elderly resident of a bustling city who had previously walked her now-deceased dog in the camaraderie of other dog-walkers in a neighbourhood park (Eason, 2011). She remarked sadly:

> I went to the park alone after she died. People with their dogs came up to ask where my little dog was – they're well-meaning but it's too painful. I won't go back to the park anymore. I'm too old to have another dog, my sight's failing and I can't risk falling again. But I do miss the companionship.

Those few words exhibit the loss of social friendships, both human and nonhuman; the loss of exercise; emerging signs of physical frailty and emotional isolation; and the destructive loss of reason to care.

Lynette Hart (1995: 166) and Leslie Irvine (2013) are among researchers citing a study by Adell-Bath et al. (1979) in which 83% of 259 Swedish dog owners agreed that 'my dog gives me the opportunity of talking with other people' and 79% also agreed with the statement 'the dog makes friends for me'. Hart avers that 'dogs seem to display an inexhaustible willingness to form and sustain partnerships with humans' (1995: 167), illustrating this with an example of the partnership between service dogs and people in wheelchairs 'who come to be seen by other people as a team, more predictably together than any mother and child, marital couple or pair of siblings' (Hart, 1995: 167). This shared identity – exemplified above by participants Terry and his curly-coated assistant, Jim, and the always-present but unnamed wheelchair – will be returned to later.

Introduced more fully at the end of this chapter and similarly viewed as teams are the participating interspecies dyads who occupy the time and space of their everyday existences weighed down by the dominative burden of chronic illness. Good management of this largely invisible load is intrinsic to the human's survival, and in certain respects to the dog's health and welfare, too. There is reciprocal responsibility in catering for effective mutual care. These canine–human partnerships are compelled to take ownership of the chronic illness that is Type 1 diabetes, to care for it, enact its routines, carry it from room to room, from home to work, to shopping mall or medical institution, to draw out blood and replenish insulin to assuage its needs and stresses; to be conscious of its fluctuating symptoms and pay homage in the form of insulin donation and calorific balance. Inept lifestyle management is not to blame for a Type 1 diabetes diagnosis, a lifetime Sword of Damocles which requires consistent care and attention to preclude its fatal downward trajectory.

Essences, ethics, and practices of care guide or direct much of the social interactions in life, whether in school, home, institution, or workplace: who and what we

Multispecies care in chronic illness 9

care about, for, and of (Haraway, 2008; Mol, 2008; Mol, Moser and Pols, 2010; Pols, 2012; Van Dooren, 2014; Taylor, 2014; Coulter, 2016b). Material goods and ethereal yearnings, the animate and inanimate causes of pleasure and pain, variations on Maslow's hierarchy of needs (Maslow, 1943) motivating survival . . . the power in ecologies and in governments.

If we fail to care about or for our fellow human and nonhuman animals – and there are of course those who pathologically find regard or respect for others impossible to express within acceptable social norms – there would be little point in continuing to journey through our seemingly brief spell of existence. Care becomes a prominent feature when traversing our own lifescape, providing opportunity to investigate other lives, to excavate and interpret illness and its attendant biopsychosocial requirements and practices. Ethics guiding moral care practices, and mutual performances of care actively conducted in symbiotic relationships, are investigated more fully in a later chapter, much of it integrating the research of Adams and Gruen (2014), Coulter (2016a, 2016b), Taylor (2014) and Zamir (2006).

Multispecies cooperation

'To succeed in life, you need to work together – pursuing the struggle for existence, if you like – just as much as you strive to win the struggle for existence', stress Nowak and Highfield (2011: xvii) in urging global cooperation. And it is to encourage multispecies cooperation, and human understanding of such collaboration in this struggle for existence and success in life, that is the endeavour of the following pages.

Hamilton and Taylor (2013: x) research 'the "hows" of daily life spent working with animals – in relation, among other contexts, to experiences of farming and slaughter, safe places for the unwanted, and veterinarians who care for the welfare of small animals – by examining the 'complex steps, interactions and negotiations' necessary for a better perspective and understanding of how animals matter in diverse places of work. In a similar vein, Coulter (2016a: 146) draws attention to the way in which nonhuman animals can become 'partners and friends' and/or 'useful commodities or tools' when they are perceived as workers. Their lives may improve or may not, dependent on 'context' (2016a: 146) and on the ways in which they 'matter' and are recognised and integrated into multispecies society or are rejected.

Prepared separately for a meeting that may join them almost literally 'by the hip' for their future coexistences, once 'matched', and only from that moment of onward bonding, the interspecies dyads become what Higgin (2012: 74) terms 'works-in-progress' and members of Haraway's 'lively knottings' (2008: vii). Although conventional medical technologies and laboratory-derived medications have position and purpose in these species' managements of daily life, it is the warm-blooded intertwined care of and by each being – framed by innovative biomedical technology and structured within the values and guidelines of a code of symbiotic ethics of care – that is analysed under the ethnographic microscope.

Assistive inanimate technologies – for example, the test strip, insulin pump, or glucose monitor, or the white stick aiding visually impaired individuals with

10 *Multispecies care in chronic illness*

Type 1 diabetes – all facilitate life compromised by chronic illness. However, when examined alongside the dog's exceptional olfactory abilities and companionable behaviours, which do more than merely facilitate the diabetic person's continuing aliveness, it becomes evident that this animated resource leads to far greater enhancement and enrichment of the human's hold on life and being well.

When beginning this project, I imagined that the human participants would fall under the 'disabled' label, a classification freely and stereotypically bandied about in 'Western' society. I prepared readings from 'disability studies' relating to minority groups of those disenfranchised and ignored because of bodily malfunction (refer Tom Shakespeare, 2014: 101–106, who expands research on challenges to disability identity), or because they were born nonhuman, sentient but suffering from condemnation under human social norms and constraints.

But when I met those who volunteered to participate as human–canine partnerships in this research, anticipated images seemed ill-fitting with respondents of either species. Instead I learned that, as one human participant succinctly put it, 'this is normal for me, this is my normal way of life'. Shakespeare (2014: 102) cites Linton (1998: 12): 'The question of who "qualifies" as disabled is as answerable or as confounding as questions about any identity status. One simple response might be that you are disabled if you say you are'. Despite difficulty with aspects of mobility, this participant is by no means unable and has altered and ordered his environment to suit his abilities and preferred lifestyle, while deploying best practices to satisfy the needs of the human and canine companions sharing his home. Similarly, the blind lawyer cited by Rod Michalko (1999: 118) describes his condition:

> I don't think of myself as disabled. I'm like everyone else. I just happen to be blind. Blindness is no big deal. All it is is a nuisance and an inconvenience. Like any other nuisance, it can be overcome. There's lots of technology around, especially nowadays.

For Michalko, the technology is his guide dog, Smokie; for others, it may consist of a white stick or walking frame, and for participant Terry, technology involves both a wheelchair and a medical alert assistance dog, Jim. The two pieces of 'equipment' enable him

> to go on my own to the football because I don't need anyone – I mean it's nice to take a carer and have somebody else to talk to, but it's also nice to just go out on your own, to have the freedom to go out on your own, which I had lost.

Although Terry is lauding Jim's companionship and the scenting abilities that give him 'freedom', he also seems to appreciate going out 'on his own' as if Jim is a useful instrument or an invisible chaperone rather than 'someone', albeit that this someone lacks vocal speech comprehensible to a human ear. The concept of companion animals as tools or technologies is discussed later.

As Charmaz (1995: 657) explicates, adaptation to living with impairment calls for changing 'life and self to accommodate to physical losses and to reunify body and self accordingly'. Life and self-adaptation enable a becoming-normal that concurs with Schillmeier's (2014: 1) suggestion that the cosmopolitics of illness make us conscious not only of the normativity of embodied social relations, but also of the practices and procedures shaping 'normal bodies':

> The experiences of illness trouble the practices and relations of our embodied life, the more so if these illnesses are life threatening, infectious, and/or resist to be [sic] curable.

Schillmeier (2014: 1), in the introduction to *Eventful bodies: the cosmopolitics of illness*, contends that these cosmopolitical events lead to conscious visualisation of 'the unsettlement of embodied human life' and provide insight into 'the complex and powerful practices of *normalizing* embodied human relations' (italics in text).

Other members of society might observe disablement or impaired ability as reasonable causes of anger or frustration but, to the 'owners' of a chronic illness, difficult circumstances are the norm, not the extraordinary, and issues of risk or hazard inherent in their illness tend to provide challenges but do not necessarily provoke continual rage or depression. A sense of purpose and an ongoing mindful determination accompany participants in this research who live life differently after a 'hypo-unaware' Type 1 diabetes label is affixed to their medical records.

Sara was diagnosed with Type 1 diabetes when in her 30s. Describing her chronic illness, she shrugs her shoulders as if attempting to shake it off:

> Well, you have to learn to cope, don't you? You can't not; you can't take it off and put it in the bin and say I'm finished now. It doesn't work like that.

Similarly, Janet, a long-term possessor of a variety of severe health difficulties including Type 1 diabetes, has become resigned to the vicissitudes that upset routine and best practice:

> A lot of it was (*done*) on autopilot. The one thing with having a long-term condition is that you get used to having lots of knockbacks and you just think, right, I'll get myself through it . . . find a way.

Despite the many 'knockbacks', participants speak openly and candidly about their efforts to navigate the complexities of life with Type 1 diabetes as well as their endeavours to swim through riptides of institutional bureaucracy and to surf waves of internal discomfort. The pitch of their voices rises and falls, the pace of their speech quickens, dawdles, halts, and speeds up again as they recollect good days and bad times. They relive experiences with gestures and facial and vocal expressions, and the companion dogs sit and listen, watch and wait, tip their heads

12 *Multispecies care in chronic illness*

to one side or other, raise a questioning eyebrow, or occasionally sniff and nudge to remind the human partner to test their blood sugar levels.

Often exhausted by the daily physical and mental battering that generally is concomitant with chronic illness, the human participants appear resolutely determined to perform to the best of their abilities to attain goals and standards of life that realistically may only become achievable through the assistance of their medical alert dogs.

Why write about dogs and diabetes?

It is 'common knowledge' that diabetes negatively affects the living of human and nonhuman lives, but there is less knowledge of the different categories of this illness that are clumped under the 'diabetes' title. So, by looking at the UK's much-favoured household companion and at the role now played by the dog in improving human life management, it is hoped that awareness of a potentially fatal, rarely visible, chronic illness – Type 1 diabetes – is better and more widely understood. The human–nonhuman animal interactions and experiences within medical and social contexts are viewed against the tempestuous, odorous symptoms of illness which are consistently revealed to canine olfaction, but fail to present many Type 1 diabetic people, or their human companions, with recognisable signs warning of an approaching hypoglycaemic episode that may result in emergency hospitalisation.

A more particular objective is to draw on aspects of the conceptual approach developed by Mol and Law (2004: 16), who examine hypoglycaemia in terms of 'the body we *do* '. Their approach points to self practices which are enacted by the chronically ill in order to evade an unwanted early demise: 'one does not hang together as a matter of course', they remind (2004: 1). Such necessarily active self practices are conducted to prevent the body collapsing, to keep the individual's unpredictable world whole and any errant corporeal pieces glued together to avoid 'leaky' boundaries (Mol and Law, 2004: 11). If the required self practices and behaviours fail to be performed effectively, death may result.

The practices of multispecies data collection and ethnographic analysis, exemplified by Kirksey and Helmreich (2010), are revealed through an anthrozoological lens magnifying familiar domestic coexistences: the lives of dogs and their companions in human-structured homes. Such revelation uncovers the choreography balancing and unbalancing human–nonhuman performances within chronic illness; a choreography of practices chiefly directed by canine olfactory sensitivity. Within this are dances embellished with attendant artefacts – the blood test kit, the insulin pen, the packet of Jelly Babies, the dog treats and the illness-identifying jacket, the music of the beep-chirp monitor, the whine or bark of the alerting dog, the thump-hiss of the fridge door and the pop of an opening sample-jar lid used in training, or the human sigh of relief or annoyance at the monitor reading of blood glucose levels. All these are familiar environmental features surrounding the human–canine partners as they weave their essential patterns for life.

Multispecies care in chronic illness 13

A further intention is to discover the active efforts made by nonhuman animals to communicate with their human companions, and to examine the discourses contributed by the human element in conversation with members of these partnerships who do not share a common language.

James Clifford (1986: 108) writes of the different 'voices' that emerge from an ethnographic discourse; voices that agree with or counter others' dialogical pathways, providing concurring or contrasting commentary. Such voices belong to MDD clients who live with Type 1 diabetes and are knowledgeable through past and present experiences; individuals whose existence is embodied in discourse, in lifestyle management, and in the reactions of human and nonhuman others. Their narratives recount the chiefly positive influences gained by living with an assistance dog, in terms of medical support and companionship, and relate the value of publicly recognised social integration when contrasted with former social disenfranchisement.

Voices also emerge from the active communications presented by the diabetes alert dogs whose coembodied presences and performances highlight chronic illness to a less-knowledgeable human public. As Irvine (2013: 165) explains, in her examination of the 'hidden' population among the homeless, she studied 'pet owners in order to introduce another set of voices'; voices who 'in speaking for' their animals, 'help to establish the identity of the animal' (2013: 15). In listening to and questioning the human participants of this project, who are used to the invisibility of their diabetes, there emerge other relational interspecies voices narrating stories of their lives and situations, while simultaneously opening paths that give space to self-reflection, to my thinking and experiencing of their symbiotic relationships and complex existences.

My interest in the ability of dogs to detect human illness through their acute sense of smell was first stirred by news media commentary on a proof-of-principle study as to whether dogs could be trained to scent the odour of malignant cells in bladder cancer from urine samples. This study, researched by Willis and colleagues, was published in the British Medical Journal (2004) and attracted worldwide attention.

Prior to the bladder cancer study, the organisation 'Cancer and Bio-Detection Dogs' had been formed by Claire Guest, with scientists and medical practitioners in the United Kingdom, to research multispecies collaborative exploration into illness odour detection and to discover whether anecdotal data could have scientific foundation. The organisation gained charitable status in 2008, and in 2011 the name was changed to Medical Detection Dogs because the range of illness conditions that the dogs were learning to detect from human breath and odour samples was expanding. Not only in the United Kingdom but also internationally, dogs are now being trained to discriminate among the odours of serious illness: see, for example, studies from Japan published by Sonoda et al. (2011), and Cornu et al. (2011), who have conducted canine odour detection research in France.

Cornu and colleagues (2011) indicated the possibility that dogs might become useful instruments in future screening for prostate cancer, a possibility which is becoming a reality as the MDD charity and the Milton Keynes National Health

14 *Multispecies care in chronic illness*

Service (NHS) Hospital Foundation Trust are currently, according to information on the charity's website, conducting an 'NHS ethically approved study' with the help of trained cancer detection dogs 'to find an early, accurate, noninvasive method to test for prostate and other urological cancers', thereby avoiding biopsies which could become interventions 'of last resort in many diagnoses'.

Research into canine detection of cancer odour is ongoing and a paper by Elliker et al. (2014) accentuates the need for robust double-blind testing to ensure confusion does not arise over the dogs' abilities to discriminate particular odours. In this research, an investigator was isolated in one room and the dog and handler were isolated in another, both observed by an independent referee. The investigator placed urine samples in an array and was then isolated, after which the dog and handler approached the array where the dog would sniff and select a sample containing the cancer odour. The researchers concluded that trained dogs might be able to remember individual scents in large quantities of training samples rather than generalise on a common odour; their results suggested that dogs could be trained to detect prostate cancer, which is the focus of MDD's current research. Dogs are being trained to work on the detection of urological cancer using samples of human urine in double-blind trials. The charity also plans to conduct molecular biomarker analyses to attempt to identify and isolate the volatile organic compounds detected by the dogs.

Sonoda et al. (2011) researched the scenting abilities of trained dogs who were employed in the olfactory detection of colorectal cancer by means of breath and faecal samples and their findings, also noted by Guest (2013: 290), revealed that 'canine scent detection was not confounded by current smoking, benign colorectal polyps, inflammation or infection' (Sonoda et al., 2011: 117) nor was there any 'correlation between canine scent judgement and human haemoglobin or transferrin' (Sonoda et al., 2011: 118), the latter being a serum protein carrying iron to bone marrow for red blood cell production.

Sonoda et al. (2011) further contended that cancer has a specific odour as do other illnesses such as the apparent acetone or pear-drop smell of diabetic ketoacidosis (DKA), a serious complication mentioned by participants in this research and explained in Chapter 3.1. Terry agrees with the pear-drop smell but says there can also be a strong smell of almonds and he recalls Jim's acute interest in Christmas cake ('he goes bananas') because of the almonds making up marzipan:

> The only thing he's ever gone to eat is Christmas cake and I'm convinced it was the marzipan because he didn't bother with anything else. You can even leave ham on the table and he won't take it. He'll put his nose up and he'll look, but he won't take it. He was trying to pick up the Christmas cake and bring it to me: 'this should be yours. The smell is yours so why is it over here?'

Terry's explanation may be based on an egomorphic (Milton, 2005) perception of knowledge gained from personal experience and understanding, rather than from the more distancing concept of anthropomorphism, and this allows him to make sense of Jim's unusual behaviour and the reason behind the dog's effort to communicate.

Multispecies care in chronic illness   15

Terry can thus tell me the content of Jim's actively produced, silently transmitted information without leaving his chair, in vocal speech that I can understand. An action performed in the past by Jim, the dog, is recognised, comprehended, and passed on by Terry, the human, in intelligible terms through time and space to me, who, knowing the smell of almonds and marzipan from Christmas experience and seeing both dog and human before me, can perfectly imagine.

As a result of Jim's attempt on the Christmas cake and their reasoning of it, Terry and Nick try never to have anything 'almondy' in the house so that Jim won't be distracted from detecting Terry's changing blood sugar levels. Nick comments that the smell of almonds is also associated with the plastic explosive, Semtex, which bomb-detection dogs can identify through olfactory sensitivity; he adds: 'dogs don't just work with human beings, but with inanimate objects as well'.

Additional research purpose

Researching the symbiotic lives of humans and dogs involved in revealing the canine olfactory sensitivity that benefits people with persistent and sometimes terminal illnesses, has allowed the opening of a channel for a more positive form of grieving over the death of my elder son from cancer. Similarly, it has enabled remembrance of my closest childhood friend, who was compelled to leave our boarding school to be cared for at her distant home after developing Type 1 diabetes – she too died young.

The writing style of this book will thus incorporate auto-ethnographical musings and reflections that surface because of the activities and behaviours of the interspecies research participants who sometimes mirror aspects of life that are wholly familiar and not always comfortable to recognise. Leslie Irvine's definition of participant observation, as requiring 'full immersion', has enabled lapses from 'academic' writing to more personal interjections when deeper, more emotional reflections bubble up. Borrowing from Irvine (2004: 3–21), 'although some of my arguments might well apply to other animals, I have studied only dogs', although keen-scenting or macrosmatic olfactory ability applies to most animals on this planet, with the exception of humans and most primates.

Like Keri Brandt (2004: 303), 'my recent biography and personal history' have become meaningful in terms of how and where this project is situated. Childhood life was spent among ponies and pigs, chickens and dogs – there was a division between the 'named' and 'unnamed' members of the so-called domesticated nonhuman animal species. Mary Phillips (1994: 123) draws attention to 'proper' names being given to laboratory animals as signifying 'the social emergence of personality', thus acknowledging their 'unique characteristics' (1994: 121). Similarly, Sanders (2003: 411) remarks that the designation of human names for dogs signifies their establishment as 'virtual' persons, and Irvine (2012: 129) posits the influence of 'individual characteristics or behavioral tendencies' on the choice of human name for a dog. An example of this became visible when I cared for 'holiday' dogs – at one stage, more than a dozen Staffordshire bull terriers from a variety of homes were in residence: all looked 'tough' and were named Rambo,

16   *Multispecies care in chronic illness*

Tyson, Brutus, and similar, but I cannot agree that their behaviour complemented their names. Rather like 'Ferdinand' (Leaf, 1936), the Spanish bull who wished to sit in the sun and not fight in the bullring, they appeared much happier playing and 'smelling the flowers' than in planning assault.

Sincere mourning was felt on the farm at the death of the named of any species who were identifiable from their 'unique characteristics', and an opaque sadness fell among us when the unnamed went out of the farm gates. It was a sheltered childhood in which words such as 'suicide' or 'cancer' were enunciated letter-by-letter by adults and funerals were not attended by children. This encouraged much poring over dictionaries and feeling scared and slightly guilty at unexpected glimpses of oddly menacing, behatted, all-in-black figures silently walking up the church path.

Poppet, a coal-black pony, came from the era of 'docked' tails and the often-given, kindly intended present of *Black Beauty* (Sewell, 1877), the harrowing tale of animal abuse and cruelty to horses that anecdotally has elicited graphic nightmares from myriad children since its original publication. She was a gentle companion, living up to her name; piglets played uninjured around her legs and she once carried a hen's new-laid egg across the fields to show us – her lips were so soft, there was not a crack in the shell. She had a stroke, after which her left ear and lower lip drooped, but she maintained her kind nature until the day I found her lying breathless in the grass. Her unspoken lessons on multispecies cooperation and the need to care and show concern for the lives of others were exemplary.

More recently, health, illness, and the unethical treatment of multiple non-human animal species again became central to my being. The global abuse of animals by children: live hamsters cooked in microwaves or guinea pigs thrown out of upstairs windows, tin cans or fireworks tied to cats' tails, dogs peppered with lead pellets or shut in crates and poked with burning sticks – the list of cruelty is endless and the above-mentioned violent maltreatment of companion animals excludes the wild nonhuman species used as target practice or trapped to be taunted and tortured. These activities have a variety of potential causes and reasonings (Kellert and Felthous, 1985) and may result in increasingly abusive behaviour towards human and nonhuman animals as the child becomes adult (Ascione, 2005).

There is difference between curiosity and malice when nonhuman animals fall victim to young human predation. I studied psychology to discover whether – and if so, why – childhood abuse of animals might lead to domestic violence and animal cruelty in adulthood and then turned to studies of canine psychology and ethology, and to the importance of dogs in triadic animal-assisted activities.

Research into the lives of domestic animals fired interest in the deaths of companion animals and to methods of remembering them that might reduce the social isolation felt by bereaved humans – those whose sole affection had been directed at someone who never judged and never argued, who always willingly offered an apparently caring affection in return for human hospitality. 'It's only a dog' is a harsh sentence when addressed to an individual bereft of a close animal friend, one who might also have been the last living link to a loved and previously deceased human companion.

Multispecies care in chronic illness 17

Interest in the discrimination and stigma that afflict multispecies minority groups, alongside existing 'on a different plane' during my son's terminal illness, guided research into early stage diagnosis of illness and the arrogant invasiveness of the serpentine cancers. This in turn led to knowledge of the lack of privacy and the possibility of pain and embarrassment during investigation preceding their discovery.

Finding innovative, noninvasive, and less-expensive methods of diagnosing serious human illness in its early stages is the ongoing endeavour of Claire Guest, CEO of the charity MDD and former possessor of a deep-seated breast tumour which might not have been discovered until too late were it not for the behavioural changes in her dog, Daisy. Such was the intensity of her dog's unusually anxious behaviour, not wanting to leave her and jumping up against her, that Claire went for health checks leading to the eventual discovery of an early-stage, but deeply embedded tumour. After this was medically treated, Daisy became more relaxed and returned to her former joyful way of being.

Claire learned of others, however, whose dogs had changed behaviour towards them, dogs who incessantly tried to lick moles; barked, whined, and became distressed when they never had been so before; or who nudged at places on their companions' bodies where carcinogenic material was later found. Certain that Daisy had sensed the malformation in herself, Claire gathered anecdotal data and spoke to members of medical professions, including John Church (1996, 1999, 2013), a surgeon with interest in biotherapy. What began with a few individuals working in a small building without running water has become a recognised, well-established charity, now patronised by the Duchess of Cornwall and invited to share its medical discoveries in Palace and Parliament.

When I first visited the charity, there were three offices, fewer than 10 staff members, and a room in which Daisy and one or two other dogs were trained to scent urine samples on a carousel and to sit pointedly in front of the one containing an affected sample. I met other dogs learning to recognise, through sniffing, rapid changes in volatile organic compounds (VOCs) in the breath of people with Type 1 diabetes. The client waiting list for a diabetes alert assistance dog is around three years despite the increasing number of MDD staff now involved in training the dogs and matching them to appropriate human companions.

However, public enthusiasm for canine scent detection of illness symptoms has increased to the extent that the charity has gained planning approval for extensive new buildings to be constructed from donations which will provide, according to the charity's website (December 2016):

> Two new Bio Detection areas, a client area for the Medical Alert Assistance Dogs, space for our specialist dogs to relax, dog washing facilities, a lecture theatre for our visitors, private rooms for client interviews and additional parking spaces . . . these new buildings will give us the space to increase the annual number of Medical Alert Assistance Dogs placements to up to 50 by 2019/20. We will also be able to expand on our existing urological (including

18 *Multispecies care in chronic illness*

prostate) cancer and malaria studies to include new projects such as colorectal cancer and Parkinson's disease.

A current research study, 'Using medical detection dogs to identify people with malaria parasites', incorporates an innovative use of canine olfactory sensitivity and involves Durham University, MDD, the London School of Hygiene and Tropical Medicine, and the Medical Research Council Unit The Gambia. A statement on the MDD website identifies the project's purpose as finding a way to 'detect malaria that is non-invasive and can be used to test a large number of samples at a time. Current tests require finger-prick blood collection and laboratory screening. In contrast, the dogs are portable and rapid'.

Starting with the bladder cancer proof-of-principle study, the charity now works with dogs in the detection of other cancers and is continuing to develop the adjacent branch in which staff members train dogs to use their scenting abilities in the detection of early signs of hypo- or hyperglycaemia in clients who have Type 1 diabetes or Addison's disease or who are allergic to the smell and/or taste of nuts. This area of canine olfactory sensitivity has become the focus of my research.

Canine olfactory capability allows early, noninvasive detection of extreme fluctuations in the blood glucose levels of people with chronic Type 1 diabetes so that medical care practices can be performed to evade hypoglycaemia and collapse leading to coma and thus prevent urgent and frequent calls for an ambulance. An extensive list of symptoms of hypoglycaemia reported by hypo-aware respondents appears in a study by Wells, Lawson, and Siriwardena (2008: 1238).

Wide-ranging roles are opening for dogs trained in olfactory pursuits beyond the already-known ability to sniff out drugs, bombs, and buried human remains. A macrosmatic or keen sense of smell is active in multiple species and contrasts negatively with the feeble-scenting (microsmatic) sensibility provided by the human nasal structure (Bradshaw, 2012; Craven, Paterson and Settles, 2010; Helton, 2009; Horowitz, 2016; Smith et al., 2004). Wishing to explore the phenomena surrounding canine olfaction in human health more extensively in terms of theory and practice, MDD provided an opportunity to observe multispecies education, play activities, and rapport gained with one another: human–human, human–dog, and dog–dog interactions.

Examined here are the care practices performed by human–canine partnerships to improve 'personal' health, welfare, domestic, and social life within the limitations of Type 1 diabetes. How the interspecies dyad adopts or adapts the practicalities necessary to effect safe and mutualistic coexistence is revealed within intersubjective and essential strategic activities that maintain well-being and coherent management of lives under constant threat. As Schillmeier (2014: 3) suggests, experience of serious illness that '*breaches* the general norms of health and related practices, introduces novel norms of illness . . . that have to be accounted for in a pragmatic sense' (italics in text). New norms are introduced and practiced when dogs undertake care work that assists in hypo-prevention and involves altered or altering procedures emerging from the effects of coincidental illnesses.

Multispecies care in chronic illness   19

Care practices and problems

> The overall aim of a multi-voiced form of investigative story-telling need not necessarily be to come to a conclusion. Its strength might very well be in the way it opens questions up.
>
> (Mol and Law, 2004: 17)

On occasion, corporeal 'leaks' undermine composure. Participant Paul has lived with chronic illness since childhood and his discomfort with a malfunctioning body becomes apparent:

> My whole body just doesn't feel right, you don't feel like you're in the right skin; nothing wants to settle. It's like nothing's moving but it feels like everything's going; it's all vibrating; all your nerve-endings are firing off but it doesn't settle.

He adds that the cause of his bodily 'unsettlement' might not only arise from Type 1 diabetes but could originate from one of the attenuating 'tightly intertwined' complex issues by which his health is perpetually hampered. Autoimmune diseases are numerous and as yet cannot be prevented or cured; causes of the immune system's malfunction, according to information available on the Diabetes.co.uk website, may include 'bacteria or virus, drugs, chemical or environmental irritants'. Because autoimmune disorders can affect different parts of the body simultaneously – for example, joints, red blood cells, muscles or skin – it is possible for someone who has Type 1 diabetes also to have additional problems from rheumatoid arthritis, Addison's disease, coeliac disease, multiple sclerosis, to issues of hyper- or hypothyroidism (Diabetes.co.uk, 2016).

In taking an 'inter-species' approach to Mol and Law's ethnographic view of people dealing with hypoglycaemia and the misbehaving body, this project investigates the place, role, and 'otherness' of a medical alert assistance dog becoming coembodied in a chronically ill person's understanding and enactment of the body they *do*. Mol and Law (2004: 16) reflect that 'keeping ourselves together is one of the tasks of life', a necessary occupation to maintain survival. However, in this instance, the multispecies coembodied entity works as a 'two-in-one-self' to achieve this – the dog, who alerts the human partner to take external steps to prevent the internal lack of insulin becoming a hazard to life, is in turn rewarded many times over by the human for vital assistance in their continued survival. As Adrian Franklin (2006) writes, in the context of what happens and what is done in 'almost every home in the western world and beyond', homes become 'home to humans living very closely and purposefully with other species, particularly with cats and dogs' (2006: 138).

Avoiding the threatening complications that commonly adhere to life with Type 1 diabetes calls for significant care methods and practices by the individual, under instruction from what may be a very distant (in terms of mileage and travel time) team of diabetes health care professionals. None of the participants in

20 *Multispecies care in chronic illness*

this study lives within walking distance of a hospital, and as the majority are no longer – if they ever were – licensed to drive, they and their medical assistance dogs become reliant on others to reach medical appointments or consultations.

When talking about institutional caring, Mol suggests that 'care is not attractive . . . even good care is not attractive' (2008: 28); it may be painful, invasive, boringly essential, and time-consuming, an unwanted addition to the 'daily grind' of managing life's progression through illness. And there is need for the human and canine partnership, coexisting within the boundaries of chronic illness whether at home or in social environs, to work hard – separately, together, as a team, as a dyad actively striving for health within a community of similar practitioners – in order to maintain a daily routine of mutual caring – however dull, however stressful or painful, however sometimes unattractive to the self and others – that will attain optimum standards of care and demonstrate a body being well 'done' in both public and private settings. And the settings themselves need ordering and organising to facilitate best practices of care.

Kendra Coulter (2016b: 199) explicates the concept of care work, including that done by nonhuman animals, as being 'tasks, interactions, labour processes, and occupations involved in taking care of others, physically, psychologically, and emotionally'. The work necessary for the sometimes challenging and complex delivery of care calls for 'skill and multifaceted communication' (2016b: 204) at a time when distraction must be ignored, no matter its attraction.

Blood, hygiene, and biotherapy

In this interspecies skilled delivery and 'doing' of care in chronic illness, blood activities become silently prominent: 'taking your bloods', giving blood, blood testing, blood glucose levels, and blood transfusions. Into this constant manipulation of blood cells swerves Mary Douglas's anthropological thinking on sullied contexts, dirt as 'matter out of place' (2002 [1966]: 44) and the dangers of pollutants, bringing contrast to medical enthusism for cleanliness in care and treatment practices.

Thoughts of zoönotic disease, health risk, and lack of hygiene at times when blood testing and insulin injection require 'purity' in the environment may inspire caution before preparing to care for, and be cared for by, a nonhuman animal sharing life day and night. Education in canine welfare and the use of efficient hygiene methods to control disease transmission between species can reduce health risk (Hart, 1995) as well as diminish fear at the prospect of an unknown or complex infection or illness.

However, looking at hygiene and disease from a different perspective, Elliott and Weinstock (2012: 551) find growing evidence that 'highly hygienic living conditions create risk for developing immune-mediated disease such as inflammatory bowel disease (IBD)'. Parasitic worms (helminths), for example, human hookworm and porcine whipworm, living in a symbiotic relationship with their hosts, become enabled to 'activate cells of innate and adaptive immunity that suppress inflammation' (2012: 551). It seems the more industrialised and

Multispecies care in chronic illness 21

socioeconomically advanced a country becomes, the more likely are its inhabitants to develop IBD; so, they conclude, exposure to helminths may offer new ways to treat IBD.

Elliott, Pritchard, and Weinstock (2013: 186) suggest that 'over the next few years, *T. suis* (porcine whipworm) will be tested for efficacy in many of the major autoimmune and immune-mediated inflammatory diseases like psoriasis and Type 1 diabetes'.

Other creatures reconsidered as beneficial to human health in recent decades are leeches, whose application in hirudotherapy to draw blood for 'curative purposes' is thought to have been effective since the Stone Age (Gileva and Mumcuoglu, 2013: 31). The researchers suggest that the usefulness of the leech in 'reconstructive and plastic surgery, and traumatology' and in other contemporary medicinal fields might assist in the creatures' protection and conservation in 'nature' (2013: 69), resulting in another form of symbiotic existence.

Biotherapy is defined as 'the use of living organisms for the treatment of human and animal illness' (Grassberger et al., 2013: v) and the increasing number of multidisciplinary practitioners and researchers in this field indicates growing acceptance of maggots (Bowling, Salgami, and Boulton, 2007), the 'most commonly employed larvae have been those of the green bottle fly (*Lucilia sericata*)' (Sherman et al. (2013), bees (*Apis mellifera*) (Molan and Betts, 2008), and leeches (*Hirudo medicinalis*) (Gileva and Mumcuoglu, 2013). Fish or ichthyotherapy involves, for example, the reddish suction barbel (*Garra rufa*) in therapeutic treatments (Grassberger and Sherman, 2013); more widely acknowledged is the ability of larger domesticated mammals, for example, dogs (*Canis familiaris*) and horses (*Equus caballus*), to aid mental and physical human corporeal complications (Levinson, 1969; Chandler, 2005; Fine, 2010). Church (2013: 4) suggests that instead of attempting to discover stronger antibiotics at a time when superbugs are showing firm resistance to current antibiotics, a burgeoning search for 'probiotics' should be encouraged so that natural mechanisms can be 'harnessed' towards preventing and managing disease, alongside care for the welfare of our environment.

According to Church (2013: 4), biotherapy is 'challenging and demanding, but it is efficacious, relatively safe, low tech, low cost, and eco-friendly' and the human–nonhuman animal collaboration involved in the diagnostic achievements of MDD exemplifies his contention.

Commodification and the ethics of care

The medical alert dogs became the 'other' species who caused my questioning of their cognitive abilities, their sensory perceptions, and their ways of being in our shared world. They show no artifice and little deception in the actions they perform with and towards their human caregivers. Chapter Two examines anthrozoological and sociological perspectives, raising ethical issues involved in the human use of other-than-human animals since the entwined strands of the human–dog symbiotic coexistence also are subject to issues of morality. Malamud's (2013: 34) forceful statement – 'service animals; serve us animals; serve us, animals' – sadly

22 *Multispecies care in chronic illness*

reflects our generally anthropocentric attitude to those sentient providers who are compelled to donate their lives to the supply of human foodstuffs, and to the burdened, scrutinised, and experimented-on subservient 'other' bodies we make use of for ourselves.

Josephine Donovan (2006: 305) elucidates the thinking behind the feminist animal care theory which stresses the need to listen to animals, to pay them 'emotional attention', to care about the content of their communications. Her approach counters the utilitarian argument of 'mathematical balance' – killing one to save the rest, as seen in the UK during the foot-and-mouth epidemic in which herds of cattle were destroyed on some farms to save others on neighbouring farms.

John Law's (2010: 57) 'care and killing' chapter on the 2001 slaughter, the results of which made distressing public viewing on television news channels, brought the pain of those carefully arranging the deaths into a world view. Farmers and veterinarians, who could be disparaged via social media as cruel administrators of this destruction of a trusting species, sometimes became known as unexpectedly caring and feeling enforcers of death for the betterment of others (in line with the government injunction) and themselves were perceived to suffer to the extent that some ignited their own manner of death. Zinsstag and Weiss (2001: 477), in an editorial comment on livestock diseases and human health which referred to healthy herd culling resulting from the foot-and-mouth outbreak, wrote that 'the psychological effects on farmers' well-being and mental health include enough human fatalities by suicide that coroners have recommended suicide prevention measures to farmers' unions'.

Hamington (2008: 177) proposes that we can learn ethics from meaningful relationships with animals by realising that quality interactions with other-than-human animals 'can stimulate the imaginative basis for the care and empathy that are crucial for social morality': through the use of the 'moral imagination', care can be universalised from one human or nonhuman to the many. His research on embodied care is significant in relation to mutualism and the co-practices of care performed within chronic illness.

The ecofeminist theory of care, discussed in articles collected and edited by Carol J. Adams and Lori Gruen (2014), has become a viable approach to aspects of this research with its emphasis on 'the importance of care as well as justice' (2014: 1). Contributing to their collection, and discussed more fully in future pages, is a paper written by Sunaura Taylor (2014), whose incisive approach to the interdependency of animal species brings the ethic-of-care theory to life when facing her own, and others', dis- or inabilities and society's reaction to them.

Accepting that compassion and empathy are crucial qualities for social morality relating to the human–canine relationships under focus here permits belief in a cross-species embodiment of moral interdependence that also succeeds in extending the biomedical armamentarium.

Prominent among researchers of multiple species' interactions are Frans de Waal (2006, 2010), who is visibly proactive in encouraging empathy to express and foster multispecies tolerance and understanding, and Lori Gruen (2015), whose

Multispecies care in chronic illness 23

writing concurs with the need for empathy to reduce or resolve human–human and human–nonhuman animal conflict in ways that can be considered moral.

Symbolic interactionism is among perspectives taken in order to understand the significance of a human–nonhuman animal collaboration that enhances the quality of life for individuals who may be rendered physically and/or socially isolated by chronic illness. Symbiotic relationships are examined in terms of commensalism, mutualism, and parasitism, with mutualism being identified as best suiting the human–canine partnerships under observation.

Foregrounding this research is the sense of smell and the outstanding olfactory ability of dogs and most other animal species. Chapter Three is devoted to olfactory perception, how aged memories are evoked by current and sudden pungencies, and how canine nasal architecture enables accurate odour detection and discrimination and the retention of scents.

In Chapter Four, focus centres on the ways people manage long-term corporeal dysfunction, highlighting Type 1 diabetes and its needs and complications (Diabetes UK, 2014; Juvenile Diabetes Research Foundation (JDRF), 2013a). The practical assistance given by the diabetes alert dogs at home and in public is made prominent, and their human partners provide narrative illustrations of the complexities involved in 'doing Type 1 diabetes'.

The controversial use of domesticated nonhuman animals as devices manipulated for human benefit – in this instance, dogs as biomedical resources and animate instruments – is the topic of Chapter Five in which such animal commodification may be considered tenable or exploitative. Addressed here in terms of theoretical evidence and practical application, is the question of whether these 'working' animals are health technologies, and their activities seen as similar to those performed by inanimate tools and assistance devices, so they 'become' equipment as well as autonomous assistants.

The meaning of care and its placement in contemporary language opens Chapter Six, which then highlights interspecies responsibilities and interdependencies and the role of mutualism, trust and respect in care practices. Coulter's (2016a) concept of an interspecies solidarity encourages a symbiotic ethic of care and moral justification for dogs' assistance work and contingent behaviours, activities in which emotion and empathy are vital drivers of concern for another's wellbeing. Flowing interspecies communication, involving circulation of silent yet graphic intention and meaning, becomes an essential part of daily life in which neither species seems conscious of a need for spoken words. However, the health and welfare of the canine partner are of primary significance to the chronically ill human colleague who must ensure the working dog has constant mental and physical ability and agility to perform regular routines and active alerts.

In conclusion, Chapter Seven, 'Endings', investigates 'what happens next' to the no-longer-working diabetes alert dog and to the unwell human when their biomedical partnership dissolves, and what it means from their perspectives to collaborate and coexist; more broadly, what cooperation in biotherapy and biomedicine will bring to illness detection through the sniffing prowess of nonhuman animals for the benefit of multiple other species.

24 *Multispecies care in chronic illness*

The multispecies storytellers

If everyday mixed-species living behind the front-door is to be revealed fully and accurately in descriptions and analyses that convey reliable human and nonhuman perspectives, findings should also be interpreted and reflected on in ways that are sensitive to the vulnerability of the multispecies storytellers. To aid confidentiality and privacy, names of both dogs and humans have been changed and no mention is made of the regions in which they reside. However, no matter how careful the attempts to disguise identity, the charity's human-alerting dog partnerships are not yet numerous, so participants may recognise one another from narrative excerpts, events, or experiences they mention that others may have witnessed, from talks they give to public audiences or from participation in media interviews. Their generosity of information lends credibility and impact to this exploration of chronic illness management.

The participant narrators, choreographing dances with dogs and chronic illness, are now introduced:

Sara and Apple

Sara lost her hypo-awareness after being ill with shingles and finding herself falling indoors and outside the school where she taught. She was close to losing her employment as a teacher because of her frequent collapses during school classes and the resultant need for 'time off' to make hurried visits to Accident and Emergency departments. After discussion with her family and with members of medical and educational institutions, she is now able to continue teaching classes with her alerting CockerPoo companion, Apple, in close attendance. 'He takes it all in his stride; he's used to 2000 pupils – kids and noise and that sort of environment doesn't faze him at all'. Apple was the family's first dog because Sara and her husband both work and had agreed that leaving a dog at home all day was 'not fair'; now Apple is her fulltime medical alert associate and is never left behind.

Terry and Jim

Terry has the brittle form of diabetes in which fluctuating blood sugar levels are more sudden and extreme, but he is helped constantly by Jim, his quick-witted and multi-skilled working dog. Jim displays his olfactory alerting sensitivity to Terry; he also collects and returns items such as the pen that fell unnoticed onto the carpet, which he carefully picks up and drops into my hand; he demonstrates how he attracts the attention of someone else to his human companion's health issues by jumping up and putting his front paws on their back (the only time he may jump up), and he fetches medical equipment when needed. 'We have a job to stop him working', claims Terry.

Richard and Higgins

When I first meet Richard, who lives and works in an urban environment, he tells me that he has never shared home life with a canine companion either as a child

Multispecies care in chronic illness   25

or as an adult, and he is awaiting the arrival of Higgins, his future diabetes alert dog, with some excitement and slight trepidation. He tells me that Higgins, a small CockerPoo, stayed with him for several days as a 'practice run' to see how they interacted and to find out whether Higgins would settle comfortably into Richard's way of life.

> He fitted in very well, was much liked by everyone and wasn't a problem in any way. I took him to a jazz restaurant where we sat at the front and he was absolutely fine.

Eighteen months later, Higgins has taken up permanent residence with Richard. We walk through a city park active with children, dogs, and bicycles, where Higgins runs free from leash restriction, sniffing tree roots and other items that call for investigation. He dashes back and forth, ears flapping and tail seeming to rotate and propel with undisguised joyfulness. While we talk, Higgins performs an alert by jumping up and scrabbling at Richard's knee, so Richard checks his blood sugar levels. 'Yes, I'm 6.5 and he knows that it's coming down as it was 16.5 mmol/l, a lot higher, at breakfast a couple of hours ago. It's going down but not to the level where I need to have a Jelly Babies boost'.

Paul and Nero

In an interview with Paul, who is vision impaired and has Type 1 diabetes, we discuss the quotient of successful canine alerts predictive of dropping blood sugar levels, and I wonder aloud if he is happy just having Labrador Nero as a companion, regardless of his alerting prowess. Paul blows out his cheeks, 'well, 90% of the time', and laughs. 'There are days . . . but having him gets me out, it gets me walking. I used to love walking and I still do', so they generally leave home, linked by a leash, and walk for about an hour every morning, and 30 minutes to an hour in the evening.

Janet and Alfie

Janet was diagnosed with Type 1 diabetes at the age of four. After several successful years of fulltime employment in the health professions, she became hypounaware and was no longer able to fulfil her work commitments. She has recently given birth to her first child in hospital, and with the support of her health care team, Labrador Alfie was permitted to stay in the ward for the days preceding the baby's arrival to maintain pre-hypo alerting and to ensure neither member of the partnership suffered additional anxiety or stress in the absence of the other.

Tina and Harley

After her parents died, Tina – who has had Type 1 diabetes for over 30 years alongside other autoimmune illnesses – and her four-month-old black Labrador

26 *Multispecies care in chronic illness*

puppy, Harley, were taken into sheltered housing: 'when you're in your late 40s, it's the last thing you want'. She searched online and found and applied to MDD. Her consultant and doctor were supportive, because every other option was 'dead'. Harley then received training in hyper- and hypodetection at the MDD centre so that he could become Tina's fulltime alert assistant:

> He alerts me to my highs, he alerts me to my lows, he also alerts me if I'm dropping quickly which I tend to do. I can be in the 20s and then drop to nothing. Now I can catch a bus, come to work, go shopping, go on holiday, go into hotels, go out for meals, do anything.

Mel and Gemma

> They call the dogs who work with the children 'Team Dogs' because they work as part of the group with the adult who cares for the child. The dog forms part of that team; the dog and the child don't work on their own like an adult partnership would. They call them 'Team Dogs' because the families are very much involved.

Mel's son, Mark, was diagnosed with Type 1 diabetes at the age of three, and has benefitted from the assistance given by Gemma, the family's canine companion, now trained in hypoalerting by MDD instructors. Mel describes Gemma's alerting practices:

> She's amazing at night. She sleeps on the bed with him and if there's a problem, she comes from his bedroom doorway to mine. If I'm only sleeping lightly, then I'll hear her claws coming across the floorboards and she'll greet me with the meter in her mouth. But if I don't wake up when she does that, she goes back into his room, comes back through our doorway, goes back into his room, comes out again and goes back – and then she barks. That seems to be the pattern.

The diabetic alert dogs are fully appreciated by the individuals with health issues whom they assist, but whether the people they meet socially recognise and comprehend the degree of assistance available from and given by another species, is less certain, since so much of their sensory work is invisible to public observation. The similarity is striking in terms of the invisibility of the two minority groups here: there is rare public recognition of the immensity of the dogs' sensory assistance and, in general, there is no social awareness of the human partners' chronic illness and inabilities. Sara comments on the invisibility of diabetes: 'it's a very hidden disability, isn't it?'

The illness condition Type 1 diabetes has no cure or clinical treatment to prevent its development, so innovative procedures to improve self-care practices and strategies, augmenting lifestyle management, are crucial requirements for day-to-day living and for the social integration of individuals with this illness, who may have to endure a lifetime of specialised behaviours. How these care strategies are embodied in individual and collective health practices and routines is learned from observing the daily activities and behaviours of people with Type 1 diabetes who share their lives with medical alert assistance dogs and by listening to their significant personal narratives.

Research by Annemarie Mol (2008) has influenced this study insofar as her intentions of writing to 'articulate the specificities of good care' within the parameters of diabetes 'so that we may talk about it' (2008: 2), perhaps may resonate effectively in this examination of care practices conducted within the mutual coexistences of medical alert assistance dogs and their human companions with Type 1 diabetes. In so resonating, this will inform members of society who may currently lack knowledge of symptoms, side effects and treatments for this complex illness and may be unaware of the efficient interspecies collaboration that can prevent the unpleasant effects of hypoglycaemia.

In the recent past, anthrozoology has 'prioritized' (Hurn, 2010: 27) the human-observed aspects of trans-species interactions, objectifying the nonhuman animals under focus. But today's researchers are more likely to observe and accept nonhuman animals as 'social actors in their own right' and, like us, as doers of their own thing. Further, compassion and empathy may now be incorporated in human endeavours to take up, as far as possible, the nonhuman's sensory perspectives so as to see, hear, smell, taste, and touch aspects of their worlds in order to better comprehend them and those who inhabit them, what they do and how they react, how they impact their environments and experience their surroundings.

2 Anthrozoological and sociological perspectives

This study endeavours to project the moral values to be learned and social life-style benefits to be gained by two minority groups as a result of interspecies collaboration and coexistence, actively applied to good effect with the biomedical knowledge and canine training skills of staff of MDD.

Also for discussion is whether such a symbiotic coexistence might occasionally fail to benefit either species or might cause unanticipated difficulty in terms of health and welfare since there is no way to avoid the ethical whirlpool in which the human use of nonhuman others is directed towards human health benefit, and such usage may be condemned as morally wrong by animal rights advocates and others. This is not the issue of bovine tuberculosis or the culling of badger populations, nor the fight for survival of foxes in town and country. It is not related to the grave matters of puppy-milling, abandoned 'Christmas present pets', or underground illegal dog fighting, all of which urgently require continuing in-depth research and applied solutions. As mentioned later in the context of animal exploitation, this research is not about intentional cruelty to domestic nonhuman animals nor about laboratory experimentation on caged species but it does investigate the moral dilemma of using animal 'others', however kindly, as commodities for bettered human lives.

Disability brought about by chronic illness can enforce a bounded way of life – an occasionally oppressive need for the security of routine and control tied into the frustration of needing to need – onto individuals requiring assistance to perform essential daily practices. This produces a social minority group entitled to, although sometimes disenfranchised from, what are termed 'human rights'. The multispecies search for 'rights' to freedom of access, for example, becomes an entanglement such as that described in the writings of David Nibert (2002: xiii), who claims that

> The oppression of other animals has been devastating for the cultural, spiritual and economic well-being of the vast majority of humans . . . the oppression of devalued groups of humans has been, and remains, disastrous for other animals.

Nibert presents challenges to the customary definition of two terms 'minority group' and 'speciesism', both of which have significance for the human-nonhuman

Anthrozoological and sociological perspectives 29

partnerships central to this study. Nibert contends that 'minority group' was a term used to define groups which 'differed from the one that controlled society' (2002: 6) and that it became commonplace for sociologists to consider minority group members as different or 'special'. As a result, he finds 'oppressed group' to be more accurate than 'minority group' in that the term avoids 'the human-centred concept of minority groups and helps challenge the prevailing view that human use and mistreatment of other animals lies in the realm of "natural affairs" ' (2002: 7).

However, 'minority' rather than 'oppressed' will be used here to describe the two marginal groupings of humans with Type 1 diabetes and the assistant dogs who collaborate in care provision, since it is their minimal number and their changing social identities and status that feature most prominently.

Qualified medical alert assistance dogs, as is the case for other accredited assistance dogs, have been granted legal rights to access shops and institutions, public transport, theatres and cinemas, hotels, and university lecture halls. Their animal 'rights' are reflected in human disability rights' imperatives – members of both species are constrained under the minority group banner of individuals requiring 'rights' – a label which continues to invite condescension, prejudice, and devaluation despite improved social awareness, advocacy, and activism. Nocella, Bentley and Duncan (2012: xvi) strive for an eco-ability approach, a meshing of ecology and ability among human and nonhuman animals and nature, that 'argues for the respect of difference and diversity, challenging social constructions of what is considered normal and equal'.

Literature investigating the advantages of animal–human interactions in the context of health and wellness has increased nationally and internationally over the past 50 years. Levinson (1969), Fine (2010), Friedmann, Son and Tsai (2010), and Wilson and Turner (1998), are among the interdisciplinary researchers whose studies are well-cited. Lynette Hart draws attention to the value of 'pet' animals in enhancing human quality of life 'that can stem an unravelling decline into disability or disease'; but she adds the significant rider: 'they only rarely offer a pathway to curing disease' (2010: 63). Although trained medical alert assistance dogs are regarded both as working dogs and as companion animals, there is no pretence that they can provide a cure for diabetes. However, their exceptional olfactory prescience can dramatically enhance quality of life and enable the provision of an acceptable and more secure standard of living it, when viewed from both medical and societal standpoints.

Much has appeared in the media over recent decades that relates to assistant animals and their human carers and to the dogs who guide humans with visual impairments through life. Contemporary sociology frames research and writing, by Krieger (2005, 2010), Michalko (1999), and others whose vision is partially or wholly impaired, which draws attention to the ways their assistant dogs have made significant, positive differences to their lives. However, there is sparse research, beyond media investigative reporting, that examines the day-to-day lived experiences of scent-detecting dogs and the significant impact they have on humans with malfunctioning internal organs.

30 *Anthrozoological and sociological perspectives*

Disenfranchisement because of disability frequently isolates the chronically ill, so the company of a dog bolsters safety in public venues while aiding social integration and shoring up self-confidence in knowing the dog can act promptly in bringing medical assistance and equipment when required.

The dogs themselves were the 'other' species who made me question their cognitive abilities, their sensory perceptions, and their ways of being in our shared world. They show no artifice and little deception in the actions they perform with and towards their human caretakers. The communications 'flowing' between each species allow for external physical intermingling and internal mental porosity, and this appears to result in caring engagements. The dogs act as beings who help and are worthy of help. Symbiotic relationships flourish, and good companionship and mutual understanding are offered and accepted without much use of spoken language.

Reviewing research sourced principally from the disciplines of anthrozoology and the sociology of health and illness, it appears that human–nonhuman animal cooperation can offer significant multispecies welfare benefit. Rock and Babinec (2008) offer an example supporting this collaboration, in relation to diabetes in people and in their domesticated companion animals. The fact that diabetes also is a condition affecting dogs and cats, who therefore require similar medical treatment to that needed by humans, produces what Rock and Babinec (2008: 325) term 'intricate' multispecies 'interconnections'.

There is an essential closeness in such complex and intimate practices. During the years spent caring for 'holiday' dogs, a small, wavy-coated elderly dog came to stay regularly, bringing her case of syringes and needles, insulin vials, and specific food items; her agenda for treatment was exacting. Meals were served to her three times a day, with a precise number of hours between each, and an injection into the loose skin on the back of her neck was to be given before she could eat, according to written instructions. Seemingly simple, it proved not to be so when other domesticated species also required caring attention: she travelled with me to collect prescribed food from veterinarians, to deliver dogs to their family homes, and on other similar journeys, in order that any delay on the road would not disrupt her diabetes management. Her medical bag and weighed food came too and we sat in car parks and roadside lay-bys following the rules of time and insulin donation. As a result of our intricate and, to my mind, mutually empathic interconnection – her patience with my tapping of the syringe to remove any air bubbles and fiddling to find space on the back of her neck that was not thickened by years of injection – my appreciation of her stoicism and tolerance grew into attachment. She became a friend because of the 'intricacies' of her illness.

The medical alert assistance dog is a working animal companion, treated for the most part as a family member who has a keen olfactory talent for helping human health to improve. Rarely do the human partners label their canine companions 'pets' unless in answer to an enquiry asking for clarification of the dog's identity in their minds as 'piece of equipment' and/or 'pet'. In recent decades, since the interspecies initiatives taken by Arluke and Sanders (1996), Bryant (1979), and Levinson (1969), 'pet' has taken on problematic connotations of dominance and hierarchy in human–human and nonhuman–human animal social engagement.

Anthrozoological and sociological perspectives 31

Belk (1996: 139) suggests that 'it is their metaphoric status as loved ones that keeps pets from being regarded as mindless machines, programmed computer games, or even livestock'. Because pets are considered to be 'more than machines' but 'less than humans', Belk contends that it is this incomplete human status that 'places pets in presumed need of our care' and at the same time grants us 'impunity in treating them as subhuman' (1996: 139). Earlier, Belk (1988: 139) examined the relationship between 'possessions and the sense of self', a concept appropriate to UK legislation which considers domestic animals to be property of their 'owners' (refer to Animal Welfare Act, 2006).

Nobis (2016), for example, pinpoints the use of the word 'pet' as signifying ownership, and thus property, which can for the most part be manipulated or destroyed without criminal liability, an aspect of law that requires amendment particularly in the context of domestic abuse where animals may be injured or killed to wreak malevolence on a human partner who has no recourse to law when the abuser resides on the property and the abused nonhuman animal is 'owned' by the abuser. If an animal is considered to be an 'owned' pet, rather than a nonhuman animal companion, the consequence may be a worrying avoidance of the need to consider or care well for the owned creature, and invites recollection of Descartes' mechanistic animals which, rather than *who* in this context, have no conscious awareness and can thus be treated as insentient objects. But Coppinger and Coppinger suggest, with reference to domesticated companion animals, 'we do not think of owning them any more than we would think of owning a child, even though we pay all the bills' (2016: 129).

A 'pet' or 'to pet' may not only lead to contexts of objectification and thoughts of superiority and control but can also involve considerations of bestiality and zoophilia. Heidi Nast (2006: 301) recollects the research of Marc Shell (1986: 122) in which he explored the sexual, familial, and social role that the 'institution of pethood plays in contemporary politics and ideology'. She continues:

> As an anthropologist, he (*Shell*) wanted to explore the limits of that familial relationship, both ideologically and in practice: can one love or marry a pet (leading to a discussion of petting, puppy love, Playboy bunnies, and so on); and would physical love with a pet (especially dogs) be akin to bestiality? Incest? Or neither?
>
> (Nast, 2006: 301)

Bearing in mind Haraway's (2003: 11–12) claim that dogs 'are not a projection, nor the realization of an intention, nor the *telos* of anything. They are dogs; i.e., a species in obligatory, constitutive, historical, protean relationship with human beings', Heidi Nast (2006: 325) explicates contemporary inferences relative to 'pets':

> Pet animals have become variably positioned screens onto which all kinds of needs and desires are projected; they co-habit with humans; their production and investment is tied to globalized pet industries and genetic engineering;

32 *Anthrozoological and sociological perspectives*

and the ethics of pet–human encounters is riven with complexities and specificities that few have explored.

Similarly, Hurn (2012: 110), noting that pets can be 'companion animals, working animals and friends, mascots, accessories, mediators and victims of human control', also remarks the 'fluidity' of the 'membership criteria for the category "pet"'; thus, my concern at using the word 'pet' despite its still-common usage in conversation. However, exchanging 'pet' for the term 'companion animal', preferably 'friend' (Hurn, 2012: 110), allows opportunity for a greater interspecies equality and at least a human recognition of another species' socioemotional worth; and perhaps removes one thin layer from the onion of domesticated animal commodification.

> Companion animals can be horses, dogs, cats, or a range of other beings willing to make the leap to the biosociality of service dogs, family members, or team members in cross-species sports. Generally-speaking, one does not eat one's companion animals (nor get eaten by them).
>
> (Haraway, 2003: 14)

Symbiotic relationships

Fuentes (2010: 600) reflected on the entwined lives of humans and monkeys in Bali to demonstrate that 'both species are simultaneously actors and participants in sharing and shaping mutual ecologies'. They may be partners in complex relationships, sharing histories and social behaviours and co-creating their practices and environments. Co-creating care practices and domestic environments around their already-domesticated selves are the medical alert assistance dogs and chronically ill humans who spin and weave their interlacing existences around Type 1 diabetes.

Coppinger and Coppinger (2016) disentangle the imbricating layers of commensalism, mutualism, and parasitism involved in symbiotic relationships. They talk of 'overlapping' and 'changing' niches which require species adaptation, and the advantages, or lack of, to be gained by 'living in proximity' (2016: 130). Reliance on and responsibility for the self and other are essential elements of companionable relationships, so interspecies trust becomes implicit to conducting symbiotic partnerships and to demonstrating successful ways of living together in chronic illness.

An Acarine tick of the genera *Rhipicephalus* or *Amblyomma* has long been considered to have a parasitic symbiotic relationship with, for example, the buffalo (*Syncerus caffer*) on which it feeds since the burdened animal gains nothing but skin irritation and possible disease. On the other hand, the red-billed oxpecker (*Buphagus erythrorhynchus*), perched on the buffalo and removing the blood-sucking ticks, does have a mutualistic relationship with the host animal – the latter is cleansed of disease-donating ticks and the bird gains nutrition – neither harms the other. However, research by McElligott et al. (2004) suggests that this bird, in searching for parasites and larvae, frequently opens old scars and creates

Anthrozoological and sociological perspectives 33

new wounds on the host animal, causing increased bleeding and irritation; so the oxpecker then becomes a less-than-equal partner, one whose behaviour verges on parasitism and not mutualism – and the buffalo remains host sometimes to a mutualistic symbiont, sometimes to a parasitic one.

There are flexible shades of meaning overhanging these symbiotic relationships. 'Even though the different organisms are not in constant physical contact, the parties involved rely upon the association to fulfil a major part of their life cycles', suggest Leung and Poulin (2008: 107). They propose that where the host and symbiont reciprocally benefit from the relationship, the association represents mutualism, whereas if the symbiont utilises the host without benefitting or harming it, it is considered as a commensal. If, however, the symbiont (for example, the oxpecker) is using the host (for example, the buffalo) as a resource and causing harm as a result, then the bird qualifies as a parasite.

There are further intricacies within mutualistic relationships involving obligatory and facultative dependencies: obligatory organisms cannot survive in the absence of the other partner, whereas facultative organisms are able to exist independently. Coppinger and Coppinger (2016: 131) flag up the hummingbird–flower image of obligatory mutualism whereby the hummingbird (*Trochilidae*) cannot survive without the flower because its 'designer bill' has evolved to enable the bird to reach needed nectar from that plant, but conversely, the flower cannot survive if pollen is not transferred to others via the bird's bill.

A complex example of a multispecies mutualistic relationship in sub-Saharan Africa, is that of the greater honeyguide (*Indicator indicator*), who is known to give a loud and distinctive call to 'solicit the assistance of a symbiont', human or honey badger (*Mellivora capensis*), in opening wild bees' (*Apis mellifera scutellata*) nests (Hurn, 2012: 115). When the human recognises the call and follows the honeyguide, the bird will lead the way to the nest; the human honey-hunter retrieves the honeycomb required and the bird is rewarded with a safely-opened nest and the remaining honeyless waxy combs – collaborative foraging highlighting mutualism on a grand scale. Budiansky (1997: 47–49) similarly draws attention to the Boran people of northern Kenya who 'still collect wild honey following the practices of their ancestors'. The Boran honey collectors watch the flight patterns and listen to the vocalizations of the honeyguide which informs them of the 'direction and distance to a nest, guides them to it, and alerts them when the nest is reached' (1997: 47).

Spottiswoode, Begg and Begg (2016) ascertained further that the honeyguide recruitment and foraging collaboration could also be initiated by the human. They report that Yao honey-hunters in northern Mozambique use a loud trilling and a particular grunting sound, learned from their fathers, to attract the honeyguide's attention and so increase the probability of finding a bee's nest. Spottiswoode, Begg and Begg (2016) suggest these results provide experimental evidence that a wild animal in a natural setting responds adaptively to a human signal of cooperation.

As these researchers contend, humans use many species, for example, hounds or cormorants, to find food, and these co-opted 'companions' are trained to

34 *Anthrozoological and sociological perspectives*

collaborate in the hunt for prey. Alternatively, Miklósi and Topál (2013: 5) suggest the rat (*Rattus norvegicus*) exemplifies a 'competitive inter-specific relationship' wherein the human may 'actively act against the intruding species'. Over millennia, a human home may have become the natural setting for dogs as companion species, and an adaptive, well motivated, and domesticated canine may find the lived-in accommodation to be worthy of interspecies coexistence (and even that mutual cooperation with a human symbiont might be sufficiently rewarding), but it cannot be said that a human home is a natural 'wild' location or situation for a dog vis à vis that of the 'village' dogs of the world (Coppinger and Coppinger, 2016).

Continuing the theme of divisions in symbiotic relationships, Coppinger and Coppinger disparage the 'stories full of euphoria' about useful and helpful working dogs, and the assumption that 'dogs and people live together for each species' mutual benefit' (2016: 224). They give an example of the connection between 'guide dog and blind person [that] is not exactly mutualism because it doesn't have much if any benefit for the sterilized and constantly controlled dog' (2016: 224). However, from the small sample of assistance dog–chronically ill human partnerships I have observed in this research, in guide dog and vision-impaired human relationships viewed previously, and from personal research conducted by Michalko (1999) and others, it appears that a mutualistic coexistence can offer benefit to both. The domestic dog, living alongside the human animal species for thousands of years, has perhaps become accustomed to working for human-given reward. It may be a very different lifestyle to that of their village-residing kindred, but the human partner of an assistance dog is willing to pay and provide optimum welfare, care, and attention that includes daily off-leash 'free-running', in return for an attentive sniff or safe guidance around unseen hazards.

Coppinger and Coppinger consider the dog–human symbiotic relationship in terms of 'obligatory' commensalism (2016: 134): if dogs were removed from the relationship, people would survive, but, they assert, if humans left the equation, dogs would not. 'Wilderness niches' adapted to the lives of 'wolves, coyotes, jackals and foxes', would be unavailable to dogs suddenly forced to hunt for food, they suggest (2016: 133). However, their very adaptability to experiences and environments, their capacity for social learning 'by observing conspecifics' (Miklósi, 2009: 191; Pongrácz et al., 2003) might ensure they would create new niches and increasingly large communities (safety in numbers and wider choice of hunting dogs) within very brief moments of time.

Leung and Poulin's (2008) exploration of the symbiosis continuum, along which parasitism, commensalism and mutualism shift and 'overlap', reviews investigations in which symbiotic interactions are argued to be 'highly plastic across circumstances and timescales' (2008: 107). Their study details 'how easily symbiotic associations can switch between mutualism and parasitism in response to even the slightest environmental change' (2008: 107). Although the subjects of the studies they review are chiefly marine organisms, plants, and insects, and symbiosis is generally used within biological and ecological research, this umbrella term covering parasitism, mutualism, and commensalism can also be opened to

Anthrozoological and sociological perspectives 35

include multispecies human–nonhuman plastic interactions that make up the ever-changing coexistences of diabetes alert dogs and humans with Type 1 diabetes.

Commensalism is an association between two organisms in which one benefits and the other does not, but neither is the latter harmed (Leung and Poulin, 2008; Miklósi and Topál, 2013: 5; Coppinger and Coppinger, 2016: 133–135). So that fails to describe the interspecies relationships referred to here, since both species gain some benefit from their partnership and neither of them harm nor is intentionally harmed by the other, if the human domus were to be considered natural habitat to the long-domesticated canine companion.

Chimpanzees (*Pan troglodytes*) (Hare, Call and Tomasello, 2001, 2006; Hare et al., 2000; de Waal, 2010) and corvids (*Corvidae*) (Emery and Clayton, 2001) are among species now considered to possess aspects of a 'theory of mind', and able to recognise the mental states of other beings. The dog in this context is considered to have the capacity for intention, even 'a precursory theory of mind' (Reid, 2009); there may not be 'thinking or planning' as those concepts are understood linguistically, but dogs do organise their living in multiple ways so as to obtain the food, shelter, mates, and playmates that they require beyond the present.

It is this notion of interwoven, flexible, mutualistic coexistences that supports research into the shared lives of the agentic medical alert assistance dog and a person with chronic Type 1 diabetes. The canine-human partnerships involved in this study restructure their former ways of being and living into synchronised performances of mutual care; performances similar to those coembodied inter- and intra-active roles played in the human–horse relationships described earlier by Maurstad, Davis and Cowles (2013).

The working dog

The following examination of the recent history of the working dog is supported by a review of canine domestication (Clutton-Brock, 1995) and Helton's research into canine ergonomics (2009). Also discussed here are methods of training 'working' dogs (Savalois, Lescureux and Brunois, 2013; Miklösi, 2009), the charity Medical Detection Dogs' concept of acceptable dog training, and discussion of the criteria enabling eligible chronically ill individuals to invest in assistive relationships with diabetes alert dogs and to develop mutually dedicated biomedical partnerships.

Domestication and history of the working dog

A brief history of the close relationship that has developed between humans and dogs over millennia is now investigated, with examination of the speculation or imagination involved in inferred conclusions as to how these very different species of animal have learned to coexist companionably.

> Man (sic) is far from the only species to practice domestication. . . . The state of dependence of one species upon another . . . is a finely-honed evolutionary

36 *Anthrozoological and sociological perspectives*

strategy for survival. In a world made up so much of competition for survival, nature has with surprising frequency cast upon the solution of cooperation.

Budiansky (1997: 17)

Clutton-Brock (1995 [2008]) observes that *Canis familiaris*, the omnivorous but chiefly carnivorous animal who is globally recognised and identified as a dog, is considered the only fully domesticated member of the canine family, *Canidae*. Listing 38 species within this family, she acknowledges earlier studies that indicate the wolf, *Canis lupus*, to be the principal ancestor of our current most favoured companion animal, notwithstanding the feral Australian dingo who is related to the pariah dogs of Southeast Asia as well as to the wolf.

Exactly when the 'domestic' dog split from its lupine relation is inconclusive and currently ranges between 150,000 years ago and 15,000 years ago. Both Helton (2009) and Miklósi (2009) highlight the contentions of Csányi (2005) and Vila et al. (1997) who argue that if the divergence of dogs from wolves occurred 150,000 years ago, this was close to the date ascribed to the *Homo sapiens sapiens'* divergence from other *Homo sapiens*, such as *Homo sapiens Neanderthals*, and therefore 'could be a pivotal point in both human and dog evolution' (Helton, 2009: 2). Adding to the evolutionary quandary is the Coppinger and Coppinger (2016) enquiry as to which wolf ancestor became the antecedent of today's domestic dog since wolves, coyotes, jackals and dingoes all fall under the Linnaeus-classified genus *Canis* and are 'interfertile' (2016: 9).

Accepted as the first animal species to be domesticated, seemingly by hunter-gatherers at the end of the last Ice Age, dogs were thought to have assisted humans in tracking, guarding, and hunting; for examples, refer to Clutton-Brock (1995), Coppinger and Coppinger (2016), Miklósi (2009) and Serpell (1995). Miklósi (2009: 96–97) provides five theories of domestication that, if combined, offer a comprehensive view of dogs' evolutionary process. He explains (2009: 103–109) the sequence of events over millennia in which bones of working dogs have been uncovered during archaeological research; research which suggests that dogs have accompanied humans for many thousands of years in terms of interspecies companionship as well as for hunting, protection, and the retrieval of fallen prey.

Estimates vary as to when human cohabitation with *Canis familiaris* began, but coexistence must have had valuable advantage over life in separate communities. Admittedly, mutual tolerance is likely to have taken considerable time to form and become a useful characteristic, just as smaller size would become evolutionarily beneficial in domestication. It seems likely that groups of both humans and nonhumans gained from interspecies cooperation and companionship as well as from competition and contest in terms of hunting guidance and resultant share of the proceeds. But as Miklósi (2009: 130) intimates, it may be 'impossible to isolate a single selective factor, a single trait, and a single causal chain for determining morphological and behavioural changes during dog domestication'.

Anthrozoological and sociological perspectives   37

Over centuries, dogs' natural wildness has been tamed and adapted to suit human ownership and their formerly liberated status has altered dramatically, turning large numbers of this species into property, mandatory in Britain, or a commodity that currently can be bought and sold, used and discarded.

Thurston (1996) writes of 'our 15,000-year love affair with dogs', highlighting the interspecies links that promoted healing as long ago as the time of the Egyptian Pharaohs when deceased respected dogs were mummified and placed in the tombs of their owners. Since Roman times, dog breeds have been developed to be functional, with the chief purpose being companionship (Clutton-Brock, 1995). The aristocracy of Ancient Egypt, Greece and Rome appeared to value their dogs greatly, wrote poems to them and erected shrines and monuments to remember them (Thurston, 1996; Serpell, 1986 [1996]).

Cemeteries in the United Kingdom, designated for companion animal interment, bear witness to valued former animal companions (Toms, 2006). An example is the Hyde Park cemetery, created in the late 1880s, which contains more than 300 engraved memorials to loved dogs, interred there within a brief 12-year span (Thurston, 1996).

A secondary result from selective dog breeding, identified by Clutton-Brock, has been to 'increase the personal status of the owner at home or in the hunt' (1995: 18). A collection of papers edited by Cassidy and Mullin (2007) lays out the evolution and purpose of dog breeding and brings the concept of genetic engineering into modern-day reproductive practices that create the 'wanted' family, sporting or working dog, or the neotonised puppy/childlike 'pet' dog. Greenebaum's family dogs, attending 'Yappy Hour' with their 'parents', are 'elevated to the status of children, or fur babies' and 'by treating the dogs like children and following traditional gender roles and expectations, the dog owners' status becomes elevated to parent' (2004: 132).

Dogs may be considered multifunctional, being purchased to boost the owner's social status, to provide company for children or to provide a sentient, live companion when family homes become 'single' accommodation. Their functioning as extensions of the human self may be seen here in their embodiment of the human-needed self-awareness of approaching hypoglycaemic episodes. Irvine draws attention to the 'behavioral flexibility' of nonhuman animals, which adaptability indicates consciousness 'because it implies monitoring of one's own performance' (Irvine, 2007: 9) and, in Type 1 diabetes assistance, the monitoring of another's performance as one's own.

Participants in this project confirm that dogs assist those who have difficulty in performing certain tasks, as well as enabling their independence and more secure home life, all of which lead to the improved physical and mental well-being of their human companions. However, based on their innate abilities and under human instruction, dogs have also become universal items of technology, learning to conduct a wide range of tasks as circus performers, hunting hounds, dogfight participants, bomb detectors, guide dogs or guard dogs, and for these efforts, they are variously appreciated.

38 *Anthrozoological and sociological perspectives*

Stray dogs and village dogs

Those of the canine species who lack human-required capabilities, who are less attractive to purchasers or 'rescuers' than others around them, or whose temperaments fail to meet the required standard, also fail to be appreciated as well-functioning members of society. Dependent on their location in the human world, they may be euthanized or discarded, passed from home to home to street where they join stray dog communities surviving on street-pickings and foraging on rubbish dumps, scavenging on middens as their ancestors have done for thousands of years. More than 50,000 street dogs were said to inhabit the city of Bucharest in Romania (Crețan, 2015: 159) until the 2013 Stray Dog Euthanasia Law established an intensive cull to purge the city of dogs who were considered aggressive to humans. Similarly concerned was the 'mayoral committee member for safety and security J P Smith [who] said the city (*of Cape Town, South Africa*) had at least 230 000 stray dogs' (Lewis, Western Cape News, 5 July 2011).

As Coppinger and Coppinger (2016) remark, dogs are ubiquitous throughout the world and number approximately one billion, although the majority of these are 'village dogs' who mostly fend for themselves and cannot therefore be termed 'pets', 'companion animals' or 'assistance' dogs.

Interesting to this project is the arrival of 'rescued' dogs from South Korea who may be considered 'village dogs', whether they were specifically bred for sale at dog meat markets or were captured while roaming for later human consumption. They have travelled across the world to take on the vastly different role and status of cancer detection dogs at the MDD training centre. Although they continue to be 'used', their employment will be in a strikingly different format to that of their prior exploitation: not only are they likely to survive and enjoy a lengthened life, they will receive constant human attention to their needs, and in return, they will be requested to perform an activity that is natural to them when attending to the significant health requirements of another species: the seemingly simple act of sniffing human odour. Importantly, MDD's cancer detection dogs live in homes as family members and visit the training centre to work on samples for short periods of time two to four times a week, so these well-travelled dogs will have opportunity to belong to a multispecies community as friends and colleagues as well as scent detection technologists.

> To promote life, biopolitics must continuously determine not only what it is to be a living thing, but also which lives are better able to be developed, which lives are worthy of enhancement, which are left to perish, and which are terminated in the name of sustaining or preserving other life.
>
> (Blue and Rock, 2011: 357)

This may convey shades of human domination and power as referred to in Ingold's (2000) research on trust and control in domestication, and which argument is countered by Karen Armstrong Oma's (2010) response urging human–animal social contracts, as first proposed by Mary Midgley (1983), centring instead on

Anthrozoological and sociological perspectives 39

'notions of trust and reciprocity' (2010: 177). In the same context, Clare Palmer's (1997) research deals with the problematic issues of inequality and lack of free consent in the creation of a domesticated animal contract.

Fijn (2011) highlights co-domestication between herders and their herds in Mongolia, examining reciprocal social behaviour and communication between humans and other animals as being important elements of animal domestication within today's cross-species communities. Distant as that coexisting collective may be from the medical assistance dogs sharing life with their human partners in urban England, the concept of a multispecies social giving-and-taking reverberates between them.

John Hartigan's thoughts on domestication, in *Aesop's Anthropology: a multispecies approach*, flag up mutuality in terms of anthropology's 'new' consideration of animals as active agents in the production of 'the companion specieshood that has so transformed the globe' (2014: 72). While agreeing with the mutuality concept, the aforesaid transformation of the globe seems still to have a long journey to travel. But Cassidy and Mullin (2007: 6) suggest that efforts are now being made to 'replace the unidirectional, progressive history of increasingly exploitative relationships with the environment, with a more halting and incomplete vision . . . [in which] . . . emphasis has been placed on mutual interaction between human and nonhuman species'. And such mutuality can result in a companionable coexistence and a collaborative friendship (Hurn, 2012) based on trust and reciprocated practices of care, easing a smoother path through what Hartigan (2014: 72) terms the 'muddled terrain "between" the human and the nonhuman, that of domestication'.

Continuing with the theme of *using* animals, we make daily use of our own human–animal physical and mental attributes for profit, be it for the education, entertainment, or welfare of others as well as ourselves. Indeed, being employed instantly places metaphorical yokes and chains around human individuals, regardless of the nature of the occupation. Self-interest that engages security and protection for the self emerges from Hobbes' (1962 [1651]) social contract theory, which signifies the transition from the state of nature to the state of civil society; a transition in which the selfish humans' 'acquisition of scarce resources, their own safety and their own reputation' is prominent (Leviathan 1(13) in Palmer, 1997: 414). There is no trust and threats to life are all-encompassing, so self-interest is a means to self-security.

However, this concept may be problematic for some, as reflected in Palmer's (1997: 411) 'idea of the domesticated animal contract', since the avenues open for human choice and accord as to suitable terms of use or employment, may be closed to any nonhuman animal agency wishing to consent or agree to it.

In Britain, dogs are considered to be possessions, the property of human owners, and if found straying, may be impounded for seven days while the owners are accessed; then if not claimed as belonging to someone, they may be 'disposed of' by finding them new homes with persons 'who, in our opinion, will care properly' for them or by 'putting them to sleep' (London Borough of Barking and Dagenham Council, 2017). A Parliamentary discussion on UK stray dog control, based on information sourced from a Dogs Trust Stray Dog Survey 2016 summary report

40   *Anthrozoological and sociological perspectives*

(September 2016: 6), contended that the number of stray dogs had dropped to 81,000 in 2016 from 102,000 the previous year and from 136,500 in 1997. An explanatory note to the Environmental Protection (Stray Dogs) Regulations 1992 No. 288, that is 'not part of the Regulations', mentions that an officer is obliged to keep 'a register of dogs "seized" by him or her' which conjures Hogarth-style images of power and pain but is hopefully a mere doffed cap to the official linguistics of a previous era. These roaming dogs became the responsibility of local authorities instead of the police under the Clean Neighbourhoods and Environment Act 2005.

Compulsory microchipping of all dogs from the age of eight weeks was mandated in the UK in April 2016, with advice that every dog should wear a collar with the owner's name and address on a tag attached to it.

The domesticated companion canine, living within a human home, enables the human–nonhuman animal bond to strengthen and intensify. These are dogs who may provide reason for human exercise, improved health, and social integration, who encourage empathy and compassion for other species, who may be perceived as surrogate children in 'empty nest' homes and who often maintain an active link between their bereaved human carer and his or her deceased partner. Their human guardians see them as family members, treat them as best they can and are anecdotally likely to settle their veterinary, animal nutrition, and welfare bills before buying their own food or paying household accounts.

Dogs living in human households have majorly altered 'Western' cultural habits for both interacting species; for example, gaining legal rights to travel on public transport and enter museums or educational institutions, or achieving the widespread availability of 'pet' medical insurance policies. But on the downside, often based on human change in socioeconomic status or alteration in life to a more penurious, even criminal, style of living, there may be opportunity for the denigration of the interspecies bond, to abandoning, selling, starving, neglecting, or abusing the creature previously welcomed and treated as a family member.

Statistics for 2018 published by the Pet Food Manufacturers Association (PFMA) claim that nine million dogs are currently inhabiting 26% of UK households, evidence which certainly appears to support the British public's alleged 'love' of dogs. These population figures were published by the PFMA after survey results, averaged over two years, gave an effective sample of over 8,000 people, and estimated that 12 million (45%) of UK households have companion animals in their homes. Wells, Lawson, and Siriwardena published research on canine response to hypoglycaemia in Type 1 diabetes patients and noted that, according to PFMA statistics in 2008, this nation of 'self-confessed' animal lovers then shared their homes with six million dogs (2008: 1235) – so the increase in UK dog numbers is substantial.

Canine ergonomics: the science of the working dog

Bearing the 'best candidate model' in mind, Helton (2009) introduces the notion of canine ergonomics, the science of working dogs, to name a new perspective integrating animal science and ergonomics. As a science, ergonomics fits and

Anthrozoological and sociological perspectives 41

matches workers to their work so that comfort and suitability are of paramount importance, and productivity is therefore expected to increase.

Suggesting that ergonomics may also be considered 'the study of entities that share human capacities in working situations' (2009: 4) – entities who in this instance are flexible and able to work autonomously – Helton underlines the value of working dogs acting as human surrogates. Incorporated into the human workplace in order to clear minefields, detect illegally transported drugs, or discover victims buried under avalanche or destroyed buildings, 'sniffer' dogs are encouraged to perform tasks in areas where human lives may be at risk or in which they are unable to achieve equivalent success.

Human and canine expertise is gained through skills training and continuous practice. Adapting Ericsson's (2001) set of behavioural determinants of deliberate practice, Helton (2009: 7) suggests that training working dogs involves four factors:

- motivating them to perform a task
- providing clearly-defined tasks to be performed
- providing feedback
- ensuring practice is repeated and purposeful

He indicates that verbalising language to enable knowledge memory may not be essential for a dog who may encode declarative knowledge in images and consequently be able to perform tasks requiring skill. However, he notes, as does Bradshaw (2012), that mental imagery in dogs is a 'very underdeveloped' research area (Helton, 2009: 8).

According to Irvine (2012), George Herbert Mead (1934) claimed influentially that animals lacked mental ability. Irvine (2012) cites Strauss's research which suggests that Mead considered animals to have 'no mind, no thought, and hence there is no meaning [in their behaviour] in the significant or self-conscious sense' (Strauss, 1964: 168). This attitude prevailed until Bryant (1979) critiqued sociologists for failing to 'address the zoological component in human interaction and attendant social systems' (1979: 339). Irvine develops Sanders' consistent portrayal of animals as 'minded participants in social life' (Irvine, 2012: s128) and, ignoring the need for language to define the 'self', highlights how 'dog training involves encouraging the dog to shape his or her behavior to human expectations' (Irvine, 2007: 8). She illustrates this with an example of her own dog's behaviour modification which she attributes to the dog's basic 'understanding of causality' (Irvine, 2007: 8) and ability to intervene satisfactorily in an action.

A similar understanding of causality, and resultant intervention, frames the unexpected behaviour modification of this researcher's cat and dog, behaviour that has intensified belief in the animal self:

> The cat lay prostrate on the dog's bed, stretched so expansively that there was no room whatsoever for the dog to lie there too. Instead of immediately pushing her off the mattress, which would have earned him the swift swipe of an

42 *Anthrozoological and sociological perspectives*

unsheathed claw, he play-bowed, whined and lowered his head submissively, looking downwards and not directly at the cat.

He slowly opened his mouth, grasped a small corner of the blanketed mattress, and gave a gentle tug – the cat remained immobile. He grumbled and pulled harder. The cat sat up and yowled at him; the dog jumped backwards and barked, crept forward and with his teeth, slowly lifted the mattress higher and higher in one corner. The cat rolled off, but retaining dignity in failure, stalked away swishing her tail; the dog lay down on his bed, mission seemingly accomplished.

However, the cat then jumped up onto a kitchen cupboard close to the backdoor, lifted a front paw, eyed the dog, and rattled the keys in the door lock. Of course, the dog leapt off the bed and raced to the door – the cat gazed at the vacant mattress for a long moment.

Did she glory in smug triumph? She looked as if she did, but that is a human anthropomorphic interpretation of what might be termed trans-species negotiation – mutual coexistence achieved without injurious aggression – and this interactive dialogue occurred between them on more than one occasion. Anthropomorphism may be derided but it seems sometimes to facilitate the human comprehension of interspecies communication of thoughts and behaviours. In this instance, however, my understanding of their behaviour and semblance of (re)-experience could more likely be attributed to egomorphism (Milton, 2005), which 'implies that I understand my cat, or a humpback whale, or my human friends, on the basis of my perception that they are "like me" rather than human-like' (Milton, 2005: 261).

S. Hurn (personal communication, 1 June 2017) elaborates, suggesting in an email that egomorphism is 'in many respects an aspect of an inter-subjective relationship (i.e., one can be egomorphic in response to another being with whom one does not have a direct or personal relationship)'. Milton's humpback whale, for example, or, citing Hurn's example, 'I engage egomorphically with those pigs on trucks bound for slaughterhouses'. With reference to the cat and dog interaction above, their relationship might be considered 'a form of intersubjectivity grounded in egomorphism' (Hurn, personal communication, 1 June 2017).

Whether it was just a game or a wily method of goal achievement, both species appear to evince minded forethought and planned action. The dog seemed conscious of the cat's likely reaction on several levels and took care in preparing successful retrieval of his bed, while the cat showed remarkable tolerance as well as knowledge or memory of canine behaviour or indeed of human behaviour when keys jangle and doors open. It is this awareness that lends credibility to the idea of animal personhood and interspecies negotiation. In terms of the medical alert dog and the diabetic human, there is broad opportunity for a shared human–canine coexistence that has value for both when resulting from well-conceived training and a comfortable closeness, and from a continuous endeavour to attain some form of mutual understanding.

The strength of the human–canine bond has been frequently evaluated in evolutionary terms. A 20-year study of breed-specific behaviour (Coppinger and

Anthrozoological and sociological perspectives 43

Schneider, 1995) focussed on the 'evolutionary mechanisms' (1995: 22) of dogs identified by the researchers as experts in their fields of work – sled-pulling, livestock guarding, and herding. They discovered the historical importance of breeding and training for temperament, and noted adolescence was the most beneficial age for trainability and adaptation to new ideas and behaviours.

This is confirmed in the training of assistance dogs who generally spend their first 10–12 months in a 'foster home', often situated in a family with children and other companion animals, so as to become 'socialised' and accustomed to travel on public transport, to walk quietly past barking dogs and shouting, running children, for example, and to learn how to be confident in the face of unexpected noise hazards, such as slamming doors, fireworks, or express trains thundering through railway stations. Once well-accustomed to the wide variety of human lifestyle management methods, young medical alert assistance dogs remain resident in family homes but visit the MDD headquarters, where they are trained by reward and encouragement, to sniff and identify odours associated with illness in exhaled human breath and to respond with an alerting signal.

Only recently (1971) did Linus Pauling discover that hundreds of different VOCs are intermingled in human breath and that, in people who are unwell, they show unique patterns based on individual metabolism; 'you are what you eat' sums up how internal bacteria behave towards ingestion and provides signposts to odours ably recognised by a canine medical detective.

Helton suggests that dogs in work are 'the best candidate models of human workers' (2009: 3). Although they lack a spoken language that we can understand and cannot hold tools in their paws as we hold instruments in our hands, they have succeeded in living and working alongside humans. Dogs have other competencies we value – and they appear to share them willingly if rewarded, or at least treated appropriately. Rewarding and enriching the life of the diabetes alert dog, and other assistance dogs, is a continuing ambition for the human partner as well as the trainer. Exploration of the mental and physical needs of these working dogs is undertaken in the research of Coppinger, Coppinger, and Skillings (1998), Rooney, Gaines, and Hiby (2009), Robinson et al. (2014), and Coppinger and Coppinger (2016). Enrichment and empowerment are essential qualities which can, with forethought, be successfully expanded to engage significant markers of canine well-being in a detection dog permanently living with an unwell human.

Narcotic detection relies to a large extent on expertise developed through canine olfaction. A study conducted by Slabbert and Rasa (1997) determined whether maternal narcotic detection behaviour accelerated later skill development and the acquisition of expertise by puppies. Early observation of working role models appeared to enhance the acquisition of narcotic detection skills. Whether puppies from expert medical alert assistance dogs would learn chemical detection skills more speedily if they observed their mothers at work, has yet to be tested, chiefly because the charity is still in its own infancy and most of the dogs in current training have been donated, 'rescued', or are family pets who have shown natural aptitude to alert their human guardians to extreme blood sugar fluctuations. Many species have been observed to pass on genetic and learned traits to their offspring or group

44 *Anthrozoological and sociological perspectives*

members to aid breed or species survival. An example are the Forest Troop anubis baboons (*Papio anubis*) who, over at least two decades, have undergone 'multigenerational culture transmission' as young male baboons adopted the behaviour of the new troop into which they transferred (Sapolsky, 2006: 645). Additionally, Irvine (2007: 16, note vii) recalls 'evidence that meerkats teach their young about hunting appeared in the journal *Science* 14 July 2006 (Vol 313 no. 5784: 227–229)'.

But despite the importance of continuous practice and training to develop expertise, there is a need for natural talent, a perhaps anthropomorphic attribution of a canine yen to fulfil the trainer's requests and find enjoyment in achievement. The medical alert assistance dog requires a temperament that allows the formation of a strong human–animal bond and a vigilant ability to sleep polyphasically or in random snatches of time so that the altered smell of changing blood glucose levels can be acted upon instantly. Both the alerting dog and the cancer-detecting dog need to have and maintain good health, mental ability and physical agility, show curiosity in training, a propensity to search by smell rather than sight, and display sufficient appreciation of the rewards offered to continue sniffing for detection purposes. But, as Michalko (1999: 138–139) stresses, relative to the matching of a guide dog to a human companion:

> All discussion of a dog's breed and breeding is put in terms of human descriptors – a dog is intelligent, confident, curious, and so on. When a dog is described as having a 'personality', it is no wonder that we often forget that it is 'just a dog'. . . . Given roughly matching levels of activity and physical fitness, 'personality' is the criterion trainers consider when matching dog guides with blind people.

Guide Dogs for the Blind and Dogs for Good are among eight accredited canine-assistance charities that fall under the banner of Assistance Dogs UK (ADUK). Dogs are recognised by ADUK if they

- have been trained to behave well in public
- have safe and reliable temperaments
- are healthy and do not constitute a hygiene risk observed over a considerable period of time
- are fully toilet trained
- are regularly checked by experienced veterinarians
- are accompanied by a disabled handler who has been trained how to work alongside their assistance dog
- are recognisable by the harness, organisation-specific coat, identity tag on their collar, or lead slip that they wear

The dogs participating in this research are accredited globally by ADUK, Assistance Dogs Europe (ADEU), and Assistance Dogs International (ADI), the latter providing an ADI Minimum Standards and Ethics document, and they are trained by Medical Detection Dogs. They are identified as keen 'sniffers' and problem-solvers

Anthrozoological and sociological perspectives   45

which aptitudes lend themselves to success in detection work achieved by olfactory ability (Gadbois and Reeve, 2014: 3–20; Bradshaw, 2012: 224–249). A study, examining the value of trained alerting dogs to people subject to glycaemic episodes, by Rooney, Morant, and Guest (2013), used structured interview sessions in client homes, comparing nine client records of blood glucose levels, assistance dog behaviour, alerting method, and further comparisons between routine testing and response testing (when the dog provided an alert). Their findings showed that seven clients recorded a significantly higher proportion of routine tests within target range after obtaining a dog; and that, 'based on owner-reported data . . . trained detection dogs perform above chance level' (2013: 1).

Dog breeds are divided into sporting and nonsporting groups chiefly for the purpose of entering category classes at shows such as Crufts, 'the world's largest dog show' held in the UK. 'Sporting' dogs include hounds who were traditionally bred to hunt prey (for example, Deerhound or Dachshund), gun dogs such as the Labrador or Pointer, who indicate and retrieve prey, and terriers (Bull Terrier or Fox Terrier) who hunt smaller animals, particularly those who live in holes, for example, foxes and rabbits. They are known as sporting breeds because they are traditionally used by people who hunt with dogs for 'sport'. The Kennel Club groups nonsporting dog breeds to include utility dogs (Dalmatian, for example), pastoral/herding dogs (for example, Border Collie, Anatolian Shepherd Dog), working dogs (Bull Mastiff, Dobermann) and toy dogs (Pomeranian), but as Odendaal (2003: 5–6) comments:

> In a certain sense, the grouping of dogs is artificial because dogs are also used interchangeably for different (incorrect?) purposes . . . nowadays the sporting breeds are seldom used for their original purpose of hunting. Labradors, for example, are used as guide dogs, and terriers as watchdogs.

Working dogs in any breed group are so labelled when 'working' and interacting with human individuals, whether in terms of rescue from landslide, scenting illness conditions, finding lost individuals, drugs or money, acting as therapeutic aides or emptying or filling a washing machine.

MDD's canine work force may have pedigreed ancestry or come from mixed-breed parentage. The majority would be categorised into the 'sporting gundog' group which includes retrievers and spaniels rather than the nonsporting working breeds; but as Coulter (2016a) and Odendaal (2003) have suggested, a working dog is likely to be working and interacting with human partners in a range of fields, so the grouping of dog breeds does indeed seem 'artificial'.

Paul considers 'the fact that the charity works with all manner of breeds and sizes is a bonus'. He suggests some charities will not 'foresee other things' whereas diabetes has many other complications 'so just having one breed of dog doesn't always work'. He is thoughtful:

> Sometimes you need a little dog, sometimes you need a big dog, sometimes, you know . . . I wanted a large dog purely because of losing sight and all the

46 *Anthrozoological and sociological perspectives*

rest of it but when another illness flared up, I was . . . like, maybe a little dog is so much easier, you can pick it up and carry it.

Savalois, Lescureux, and Brunois (2013: 77) draw attention to 'recent trends in social science advocating recognition of interactive properties in human–animal relationships' in their ethnographic investigation of herding dogs and their 'trainer-users'. 'The dog's' hunting skills are used to turn him/her into a working tool, through minimally constrained education and training'. As these researchers learned from their human participants, 'once trained, the dog should become an autonomous but controllable worker' well versed in helping (2013: 77). The effects of medical assistance dog training enable independent decision making by the dogs and in turn, learning is gained through observation of the dogs by both clients and trainers.

However, there are important criteria to be fulfilled by the prospective human member of the interspecies partnership. Because of the high number of people applying for a medical alert assistance dog (MAAD), the charity's website defines criteria for acceptance onto the client waiting list:

- those who are detrimentally affected by their health condition and have little or no hypoglycaemic awareness
- those who have made every attempt to come to terms with their condition and to manage it by other means, but still have frequent hypoglycaemic episodes
- children should be at least five years old and, if under the age of 18, have adequate parental support

The following list includes items considered when taking the decision to accept an application for a MAAD:

- the individual has been diagnosed with a life-threatening illness for a minimum of 12 months
- the current impact of the condition on the applicant's daily life; how often emergency paramedics are called out or how frequent the need for hospital admission; whether the applicant has had to stop work or, if a child, has had repeated absence from school
- whether the applicant would be willing to monitor their blood sugar levels regularly and keep detailed records of them, and be prepared to maintain records of the dog and his or her work performances
- whether the applicant could commit to attending the MDD training centre regularly to participate actively in human and canine training days and further, would be able to manage the dog correctly
- whether the applicant would be able to meet the emotional, physical, and financial needs of the assistance dog and provide a stable home environment and
- be able to understand that the MAAD is a working dog, similar to a Guide or Hearing Dog, and would wear a jacket identifying the MDD charity whenever

Anthrozoological and sociological perspectives   47

out and about in public. Applicants should understand that when they are seen in public with a working dog, they are liable to attract interest in both themselves and their health condition

More information is requested in application forms and questionnaires for those chronically unwell individuals who are eligible to apply, including those who apply for their own dogs to become working diabetes alert assistance dogs. The need for responsible commitment to the assistance dog's welfare is emphasised and applicants are asked to describe their past experiences of dog-handling and to name the person who would be responsible for the dog's daily free-running and where this would take place. An additional document, to be submitted with the application form, asks the applicant's diabetes healthcare professional to complete medical details that would assist in the charity's 'accurate evaluation' of a prospective client.

MDD has charitable status and so does not charge for training a medical alert assistance dog – current costs to train each dog are approximately £13,000 – to the sometimes exacting and essential requirements of the diabetic individual. However, a paragraph in the application form advises that:

> Once a dog is placed, you are financially responsible for the care and welfare costs (including insurance) of the dog, except in exceptional circumstances. The dog's welfare is paramount to us and the dog will at all times remain the property of Medical Detection Dogs.

Words such as 'ownership' and 'property' in terms of companion dogs and their human keepers are commonly stated in the Code of Practice for Dogs in the Animal Welfare Act 2006 and are in general parlance. This returns us to dominance and control issues, and to the use of animals as equipment managed by human means and the labelling of them as 'of unequal status'. But being a device or property belonging to another for health benefit can, as in this case, ensure a high standard of care and affection.

'Works-in-progress'

Marc Higgin (2012: 74) takes human–dog partnerships working in the field of blindness to explore interspecies 'works-in-progress' who, like the diabetes alert dogs and their human partners, are developing and learning together how to be and act as an animate assistive device. This is the becoming of a symbiotic progressing relationship in which smell is the overarching instigator of caregiving mechanisms to reduce health risks in the interspecies lives.

The 'working' dog of this research is an assistant, a skilled and caring helper to those who require expansion, extension, or improvement to an ineffectual or malfunctioning corporeal ability or element in order that they may proceed safely and successfully with worldly existence. In the context of scent detection and Type 1 diabetes, these dogs assist. They are not considered to be 'in service' in the same

48 *Anthrozoological and sociological perspectives*

manner and below-stairs hierarchy of butler or housemaid. Their human companions do not conceive them as 'trapped' (Serpell et al., 2010: 483) in servitude, dominated and oppressed, or imprisoned as slaves.

Once trained in scent detection relative to their human partner's odour patterns, the dogs work of their own volition, using independent decision-making skills, and are not situated in positions of subservience to their human companions. They are not embedded in a contract that they have 'personally' signed (Palmer, 1997), and 'they do not receive monetary pay directly, nor would they be interested in money specifically' (Coulter, 2016b: 201) for their consistent and considerable assistance. They are, however, nutritionally or physically rewarded with food, toys, free time, or play time. They have accreditation from the aforementioned national and international organisations, ADUK, ADEU, and ADI; and their human 'teachers' similarly attain accreditation from recognised dog training organisations.

The medical alert assistance dog undertakes work that involves a previously established task, for which he or she has been trained specifically. Jocelyne Porcher (2014: 7), when referring to the need for mutual recognition by farmers and farm animals, suggests 'work can only reach its potential if it is recognized' and contends that it is 'with speech and petting that the farmers recognize their animals, and it is with trust and proximity that animals recognize their farmers'. The diabetes alert dogs and their human coworkers also offer and accept tangible or spoken reward and recognition of their endeavours, for example, to nudge and have the alert signal noticed and acted upon, to be nudged and offer reward, to give and take responsibility for each other's care practices. In this work, social identities are formed, and become appreciated and accepted by multiple entities.

The work to be performed is comprehended through earlier instruction, by reward-based training that may take weeks or months of practice depending on the age and ability of each dog, leading to both an agentic way of acting and a habitual positive responding towards a future lifelong human companion. Classic conditioning or training methods stem from the days of Pavlov's work with dogs, who salivated at the sound of a bell having learnt that that noise signalled food, but such learning can result in nonhuman animal discomfort and fear. Pavlov 'helped to establish the fact that animals such as dogs were quickly able to learn the significance of artificial cues that evolution could not have prepared them for. . . . Classical conditioning is automatic; it does not involve the dog reflecting on what has just happened' (Bradshaw, 2012: 101). Although positive is preferable to negative reinforcement, both of which may have success in animal-training methods, it is instrumental or operant conditioning, reward-based training – rewards taking the form of highly desired food items, toys, praise, active affection, or off-leash play – that seems most attractive in concept and achievement for both dog and 'handler', and is the method used by the charity's training staff. Bradshaw (2012: 107) emphasises that, as for classical conditioning,

> The timing of the delivery of the reward is crucial. There must be no more than a second or two between the dog performing the desired action and

the arrival of the reward. Longer than this, and not only will the learning be slower to establish, but there is also an increased chance that the dog will make unwanted associations with something else.

Throughout the observation periods, there was no evidence of anything but encouragement to ensure training moved at a pace suited to the dog's personality, age, and temperament.

Medical detection dogs in training

During a visit to the charity's headquarters, I watch two trainers working with a young dog, Ben, who has completed the first week of scent training and is now moving on to a client's individual scent. While the dog is relaxed and ambling around the office desks, one of the trainers, Liz, puts a client's breath sample pot inside the leg of her boot and says that 'as soon as he's on it, we click and reward – the main thing is to let him find the client's scent'. They encourage Ben who seems a little confused and unsure of his purpose; he licks his lips and his eyes wander round the room. Liz says the idea is to make it a game as he's still in the early stages of training. 'We don't want him to get anxious or stressed out'.

The trainers wait patiently and gently guide him towards the general area of the sample without giving away the pot's position. They will do this up to five times a day 'but sometimes only twice', depending on the dog's degree of confidence. Rooney, Gaines and Hiby (2009: 133) confirm the need for dogs to have positive associations and gradual introductions to required actions so they are never afraid or concerned when asked to perform a behaviour.

The sample for medical alert dog training is always placed somewhere on the human body as that is the source of the scent. 'It's never visual', always olfactory detection, and the sample pot is only used once so it gives off a clear and uncontaminated odour. The training starts with a cloth placed somewhere on the trainer and the search is treated as a game, using a general odour until the dog is ready to be matched with a client's sample odour:

> Once you've got that confidence, you let him search on his own to build on the confidence, and then hold off the food reward so that a bit of frustration encourages him to want the reward – but it has to be very finely timed which is why I went straight in when he started to lip-lick and yawn, to show him he's right and not push him too far. If you lose confidence in the early stages, then it's really difficult to build it up again.

Ben has a food allergy so he's on a fish and vegetable diet. His high-reward treat is freeze-dried duck. Liz remarks that it is necessary to find the right high-value item to motivate the alert dog, and not give something they've had during puppy training. 'We have to be really careful with the choice of reward we use in training'.

However, being an animal and therefore sentient, the 'working' dog is not a mechanical robot – not of the order of the interactive therapeutic 'Paro', for

50 *Anthrozoological and sociological perspectives*

example, the robotic seal which has achieved success in care facilities since 2003 and epitomises the advantages of neoteny, having been created with large soulful eyes and a soft, furry, huggable 'epidermis'. 'It' is designed to be 'sociable' and to have 'states of mind' (Turkle, 2011: 8–9), dependent on how the robot animal is treated and how this affects its tactile and other built-in sensors.

As with the Paro seal and the AIBO robot dog, the medical alert assistance dogs provide cost savings and financial benefit to health-management organisations as well as providing health and social advantages for their diabetic carers. But neither of the former 'animal companions' can maintain the close, warm contact and agentic ability of the live diabetes alert dog.

At the charity's training centre where trainees are matched to individuals with chronic illness, the atmosphere indoors is inviting. Human and canine workers intermingle with seemingly contented, collaborative intent. Gates across doorways act as multispecies department dividers rather than as species separators. There are desk workers, eyes fixed on computer screens, who have dogs lying next to their chairs – these are trained dogs paired with humans who are themselves employed in the charity's work but who would be unable to sustain employment without the alerting interventions of their canine companions.

The diabetes assistance dogs learn a routine of alerting behaviour that is appropriate and acceptable to the human recipients who need to learn and adjust to someone sharing their home and lifestyle, someone who is likely to have habits of which they may not always approve; and, if they have never before shared life with a dog, who will take up more space and time than they could possibly have imagined. They learn how best to maintain the wanted optimal alerts through accurate and timely reward, paying due attention to the canine signals, and ensuring interspecies training continues, whether at home, in the shopping mall or open field.

A staff member, 'Val' (her name, as with other members of the MDD staff, has been anonymised to maintain confidentiality), explains the procedures involved in placing a trained dog with a potential human match. She informs me that, before an interview, all applicants are first invited to attend an Applicant Awareness Day during which information, required by an applicant to make an informed decision as to whether a medical alert assistance dog is right for them, is given. Also offered are details of the requirements needed to ensure maintenance of a future effective partnership with a medical detection dog.

Before a placement is finalised, the applicants receive training and handling sessions at a one-day 'Introduction to Assistance Dogs' meeting. After this session, the instructors advise whether they feel the applicants require further training before being placed into a dog–human matching procedure. These additional training periods may take one to four more sessions and result in a decision to proceed with matching. If a situation arises in which it is considered not viable for a client to handle and manage an assistance dog safely and confidently, the applicant would not proceed further in the matching process.

Val explains that any clients with young children are invited to the MDD centre to attend a family handling day which 'covers appropriateness around dogs and how to read the signals that dogs give to show they are happy or uncomfortable'.

Anthrozoological and sociological perspectives 51

Once applicants have carried out as much training in handling an assistance dog as is felt necessary, they attend a dog match day to find a suitable companion. Val observes that this may necessitate the applicant returning to the centre on a different day in order to work with other dogs, should the first assistance dogs they meet, not be found suitable. Once there is a potential match, the interspecies dyad attends a two-day advanced handling session at the centre, and then spends a further three days in the client's home environment.

If this is successful, scent training commences with an instructor. The partnership will then receive weekly visits for a period of six weeks following the home placement, changing to fortnightly visits for another six weeks, depending on progress. Val comments that there is always support available by way of telephone calls, visits, and if needed, a two-day refresher handling course for the client, until the human-canine partnership achieves accreditation which may take place three to six months after the dog's placement but might take longer. Thereafter, she says, the MDD instructors undertake a 'six-month' home visit to the partnerships and then annually. They also arrange and run regular refresher and get-together sessions at the training centre and in other regions, and the latter, Val affirms, are particularly benefitting partnerships residing some distance from the MDD Centre.

Medical Detection Dogs supports the concept of the 'Five Freedoms' for the good welfare of dogs in their care and in the care of their clients:

- freedom from hunger and thirst
- freedom from discomfort
- freedom from pain, injury and disease
- freedom to behave normally
- freedom from fear and distress

The Code of Practice for the Welfare of Dogs (DEFRA, 2009) applies to all dogs and is intended to 'provide practical guidance' to assist in compliance with the provisions of Section 9 of the UK Animal Welfare Act (2006). The Act stipulates that all reasonable steps should be taken to ensure that dogs' needs are met and elaborates as to how this should be done, based on the Five Freedoms. Although breach of a provision of the Code of Practice 'is not an offence in itself,' if proceedings are brought against an offender under Section 9 of the Act, the Court will look at whether the offender has complied with the Code in deciding if an offence has been committed (DEFRA, 2009). For individuals who have canine companions, whether as trained medical assistance dogs or solely as good friends, the Code of Practice gives a set of guidelines for human practices of canine care.

Medical detection dogs in work

In the study by Savalois, Lescureux and Brunois (2013: 82), there is a section entitled 'when the focused work tool becomes an autonomous worker' which may be linked without difficulty to Paul's later comment about his diabetes alert dog, Nero, being an instrumental aid. A further example can be identified in Mel's

52 *Anthrozoological and sociological perspectives*

commendation of Gemma's independent decision-making. The dog wakes Mel in the middle of the night with the medical kit in her mouth so that Mel is immediately readied to test her child's dropping blood sugar levels.

Within the bounds of their research into interactivity, in herding dog training and usage where the dogs' trainers are livestock breeders, Savalois, Lescureux, and Brunois (2013: 83) suggest that 'the trainers consider that the dog's knowledge of livestock functioning is much better than their own'. In the context under investigation here, the intention is to facilitate life with chronic illness and provide means to improve the functioning of blood glucose in the body. Although medical professionals are usually human, it is fair to say that both the charity's dog-training staff and the individuals living with Type 1 diabetes accept that the diabetes alert dogs' knowledge – or, rather, their ability to detect the impact of diabetes on the human body – is much better than their own.

Natasha exemplifies this thinking and identifies emerging knowledge and abilities of the diabetes alert dogs, confirming that:

> We all know the dogs know way more than we do, but there's only so much that is currently scientifically proven that can be worked upon; and of course when you live with one, and certainly all the partnerships we've spoken to so far, you know, they will tell you that the dogs do more than what they've been trained to do.

This echoes the words of Despret's (2008: 133) cattle breeders, who denote intentionality to their animals by commenting that the animals 'know what we want better than we know what they want', and is further elaborated in Haraway's (2016: 129) study:

> Figuring out what their animals want, so that people and cows could together accomplish successful breeding, was the fundamental conjoined work of the farm . . . the animals paid attention to the farmers; paying equally effective attention to the cows and pigs was the job of good breeders.

Haraway (2016: 129) suggests that this is an 'extension of subjectivities' for both humans and animals, and in Despret's (2008: 135) words, this is 'becoming what the other suggests to you, accepting a proposal of subjectivity, acting in the manner in which the other addresses you, actualizing and verifying this proposal, in the sense of rendering it true'.

Intersubjectivity, elucidated by Hurn (2012: 125–138), and incorporating consciousness of the self and the other (Irvine, 2007), empathy (de Waal, 2010; Gruen, 2015), flexible personhood (Shir Vertesh, 2012), and a spiritual transspecies merging (Viveiros de Castro, 1998), is reflected in the entangled relationships of the medical alert assistance dogs and their chronically ill partners.

Goode's 'general model of intersubjectivity' (2007: 90) in which matters may be 'assumed but not communicated; matters communicated but not spoken; and matters formulated into language' (2007: 89), can demonstrate how

Anthrozoological and sociological perspectives 53

'anthropomorphic description might be based upon shared aspects of dog–human intersubjectivity that are in some sense anterior to linguistic naming' (2007: 90). For example, interspecies communication that takes place through the silent language expressed through the senses and in corporeal mobility. The assistance dogs central to this research have innate and taught skills that augment the capabilities of their human companions: those less well-endowed with sensory awareness and those who are restrained by chronic illness to limited movement in the home, or whose intention to integrate in society is prevented by fear of unprepared-for dizziness or an unexpected fall on the bus, in the supermarket, or at school. There is reciprocal intention in their knowing and learning communications and in their care-workings together for comfort and improved health.

In the 'donation' of abilities and skills, the dog effectively 'becomes-with' the human and embodies the malfunctioning aspects in order to recognise them (in this instance, the extreme 'fall' in blood sugar levels made obvious to the dog in the altered odour of human breath) and create means for positive restructuring (human recognition of the dog's alert by follow-up blood testing).

Needs and complex issues in chronic illness

Turning to the sociology of health and illness, content is centred here on researching medical and sociological issues involved in chronic illness and examining the concept of disability, the study of needs and complex issues in Type 1 diabetes and the management of long-term bodily dysfunction.

When would someone identify themselves as disabled and why; when would society nominate an individual as disabled and why? How does a medical alert assistance dog make a difference to the human's self-esteem and social integration? Questions of personal and social identity formation, and the sharing of an interspecies identity, are to be investigated. Discussion is enhanced by the insights given by Tom Shakespeare (2014); by Molly Mullin's (1999: 202) commentary on the crossing of fluctuating boundaries between species and the human use of nonhuman animals to construct identity, in which she cites (1999: 211) Haraway's notion of 'polishing an animal mirror to look for ourselves' (1991: 21); and further, by considering Rod Michalko's illustration of his shared identity with a guide dog, Smokie, 'the two in one' (1999). The concept of transhumanism and a cyborgean identity highlight the extension of human wellness and ability through partially mechanical means, seen against achievement in health attainment by guidance from sentient instruments.

This section draws on research studies that explore long-term chronic ill health with focus on Type 1 diabetes, and that demonstrate how chronic illness and resultant ongoing disability may alter an individual's existence and identity in today's individualist 'Western' world of changing attitudes, behaviours, and methods of living with a long-term illness. Prevalence figures for 2017 state that more than 3.7 million people in the UK are known to have been diagnosed with diabetes (Diabetes UK, 2017) and close to a million adults and children are estimated to have undiagnosed symptoms of this life-changing illness.

54 *Anthrozoological and sociological perspectives*

Type 2 diabetes can be partially attributed to obesity and lifestyle behaviours and allows 'room for improvement' in health by the individuals themselves. Type 2 diabetes is the condition generally understood as 'diabetes' by society, whereas juvenile-onset or insulin-dependent Type 1 diabetes is a 'silent', lesser-known chronic illness that occurs when the immune system views its own cells as alien, resulting in destruction of the body's insulin-producing beta cells in the pancreas.

From the onset of a Type 1 diabetes diagnosis, care practices and practitioners infiltrate the life of the 'patient'; whether nurse or physician, parent or pharmacist, nutritionist or neurologist, teacher, work colleague, friend, or paramedic, weighing and measuring, pricking fingers and testing blood – of necessity, care is given by individuals and communities to improve ways of doing life with this form of diabetes.

The focal canine–human symbiotic relationship stems from a recently developed, noninvasive procedure to benefit people with Type 1 diabetes. The collaborative multispecies process incorporates the dog's acute sense of smell in detecting extreme fluctuations in blood glucose levels, symptoms which may fail to be recognised as needing urgent attention by the individual with Type 1 diabetes, but which may result in serious and severe reactions.

Unlike the participants with Type 1 diabetes in Mol and Law's 2004 study, respondents active in this research have, over their lifetimes, lost awareness of symptoms and the embodied ability to sense an approaching hypoglycaemic crisis. When all educational attempts and medical encouragements to continue feeling or sensing symptoms of an imminent hypoglycaemic episode, or 'hypo', fail, the chronically ill person may, on frequent occasions, become dizzy; lose environmental awareness and sense of location or situation; collapse; and, without human assistance to call an ambulance, fall into a potentially fatal coma.

However, each human with Type 1 diabetes participating in this study relies on a canine 'stand-in' for an embodied sensation. Canine olfactory acuity perceives what the human fails to recognise and intercorporeal sensitivity maintains an advance warning system to prevent a hypo. Dogs are trained to act on their olfactory detection of changes in the diabetic's odour signature in order to alert the individual so that blood sugar levels can be tested, insulin dosages adjusted, and medical treatment measures enacted appropriately.

In addition, care practices affecting canine–human partnerships in chronic illness, are examined within the boundaries of Type 1 diabetes communities, whether these are drawn from personal health teams, medical institutions, communal groups comprising participant members of this research, instruction and training group collectives, or the social groups in which the human–canine partnerships become integrated.

Nettleton avers that medicine has been 'taken to task for the way in which it treats patients as passive objects rather than "whole" persons' (2013: 5). 'Western' attitudes to the generally accepted 'medicalisation' of illness, the biomedical model in which the patient may be considered a passive anatomical bearer of disease in the hands of the medical professional, have swung towards a more

Anthrozoological and sociological perspectives   55

active process in which disease is also seen to be socially created and constructed and can therefore be affected by the patient's choices and decisions on illness treatments. As Bury (1991: 452) opines, 'interpretive sociology, in particular, has developed a view of people as agents, rather than being merely the products of the contexts in which they live'.

The current division between illness and disease allows an individual versus a collective interpretation. In the former, illness is seen as a personally owned experience, whereas disease is medically identified as corporeal dysfunction. Impairment or dysfunction then gains medical attention and professional treatment, whether it is a disabling condition or not. In this research, the condition of Type 1 diabetes can seriously hamper a desired lifestyle; unlike some illnesses, it is chronic and neither preventable nor curable. As a result, those with chronic illness learn to adapt in order to re-able aspects of their changed future; find, enact and establish new coping skills and strategies; and attempt to understand some of the complications and restrictions caused and being created by the diagnosis and ongoing treatment regimes.

Sociologists, suggests Nettleton (2013), should observe illness behaviour and attempt to understand illness action; regarding the latter, she enjoins sociologists to perceive how the experience of illness affects people, how they comprehend and interpret it, and find personal significance in it. 'The sociology of health and illness involves the study of people's interpretations of their bodily experiences and concerns the social aspects of the regulation of bodies' (2013: 9). Use of an illness narrative provides identity and meaning for the participants in this study. Experience of chronic illness is explained in discourse, buoyed by the extensive research conducted by Charmaz (1983, 1995) and Bury (1991, 2001). Bury (2001: 264) suggests that language and narrative are prominent features 'in the repair and restoring of meanings when they are threatened'.

Shakespeare develops the narrative concept in terms of academic research and autobiography in his work *Disability Rights and Wrongs Revisited* (2014). He discusses the varying effects of impairment resulting from trauma or illness and highlights (2014: 32) Charmaz's (1995: 657) suggestion that

> Chronic illness assaults the body and threatens the integrity of self. Having a serious chronic illness shakes earlier taken-for-granted assumptions about possessing a smoothly functioning body.

Charmaz's use of abusive verbs to illustrate the physical and mental turmoil that may be created by chronic illness – assault, threaten, shake – is forceful and unambiguous. The demise of a formerly flourishing self-belief can cause the unwell individual to be dragged deep into a vortex of depression, into an unedifying day-to-day downward spiral where merely to exist may be a lonely, confusing, messy, and seemingly pointless process. Kenneth Doka's (2002) concept of 'disenfranchised grief' and its challenges lends itself to bodies shaken apart and lives unsettled by chronic illness so that sorrow and regret for what might have been, become prominent and possibly destructive emotions.

56 *Anthrozoological and sociological perspectives*

Although resultant changes in lifestyle always occur, not all chronically ill individuals experience the intense psychological effects of such a diagnosis as those noted above. To wit, chronic illness involves the creation of an identity of self that incorporates the complexities of both 'living a life' and 'living an illness': what Whittemore and Dixon (2008: 177) term 'uneasy bedfellows' existing side-by-side through necessity and challenging the self to produce a personally and socially acceptable identity. These researchers employed a mixed-methods design to examine ways in which US adults with a chronic illness integrate it into their lives. Findings showed participants tried hard to integrate illness into a meaningful existence. However, the necessity to live an illness was considered overwhelming because of the frequency and unpredictability of changing symptoms, the range of emotional challenges and the essential daily routines.

'In mainstream medicine', according to Howes and Classen (2014), technology has largely usurped doctors' sensory diagnoses, 'while in treatment the alleviation of pain is often considered the most that should be done for the patient's sensory well-being' (2014: 37). Investigation into sensory perception was once the sole preserve of psychology but now includes what Howes and Classen (2014: 13) term a 'coalescence' of disciplines, for example, those of anthropology, geography, literature, and, more recently, sociology. They consider a combination of approaches has encouraged the development of a new field of sensory studies.

The prescription of alternative and complementary medicine has become more widespread as a result of the increasing Western desire to have senses and emotions, 'lived experiences' (Howes and Classen, 2014: 7), recognised and catered for in medical treatments – for example, in music therapy (De Nora, 2016), equine acupuncture (Koski, 2011), or animal-assisted therapy (Fine, 2010). These are among sensory healing remedies for multiple species now becoming acceptable in ways that were previously unheard of or merely anecdotal in the West. This change has also affected the care and welfare of domesticated nonhuman animals, with examples seen in Reiki's 'hands-on' touch therapy, in citronella-based fly repellents, and in plant-based homeopathic remedies such as 'rescue' drops for calming dogs during thunderstorms, firework displays, and similar stress-inducing events.

Although complementary therapies and remedies are now more widely available for health-giving and caring purposes, it is the employment of other animal species to help in improving human well-being that is central to this study in which research into chronic illness investigates the new identities of humans integrating Type 1 diabetes management into their lives, before and after the arrival of a medical alert assistance dog. From this, as has already been shown in the partnership between Tina and Harley, emerge shared and individual identities – the human–nonhuman animal dyad becoming socially accepted and integrated as a single united 'self' in society, contrasted with the solitary human trying to escape the self-designated long-term societal outcast label, wanting to 'belong' but frustrated by the self's inability to cope unaided.

Problematic issues can develop if continued social interaction and integration into 'normal' society are curtailed due to anxiety and the stress of anticipating public embarrassment at personal human failure. The narrative that follows from Janet, explaining her life before Alfie's companionship, exemplifies such issues.

Kathy Charmaz (1983: 170) details four sources of suffering resulting from the loss of self in chronic illness – the necessity to cope with 'living a restricted life, existing in social isolation, experiencing discredited definitions of self, and becoming a burden to others'. These issues remain prominent today in reducing both self-worth and a positive self-image among the lives of the chronically ill, regardless of age, ethnicity, gender, colour, creed, or demographic context. 'Experiences of being discredited, embarrassed, ignored and otherwise devalued' (Charmaz, 1983: 177) contribute to growing isolation and loss of self-worth.

Much self-esteem rides on the quantity and quality of support from medical personnel, family, and friends, but where such validation is unavoidably absent, feelings of depression and inferiority may take over the reins of identity formation. Diminishing control of the illness and a lack of self-efficacy can lead to feelings of failure and incapability; losses leading to a halted progression towards better health and lifestyle. Alternatively, people with chronic illness may 'gradually raise their hopes and progressively increase their identity goals when they meet with success' in their adaptation to a changing body (Charmaz, 1995: 660).

When the human self-image is devalued and social disenfranchisement becomes personal to the individual with Type 1 diabetes or other chronic illness, the medical alert assistance dog can play a highly significant remedial role. The dog is not merely an autonomous medical assistant but a sentient partner able to provide positive, visible evidence of the human's status in the world. The canine provision of respect, nonjudgemental support and willing companionship, together with an apparent desire for the other's approval, highlight characteristics that naturally boost human self-confidence.

In/dependence

The dog becomes an aid to independence, simultaneously allowing dependence – a weighty burden of responsibility that appears to be shouldered with equanimity. As a guide dog safely leads an unsighted companion around shopping malls and onto trains, so the diabetes alert dog can arrest the progress of their human partner's disorientation and confusion before a hypo sets in during a shopping trip or journey on public transport. In return, the dogs are praised and rewarded, given time out and time to play.

Loss of an independent lifestyle, complicated by an inability to function as expected and approved by Western society, can lead to withdrawal from social activities and to a perceptible lessening of healthy cognitive thinking. A young participant, Janet, who relies on grizzle-muzzled Labrador, Alfie, for support in private and in public, exemplifies this:

> I had no confidence before Alfie. I wouldn't talk to people because I'd be so worried that I might just collapse on the floor in front of them; it got to a point where I just didn't want to go out and I'd only go out with mum or my

58 *Anthrozoological and sociological perspectives*

brother – it just felt too daunting. So yeah, having Alfie, my confidence just sort of soared really.

Bury (1991) suggests chronic conditions vary markedly in terms of their symbolic significance within segments of the cultural order, affecting individual adaptation as the meanings alter throughout life stages. Changes in symptoms over time, he claims, can affect social responses and these may then affect experience (1991: 454).

Risk and uncertainty in the behaviour of those with chronic illness can cause an observer to draw incorrect conclusions – dizziness or visual impairment may lead to a wandering, stumbling gait more often associated with drunkenness, and incoherent speech encourages similar branding. A fall or loss of consciousness in public by a diabetic individual may be viewed as stereotypical of an epileptic seizure or of a lengthy sojourn in the local pub, but is rarely considered, by a public likely lacking knowledge of Type 1 diabetes, to be the result of extreme fluctuation in blood glucose levels. And then those who do recognise it as a symptom of diabetes may kindly but mistakenly offer sugar-free drinks or food whereas the need is more often for a boost in glucose intake for those suffering from hypoglycaemia.

Whittemore and Dixon commend their adult participants living with chronic illness as 'remarkably resourceful in developing attitudes and strategies to assist them in integrating the illness into their life context' (2008: 11). Bury (1991: 451–452) also comments on results from studies that have detailed 'the steps people take to manage, mitigate or adapt to it (*the burden of chronic illness*), and the meanings attached to these actions'. Such resourcefulness becomes equally apparent from interview excerpts in which this study's participants narrate their personal interpretations of life with Type 1 diabetes and with a canine medical alert assistant.

It is, of course, not only the individual with chronic illness who is severely affected by the diagnosis. There is a visible ripple effect that spreads out the impact onto others in the household, onto work colleagues, friends and in fact, all who come into contact with him or her, be they members of the personal health care team, staff in shops or institutions, or even those meeting the individual in a social setting or travelling on public transport:

> The biggest challenge now is getting on the bus with the dog and the baby and the pram. I have to pick the time of day when I know the bus is going to be quiet otherwise space is so restricted for a dog and a pram; the dog needs to be tucked under the seat so his tail doesn't get trodden on and still be within reaching distance for treats so I can reward him for being good.
>
> (Janet and Alfie)

The implications of a chronic illness diagnosis are felt personally and socially, economically and financially, physically and mentally: the results cause manifold life changes for more than the lone recipient of the diagnosis. Participant

Anthrozoological and sociological perspectives   59

Paul's partner, Natasha, draws attention to some of the diverse consequences of this chronic illness:

> When I think about it, you know the tinnitus, the partially sightedness, you know he's now broken his nose twice, he doesn't smell very well, he doesn't taste very well, he's got diabetes and another chronic illness, and you know with depression and anxiety, your mental capacity is not as astute as it used to be, and yet to look at him, you wouldn't think there was anything wrong with him; but it's that whole silent illness thing.

Chronic illness within a family context has been well explored (among relevant studies are papers by Rolland, 1987; Newby, 1996; Knafl and Gilliss, 2002; Gregory, 2005). But research has also analysed the effects of chronic illness on individuals living alone. Charmaz (2006) highlights the measuring of individual pursuits as means to assess personal health and illness, and to aid the definition of a dynamic identity. In her research, those debilitated by chronic illness took on more social, rather than physical, roles in activities they had previously enjoyed; they were able to maintain friendships and social contacts that 'reaffirmed that they had not become invalids' and thus gained significant feelings of continuity and self-worth (Charmaz, 2006: 34).

Tina, who shares her home and life with diabetes alert dog (DAD) Harley, appreciates friends at work who understand the difficulties inherent in chronic illness, who go out of their way 'to keep her within the work loop', and who are seemingly unaffected by her repetitive questioning:

> When I'm typing, I use the 18 font whereas the others are using 11. I've seen a lot of deterioration in my eyes and I think my memory's going – I keep turning up at appointments at the wrong time; people tell me stuff and then I go and ask them again.

Through the endeavours of office colleagues and the night-and-day canine alerts to possible hypos, she continues to live on her own, to use public transport, and to be employed, all of which would be impossible without the dog's attentiveness to her changing chemical odours.

Whether or not the participants in this study had shared their homes with canine companions before diagnosis, the affirmation given by a medical alert assistance dog upholds self-validation and helps to avoid prejudice and disenfranchisement. Those interviewed were able to maintain the same social standing as other people who kept dogs, walked with them in urban and rural settings, travelled distances on planes, buses and trains, attended dog-training classes, who freely conversed in social situations and, as often occurs naturally among 'dog-walkers', were fully able to discuss the merits, or otherwise, of their companion animals on human enjoyment of life.

Perspectives were therefore not so altered by the diagnosis that former lifestyle management methods had to be completely abandoned in the face of changing

60 *Anthrozoological and sociological perspectives*

social pressure. However, the age of the chronically ill person can affect the opinion of the observer, whether they are aware of such an influence or not. Bury (1991: 456) cites Blaxter (1990) in emphasising the 'continuing moral dimension of beliefs and practices surrounding different health states'. Type 1 diabetes is heritable rather than a result of certain lifestyle behaviours, so children may be diagnosed with this condition at a very young age and receive beneficial support and, likely, sympathy and consideration appropriate to their age.

Older recipients of this medical diagnosis may be considered less kindly when seen, as mentioned earlier, to stagger or to block doorways or pavements with a wheelchair. However, when the hampered individual of any age is accompanied by an assistance dog fetching a medical bag or pressing a doorbell for the hampered individual of any age, public scrutiny is immediately swayed to thoughtful concern. How flexible is our moral thinking!

Self and social identity formation

Molly Mullin (1999: 202) comments on the human use of nonhuman animals to construct identity and pertinently cites Haraway's notion of 'polishing an animal mirror to look for ourselves' (1991: 21, in Mullin, 1999: 211); a phrase which so simply emphasises the human reliance on animal reflections to gain images of ourselves and our place in the world. Charmaz and Rosenfeld (2006: 36) also investigate the mirror image when exploring Cooley's (1902) 'concept of the looking-glass self as a tool for looking at the relationships between the body, self and identity'. They point out the difficulties faced by individuals with dis- or inabilities who are compelled to struggle against 'obstacles that undermine realizing a recognizably competent identity' (Charmaz and Rosenfeld, 2006: 37).

In public, 'potentially discrediting visible characteristics . . . shape how actors manage their envisioned selves' – whether they face 'imagined comparisons with others and imagined normative standards' (Charmaz and Rosenfeld, 2006: 38) or whether they turn away from social integration.

When I ask if she has ever collapsed in public, Janet admits one particular cause of personal fear, perhaps unconsciously relating it to the stigma that can so easily be manifested by the reaction of others when a malfunctioning body determines its own behaviours:

> Not in public. I've always been so on the ball with blood-testing . . . but when I would have them (hypos) at home during the night, I make a real high-pitched shrieking noise and it's always that that's made me super, super, like I don't want that to happen in public because that would probably really scare people and make them sort of 'ooooohhh' (*laughs quietly*). Obviously with the convulsions and everything, I just thought I don't want to put anybody through it.

I remark her thoughtfulness for others and am reminded of Tina's similar care and concern for what other people might think of their illness-related 'unusual' behaviours.

Anthrozoological and sociological perspectives 61

Lynda Birke and Jo Hockenhull (2012: 2) draw attention to the ease with which we 'focus on the *outcome* of our relationships with other species, but much less on how relationships *work*, as a process, or an ongoing interaction between two or more sentient individuals' (italics in text). In this study, focus pinpoints working relationships, and relationships being worked on, within healthcare boundaries; mutualistic collaborations developing performances and processes by which human and nonhuman may cross boundaries and embody mutual attunement in a shared identity.

Richard comments on the frequency of his public identification as 'the trainer': 'maybe the dog's jacket should have "in training" on one side, and on the other, his actual job. Perhaps have "hypo-alert dog" on the jacket'. At this point, a visitor sitting at an adjacent table in the café where we are conversing, questions: 'he's very small to be a blind guide dog, isn't he?' I am surprised that the speaker seems not to have noticed that Higgins' jacket is red, in contrast to the Guide Dogs' well-known yellow identification garments and accessories, nor that neither dog or human appear visually impaired. But again, many people ask if the dog is diabetic.

Charmaz and Rosenfeld (2006), as mentioned earlier, shed light on the self's internal and external image presented to the individual as both mirrored reflection of self and visible appearance to others. They suggest (2006: 35) that increased knowledge of the body is extricated 'beyond appearance and information control about the body into the experiences of the body and to those emanating from it as they arise during illness and disability'. Charmaz and Rosenfeld claim that 'as our sensitivity increases to the unexpected gaze of others, staring into the looking-glass they hold can become increasingly painful' (2006: 36) and then that pain can fracture the mirror, refracting 'contradictory images', they write with a jarring accuracy (Charmaz and Rosenfeld, 2006: 44). However, such 'pain' may be reduced when the mirrored image portrays the two-in-one, the dyad that is 'our self', and the strength of the symbiotic partnership is seen to diffuse the critical gaze of others and magnify the visible interspecies bond.

Richard admits that he now looks less at people's reactions to seeing the red-jacketed Higgins and himself when they are perceptible to a public eye:

> I'm more focused now on what I am doing. I'm probably more aloof than I was to begin with. I used to feel that everyone was looking at me. People ask if they can stroke him. Now I'm more conscious of the ratio; that one in every ten people wants to pat him or ask a question. On trains or buses, you can't help but sit next to someone who wants to talk about what he does. I've got over the self-consciousness now and can concentrate on what the dog and I are doing.

As we speak in the parkside café, another refugee from the inclement weather comes across from a neighbouring table where he is seated with a companion:

MAN: I see your little dog has 'medical training' on his jacket. Why medical training?
RICHARD: I have diabetes and he alerts for high and low blood sugar levels.
MAN: So somebody with diabetes could have a dog like this?

62 *Anthrozoological and sociological perspectives*

RICHARD: Yes, to warn them.

MAN: That's very interesting.

RICHARD: You can look up the charity, Medical Detection Dogs.

The man thanks him and moves back to his companion. Richard ponders for a moment and says: 'that was enough, I think; you can overdo explanation'. Richard's reduced self-consciousness, newly shared identity, and way of being with Higgins may perhaps be related to Haraway's 'animal mirror' (1991: 21) and Mullin's 'mirrors and windows' (1999: 201). He seems to reflect and affirm nuances of Higgins' visible abilities and the shared benefits of 'crossing boundaries' (Birke and Hockenhull, 2012) and creating bonds.

Erving Goffman (1959) examines the presentation of self in everyday life and his glimpse of humans working in lower-order service employment can relate also to the nonhuman animal considered to have a lower social and economic ranking than the human. 'Face-to-face interaction may be roughly defined as the reciprocal influence of individuals upon one another's actions when in one another's immediate physical presence', Goffman (1959: 26) pronounces, and then continues: 'a "performance" may be defined as all the activity of a given participant on a given occasion which serves to influence in any way any of the other participants' (Goffman, 1959: 26). The alerting dog's performance is a constant activity on given occasions so that 'when an individual or a performer plays the same part to the same audience on different occasions, a social relationship is likely to arise' (Goffman, 1959: 27), one in which belief and trust in each other is affirmed daily.

Michalko (1999) continues this theme:

> From the beginning, Smokie demonstrated nothing but his desire to become my friend. He is my partner and the trust, respect and admiration we have for one another is captured even more in the idea of friendship than in that of a bond (1999: 187).

Tales of the presentation and reception of the shared identity under public scrutiny are woven through the narratives given by the human half of the participating multispecies partnerships. Tina is a long-term possessor of Type 1 diabetes and relates deep feelings of shared identity with Harley, who rarely fails to alert appropriately and never leaves her side:

> And what I like, the thing I love about him, is that we're no longer a number, we're actually an individual person, an individual being, and that's what fascinates me.

The dog's presence and abilities are communicated by body language and active participation in the relationship. In particular, the human-needed canine alert is communicated as a result of the dog's acute sense of smell verifying changes in chemical odour detected in their human partner.

3 The canine sense of smell and olfactory acuity

Perceiving dogs as animate instruments, as efficient and highly effective health-care resources, requires examination of the canine nasal structure to discover how this contributes to their exceptional accuracy in olfactory sensitivity. Low (2005: 397), having explained in his 'ruminations on smell' that smell occurs everywhere in the experience of life, suggests that discovering the role of smell in our daily routines might better be 'apprehended within the domain of a sociology of everyday life'; and in this case, its role within the everyday realities of symbiotic life in chronic illness.

Looking at the dog's sensory acuity compared to our own, in terms of olfaction, appears to be an exercise in futility since the human nose conveys merely a microsmatic – or weak-scenting – ability, much like the nose of most primates, and functions far less capably than that of the pig, dog, or rat. However, research by Zelano and Sobel 'highlights results from studying humans, whom we think provide an underutilised, yet critical, animal model for olfaction' (2005: 431). They comment on the canine ability to recognise humans through odour but 'we don't all appreciate that, reciprocally, humans can identify dogs by their odor', as suggested by Wells and Hopper (2000), and seen in the practice of human scent detection ability that is learned, conducted, and discussed by Horowitz (2016).

Sarah Pink (2015) delves into historical sociology of the senses, researching studies investigating the sense of smell and social interaction. She highlights the suggestion by Kelvin Low that 'the differentiation of smell stands as that which involves not only an identification of "us" versus "them" or "you" versus "me", but also processes of judgement and ranking of social others' (Low, 2005: 405). Our judgement of a dog may easily, and sometimes unknowingly, be affected by an unpleasantly odoriferous and unkempt coat that has been well-rolled in the intense scents left by fox, badger, or cat, for example.

Howes and Classen (2014: 38) recall historical images of the senses as 'gateways to the body': illness could cause sensations in the body while some bodily sensations could cause illness or raise good health. Low's study of smell, Pink avers, 'attempts to move . . . towards individual, lived experiences where smell may be utilized as a social medium in the (re)construction of social realities' (Low, 2005: 398).

64 *The canine sense of smell and olfactory acuity*

This research is vested in the canine sense of smell and its influential use in biomedical technologies, and therefore the study is not deemed a sensorial ethnography since the personal or human naso-sensory perceptions of the odour of volatile organic compounds are not being interpreted or recorded. However, there is no doubt that both human and canine participants are affected by olfactory experiences within their shared homes, within their communities, practices, and coembodied identities. The canine olfactory sensitivity that enables acutely perceptive and beneficial detection of symptoms of human illness at home, or in the public gaze, can be considered to have use, as Low has suggested, as a social means to (re)construct 'social realities' (2005: 398).

Irvine takes behavioural flexibility as well as multisensory integration to be indicators of consciousness (2007: 9), emphasising that the ability to integrate information from different sensory pathways allows beings to detect misinformation and respond to it. Hearing, touching, seeing, smelling, and tasting all provide detailed information for conscious processing; the alert assistance dog has a highly developed sense of smell that allows detection and prediction of possible corporeal frailties of which the human is not consciously aware and therefore does not recognise as requiring urgent attention and action.

Serpell (2010) is among previously named contemporary researchers who consider the contribution made to human health by companion animals, a theme invigorating the heart of this investigation into the impact of canine olfactory detection on chronic illness management. This beneficial sensory ability is extensively explored by Miklósi (2009) and by Bradshaw (2012), the latter providing an anthrozoological perspective on the canine 'world of smells', a world enabling prediction and detection beyond vision and audition that has profound significance for human well-being.

Smelling like a dog

Alexandra Horowitz (2016: 3) commits to training her nose 'to better conjure what it might be like to have the mind and nose of a dog' in order to discover canine experiences of smell and the odours, often beyond our ability to recognise, which guide a dog's perception and understanding. In her scenting endeavours, what Sluka and Robben (2007: 28) might term 'sensorial fieldwork', Horowitz (2016: 6) suggests 'we may also see how to return to that perhaps more primal, so-called animal state of knowledge about ourselves and the world that we have forgotten in a culture wrought of technology and lab tests'.

However, it is also in perceiving the medical alert assistance dog as a modern-day health technology that we gain increased experience of our shared identities and 'situated knowledges' (Haraway, 1988: 575–599). Haraway suggests that feminist objectivity 'allows us to become answerable for what we learn how to see' and recalls 'lessons that I learned in part walking with my dogs and wondering how the world looks without a fovea and very few retinal cells for color vision but with a huge neural processing and sensory area for smells' (1988: 583).

The canine sense of smell and olfactory acuity   65

Research into the importance of the senses of vision and hearing to humans has been and continues to be a vast arena for exploration. But, in comparison, the sense of smell has been sparsely investigated; and research relating to the canine perception of odours remains scarce. Our sense of smell is not a priority for human survival, or at least not in contemporary 'Western' society.

Consequences of scenting

Howes and Classen (2014: 4–5), in researching the importance of smell in global societies, cite Endicott's study of the Batek peoples of peninsular Malaysia, who are reported to 'classify virtually everything in their environment by smell, and say that the sun has a bad smell "like that of raw meat", in contrast to the moon, which has a good smell, "like that of flowers" ' (Endicott, 1979: 39).

Subconsciously, we evoke memories and draw conclusions based on odour, taking pleasure in smells enticing us to enter a favourite bakery or to linger in a rose-laden garden. We breathe in and, with eyes closed, can identify bruised mint leaves, the smoke from an autumn bonfire, and a steaming tarred road after heavy summer rain, or the less-pleasant, sulphurous smell of a bad egg or, worse, the noxious odours from open sewage or a decomposing carcass.

Those examples exhibit strong and distinctive scents whose pungency our sense of smell cannot ignore; all are consequential effects of where we are or what we are doing; neural messages from the nose to the brain affording future memories and related emotions. Mention the smell of rotten eggs and immediately I stand wind-blistered and sand-blasted under a leaden sky, on the shoreline between a darkened sea and the granite-grey desert of the Skeleton Coast of Namibia, watching the churning thunderous Atlantic rollers disinter seabed organisms and pump malevolent, sulphurous smells landwards – smells that evoke memories.

Olfactory memory training has been shown to assist in improving the human ability to smell odours, notably for people with Parkinson's disease who may have lost this sense (Haehner et al., 2013); furthermore, the inability to detect odours as predictive of Alzheimer's disease is also under investigation. Hummel, Landis and Huettenbrink (2011) affirm that smell and taste disorders strongly affect quality of life and suggest that the ability of the olfactory epithelium to regenerate is significant to treatment.

However, our human survival depends more reliably on the sensory perceptions of keen sight and acute hearing (Ingold, 2000: 243–287), whereas dogs survive by employing their sense of smell as primary means of identification or discrimination, to detect areas of safety or danger, food and water, family member, friend or enemy, migratory pattern or the quickest route to the best mate. Evolution as human animals has reduced our scent detection ability, both in physiological structure and olfactory capability, so we now rely more on sight and hearing to perceive and achieve wanted goals.

Ache and Young (2005: 417) suggest that 'the ability to detect and respond in an adaptive manner to chemical signals serves as the primary window to the sensory world for most species of animal', but an acute sense of smell is no longer the

66 *The canine sense of smell and olfactory acuity*

prime human survival mechanism in contemporary society. There are exceptions, of course, such as the olfactory skills of 'wine tasters and perfumiers' (Bradshaw, 2012: 226), whose professional 'noses' may be highly insured for their commercial value to fragrance producers and vintners.

The exceptional canine ability to perceive and identify odours with high accuracy, together with dogs' sometimes surprising propensity to like the company of humankind, has become appreciably useful for a range of tasks, as noted above. Their additional value to biomedical research lies in the collaborative noninvasive detection of physically limiting boundaries constructed by chronic illness – particularly that of Type 1 diabetes. People with this illness can only obtain necessary insulin through injection or infusion so have a continual struggle to maintain accurate practices of care and to conduct the stringent treatment regimens to correct and balance blood glucose levels that fluctuate dramatically according to intake of nutrition, levels of stress, barometric pressure changes, and/or exercise.

Internationally, positive results are emerging from ongoing scientific research and development technologies in this field – for example, work on types of artificial pancreas, on pump therapy and the creation of human stem cell–derived beta cells (Vegas et al., 2016). Staymates et al. (2016) experimented with the design of a 3-D printed dog's nose which could sniff and found improvement in detection which could benefit future vapour samplers for explosives, narcotics, and illness.

But 10%, of the 3.7 million people known to have diabetes in the United Kingdom, have already been diagnosed with Type 1 and this compels them to spend every day of their lives practicing the mechanics of care and performing strict treatment routines to control the effects of the illness, using whatever method is currently available to them. That those with Type 1 diabetes will look forward to new health technologies is not in doubt, but survival in the 'here and now' is the primary objective of those currently coping with the complexities of this chronic illness.

A human inability to recognize symptoms of an onset of hypoglycaemia can result at worst in death. However, the smell of changing scent signatures, the VOCs exhaled in every breath, disturbs the usual odour pattern recognised by the medical alert assistance dog, who then actively warns the human partner of an impending episode. These dogs may nudge, nibble, stare, paw, whine, scrabble, or jump up to alert the human companion. They are trained to use an alert signal that is both natural to them and recognisable as such by their partner and not seen, for example, as an invitation to play or go for a walk. I ask Liz, an MDD trainer, how the young dog she is working with is likely to alert a future partner. She replies that it depends entirely on the dog. 'Ben is quite a nudger so maybe he'll do that. It's whatever the dog offers, not what the client chooses'.

The alert behaviour needs to be of sufficient intensity to wake up a sound sleeper with fast-dropping blood sugar levels and at night is likely to be performed with increased volume and mobility when compared with more subtle alert signals in daylight (participants recall the dogs shaking their heads and rattling collars and tags, jumping on the bed, whining, and barking when doing nighttime alerts). The medical alert assistance dogs learn to give well-practiced alarm signals to their human partners when blood glucose levels rise or fall to unsafe concentrations – usually above 12 or below 4.5 millimoles per litre, although the range will vary according to the individual concerned. (Mole is the molecular weight of a biological substance in grams so that, for example, the molecular weight of glucose is 180; 1mmol glucose equals 180 mg.) People with Type 1 diabetes generally see 7mmol/l as a 'normal' blood glucose reading on their monitors.

The canine assistant may fetch the medical kit for their human companion and not leave them until sufficient treatment has been seen to have been performed. In reference to causality (Irvine, 2007: 8), the trained diabetes alert dog appears able to connect cause and effect: to have intention to act, to perform that intention, and then to wait and see the consequence of what they have done – and do more if he/she 'thinks' it necessary. As one participant confirmed, referring to her canine partner:

> In the middle of the night, obviously I'm in a deep sleep, he'll get me up and get my blood kit; but he doesn't stop there because he won't relax and let me get back into bed to go to sleep until I've had my Lucozade and something to eat – and then he'll just chill out.

Canine nasal structure

The dog's nasal cavity contains hundreds of millions of sensory neurons in the olfactory epithelium (OE), the skin which lines convoluted nasal turbinates – paper-thin, spiral-shaped bones at the back of the nose – providing an extensive area for odorant transport. Helton (2009) opines the average dog to have an olfactory epithelium of approximately 170 square centimetres compared to the approximate 10 square centimetres of OE in a human. The OE of the pig is estimated to extend to 300 square centimetres (Roura and Tedó, 2009).

Whether the porcine olfactory ability could be aligned to biomedical treatments in the same manner that dogs are trained to assist in healthcare, is not for this study; but future research into the scenting prowess and 'trainability' of other macrosmatic species could lead to a broader resource base of animals specialising in odour variation: animals who may be able to deliver increasing accuracy in the detection of illness at an early stage, both among human and nonhuman sufferers.

No mechanical system or technological equipment have yet been designed to be as effective in odour detection and discrimination as the nasal architecture of mammals such as rats or dogs. The nose of the dog serves as a model for the e-nose, an electronic nose that may eventually provide noninvasive diagnosis of serious illnesses affecting human and nonhuman animals. Gas sensor arrays, such as the LABRADOR (the light-weight analyser for buried remains and decomposition odour recognition) which is used to find concealed graves (Vass, Thompson and Wise, 2010), are among those advancing inanimate scent detection technology, but there is nothing currently manufactured and available to match the keen olfactory sensitivity of most nonhuman living creatures.

68   *The canine sense of smell and olfactory acuity*

News media and academic papers have commented variously on the exceptional scenting abilities of multiple species. It is recorded that

> Turkey vultures (*Cathartes aura*) are, according to Lisney et al. (2013: 1955) 'considered to be olfactory specialists' and 'primarily rely on olfaction to detect and locate carcasses' in forested or hard to access rural regions. When comparing the visual systems of New World turkey vultures and black vultures (*Coragyps atratus*), Lisney et al. (2013) noted that the turkey vulture has larger nostrils, a larger nasal fossa, a greater surface area for olfactory receptors, and a relatively larger olfactory bulb, and that they are able to detect carrion in the absence of visual cues; in Africa, the Giant Pouched Rat (*Cricetomys gambianus*) learns swiftly to scent and warn of concealed landmines (Poling et al., 2010) and to detect pulmonary tuberculosis from sputum samples (Poling et al., 2011); in Southern Africa (Miller et al., 2015), the olfactory prowess of the African elephant (*Loxodonta africana*) enables detection of TNT traces; in Britain (Coles, 2015). the People's Trust for Endangered Species supports research with working 'sniffer' dogs to trace hard-to-find harvest mice (*Micromys minutus*).
>
> (Coles, 2015)

Locusts, of the family *Acridae*, are also becoming instrumental in the olfactory search for explosives. BBC Technology (2016) reported that researchers are currently developing technology that may allow locusts to detect explosives using their sense of smell. According to Baranidharan Raman of the School of Engineering and Applied Science at Washington University (2016), neural signals from a locust's brain would be processed by an attached chip that could send information back to those guiding the locusts into remote areas.

Craven, Paterson, and Settles (2010: 933) suggest a dog can detect odorant concentration levels at 1–2 parts per trillion and, according to Walker et al. (2003, 2006), canine olfactory acuity is 'roughly 10,000–100,000 times that of a human'. Think of a drop of water – and two water-filled Olympic-sized swimming pools – to picture the ratio more easily. Investigating the fluid dynamics of canine olfaction, Craven, Paterson, and Settles (2010) draw attention to the fact that olfaction and respiration each have a distinct airflow path through the nasal cavity and these unique nasal airflow patterns can explain macrosmia in certain nonhuman animals.

Breathing in enables odour-laden air to be transported to the olfactory recess area of the nose, while respiratory airways take the remaining airflow from the olfactory recess towards the nasopharynx, where it leaves the nasal cavity. Craven explains that 'expiratory pathlines originating from the nasopharynx demonstrate that airflow bypasses the olfactory recess during expiration, leaving quiescent (*inactive*) scent-laden air there, providing an additional residence time for enhanced odorant absorption' (2010: 940, figure 7c), and enabling accurate detection and discrimination.

A canine alert can be given up to an hour before an episode that might cause human loss of consciousness. An example is offered by Mel, a participant whose

The canine sense of smell and olfactory acuity   69

child has had Type 1 diabetes for several years but has been able to play foot-ball because their family dog and trained canine alert assistant, Gemma, alerts to Mark's changing blood glucose levels by jumping up as she watches from the sidelines before his blood sugar drops too low. Mel explains:

> There is a respect barrier, a line of tape and posts between spectators and the players on the soccer field. Gemma will sit quietly beside me, then she will try to go over to him; she goes to the end of the lead, turns back and faces me, comes back and jumps up, paws at the bag I keep the meter in; then she goes back to the end of the lead which will be just about under the tape, and sort of jumps back and tosses her head as if to say 'come on'.

Mel then goes to the coach and whispers her request to 'get him off'. The player can be called off for a blood test, perhaps be given a swift-acting carbohydrate boost, and may then be able to resume play.

Similarly, adults can shop without fear of collapsing in the street when the assistance dogs recognise and alert to scent changes prior to a 'hypo'. Before she shared life with Apple, Sara frequently collapsed in public without warning, an often-embarrassing feature of hypoglycaemia in which blood glucose levels can suddenly drop dangerously low.

Tina, whose blood sugar levels are also inclined to drop very fast, recollected having a recent 'funny turn' when Harley jumped up as she was paying for goods in a supermarket. 'The lady at the till asked if I was alright. I said I'd get a cof-fee and sit down. I came round in the ambulance'. The next time Tina went there to shop, the staff told her how sorry they had felt for Harley: 'he was so stressed doing everything, making sure everyone was doing everything right, we thought you were a trainer'. Such nonhuman animal concern for human frailty, and such human concern for an animal's visible and invisible anxiety, evidence more than one way in which symbiotic relationships are caused and maintained. (Methods that may reduce such anxious behaviours in a working dog are addressed further on.) Tina believes the shop's members of staff like to see Harley working and, referring to her collapse, adds: 'by all accounts, he did super'.

During our conversation, Harley lies stretched out, snoring loudly, under Tina's chair. Suddenly interrupting her discourse, he gets up, stares at her, puts a paw on her leg, then jumps up and licks her face. She tests her blood sugar levels and finds them to be 23.5 millimoles per litre, far above her acceptable range. Harley is rewarded swiftly with praise and a treat. In this case the dog has alerted to hyperglycaemia, when blood sugar levels rise too high rather than dropping too low, but he has been trained to alert to both hypo- and hyperglycaemic conditions endemic to his human partner.

Dogs can retain scents, as can cats, rabbits, rats, and most other species. How-ever, the olfactory recess is 'largely absent in microsmatic primates' (Craven, Pat-erson and Settles, 2010: 933), for example, humans and rhesus monkeys (*Macaca mulatta*), and olfactory mucosa (mucous membranes) in these species are situ-ated in the upper part of the nasal cavity. The dog's exceptional olfactory acuity

70 *The canine sense of smell and olfactory acuity*

appears to 'depend on its nasal airway architecture and odorant transport by these unique airflow patterns generated during sniffing' (2010: 939).

John Bradshaw devotes a chapter of *In Defence of Dogs* to canine olfactory ability, comparing its advent to the diminution of human odour perception and the evolution of our three-colour vision (2012: 227). Excluding perfumiers and wine-tasters, who have specific verbal language to describe the odours they smell, Bradshaw draws attention to the lack of language available for human description of 'the quality of odours' surrounding us (2012: 226). Where we have the advantage in daylight vision terms but have weaker auditory powers than dogs, the latter leap and bound streets ahead of us in the scenting stakes. Not surprising, when reading statistical claims by Bradshaw and other researchers (Craven, Paterson, and Settles, 2010; Miklósi, 2009) that between 220 million and two billion nerves link the canine olfactory epithelium to the dog's brain.

So sniffing is a natural practice for a dog – air is inspired and expired both for olfactory purposes and for respiratory survival. Encouraging dogs to use their sense of smell to identify biomarkers of human disease through positive reinforcement or reward-based training appears advantageous to both species. However, ethical issues arising from the concept of 'using' other-than-human animals are for later discussion.

The following chapter, with its sizeable number of quoted and barely edited participant narrations, is strongly influenced by James Clifford's image of a wished-for 'utopia of plural authorship that accords to collaborators not merely the status of independent enunciators but that of writers' (2007: 490). The voices of participants should be heard as speaking for themselves in their own choices of language, time, and space. Clifford (2007) suggests it is only after they have been heard that a researcher should attempt to reflect, discuss, interpret, or analyse any verbal content narrated by the observed speakers in response to questions asked.

Respondents, 'speaking' here, neither evade questions nor try to change meanings. The vocal responses are communicated in human speech since the dogs achieve interspecies communication mainly through physical movement and sensory perception. The participants volunteer word-pictures of their everyday routines in Type 1 diabetes, the coembodied skills and behaviours they find compulsory to practice and make available to observation, and the mutualisms inherent in the symbiotic relationships developing from chronic illness.

4 'Doing' diabetes Type 1

Doing the daily routines of assessment, measure, and control, necessary to balance blood glucose levels and carbohydrate absorption, and performing active behaviours (doing tests and recording what, why, and when they have done, are doing, and will do), require physical and mental work, intense concentration, and a need for internal and external self-knowledge. Observing the length of time which respondent, Paul, spent enacting these routines, the question arose 'how much of the day do you spend thinking about the illness?' The answer was thoughtful:

> It's probably on your mind 24 hours a day or all the time you're awake. If *you* think about dinner, you'd just put something on; but I first need to think about what I'm going to eat, how much I'm going to inject. It may only take 15 minutes but when you sit down to eat, you think I've got to eat all of this, and then if you don't, you think I've missed that out so that's left me short on eggs, so then you've got to get something else to fill the gap.

And yet this calmly spoken complex statement fails to encompass the depth and breadth of the causes and effects of life with Type 1 diabetes and its conjoined emotional upheaval. Extracts from Paul's narrative, given during fieldwork observation, reveal many of the complicated, and sometimes confusing, requirements of Type 1 diabetes and detail the necessary 'juggling' of carbohydrates to suit the moment. Consumed 'carbs and cals' can be highly effective or completely ineffective, depending on the rate of absorption, the speed of the rise or fall of blood glucose levels, the items being digested, current 'mood', and the variety of contextual settings.

Each person with chronic illness is unique within and without, so a diet suiting one diabetic, for example, may lead to an increase in hypoglycaemic episodes in another; one type of energy drink may increase blood sugar levels almost instantly for some but make no difference whatsoever for others. Discovering similarities and differences in such care practices may afford assistance to 'newcomers' with Type 1 diabetes who are likely overwhelmed by the enormity of their diagnosis, and to parents shocked to learn of their infant's seeming lifetime medical 'sentence'.

Participant narratives expand detail and exemplify their shared lives, giving commentary on the advantages and disadvantages of mutualistic practices of care.

72 'Doing' diabetes Type 1

With emotion and knowledge relating to chronic illness being embodied in both participants and, to a lesser extent, in the researcher, the narrative gains from insight into the body as subject and as object, into the interconnectedness and engagement of the two species, and as Mol and Law (2004: 4) have suggested, into 'the body we *do*' to avoid a hypo.

Josephine Donovan's (2006: 324) call for 'a feminist animal care ethic . . . political in its perspective and dialogical in its method', pleads for the extinction of superimposed human voices over those of animals and urges recognition of their own subjectivity instead of considering them human-dominated objects. Clifford (1986: 15) introduces the concept of 'polyvocality' into our cognition; the notion of a seemingly efficient and apposite method of hearing what discussants think and feel about themselves, their illnesses, the company they keep and the existences in which they live. However, 'researcher mediation' (Emerson, Fretz and Shaw, 1995: 13) cannot avoid some degree of influence on the direction and pattern of flow before, during and even after a discourse is complete. As Hurn suggests (2012: 212), polyvocality has become expected in 'postmodern ethnographic writing', but the multiple voices heard are principally of human creation. It is hoped that Donovan's plea continues to be acted upon so that multispecies dialogues are more sensitively and correctly interpreted.

The illness, Type 1 diabetes

Formerly known as insulin-dependent diabetes, Type 1 diabetes is a medical condition in which the immune system destroys the body's insulin-producing beta cells in the pancreas. Produced successfully, insulin is a hormone that allows glucose to leave the blood and enter the cells of the body to provide energy, but once an individual is diagnosed with Type 1 diabetes, insulin injections or infusions take over and become a constant requirement.

Information from Diabetes UK (2016) suggests that diabetic ketoacidosis (DKA) may be an indication of undiagnosed Type 1 diabetes; it is likely to occur when insufficient insulin prevents glucose entering cells and results in the body burning fatty acids and producing acidic ketones for energy. High levels of ketone bodies in the bloodstream can lead to DKA, loss of consciousness, and possibly death if the individual is not treated rapidly.

Paul believes his ketone production is generally low and quite often, if he 'goes high', ketones are not registered on the monitor when testing so he is relieved not to suffer ketoacidosis. But when Nero gives strong alerts to his blood sugar levels, he wonders if ketones are being produced and decides he will start looking into this. His thoughts show him to be an 'active' rather than 'passive' patient (Nettleton, 2013: 5); one who endeavours to discover improved methods and treatments, who will trial and experiment with what is new and available:

> You don't know unless you try these things – bear in mind that like the blood monitors, years ago it used to be urine sticks and the results were 4–6 hours in arrears I think, so when you used to do your dipstick and you turn round

'Doing' diabetes Type 1   73

and find you're high, bear in mind you only had the little strips to line up, and it was this and it was that . . . four hours ago.

He is surprised that people are unconcerned with finding new or improved methods of dealing with their illness; that there is passive acceptance instead of an active, ongoing endeavour to make life more comfortable:

> Everyone's different so what affects one may not affect the next; you tend to find what works for you and stick with it. You get people who've been 10–15 years with it and they don't understand – you think surely they experiment, it's the only way of learning anything – that in certain conditions, this happens, or that happens; it doesn't always but it's more likely to.

On a visit to the charity's offices, I listen to clients talking to and learning from one another, as I am myself. They discuss symptoms of people who retain hypo-awareness, often noticed in pallor, shaking, and sweating, but those are the early signals and if ignored may lead to moodiness, aggression, or unexpected silence. One speaker, Sally, remembers teenage arguments with her mother over the need to test when 'in a mood'. I ask if she is still aware of being 'difficult' and she answers 'nowadays, no, not very often':

> My poor husband probably gets most of it now and there are times when he's woken up in bed and found me trying to smother him with a pillow because I can get quite aggressive. I joke about it but it's because my blood sugars are so low that my brain doesn't know what it's doing and I'm in fight or flight response – so I'm going to kill my husband.
>
> *(Laughter follows her comment and someone says,*
> *'but that's normal, isn't it', which maintains the*
> *humour – but as is so often the case, the humour is*
> *there to alleviate darker emotion and covers recognition of*
> *the complex issues involved in coping with Type 1 diabetes.)*

One of the medical alert assistance dog trainers, Gill, admits she never realised 'how debilitating' the illness was until she was employed by the charity.

> I knew people tested their blood, I knew they used insulin and things like that, but I was very naive about hypo-unawareness and how it stops people going out, stops people working, you know, puts a lot of boundaries in there for them.

Effects of the diagnosis

Richard relates that he was about 21 years old when first diagnosed with Type 1 diabetes. Expecting him to have been shocked and possibly depressed by the revelation, I was surprised when he said he had felt relief: 'I had the classic symptoms of having a very dry mouth and not being able to quench my thirst', so finding reason

74 'Doing' diabetes Type 1

and name for his symptoms enabled access to a community of similarly labelled individuals and eased anxiety when learning of available medical treatments.

Symptoms occurring before a hypo, and of which he is no longer aware, are listed on the kitchen wall at home and in his office so that his work colleagues can recognise out-of-the-norm behaviour and respond appropriately:

> I've broken the symptoms into groups. The first one is sweatiness, dizziness, trembling, shakiness, going pale; the second group is irritability, difficulty speaking and/or concentrating, confusion and in the third group, disorderly or irrational behaviour that may be mistaken for drunkenness.
>
> Sometimes I think I've got low sugar levels when it's the opposite, when it's very high which is because . . . you know, not really having the full inkling – it used to be sort of trembling of the lips, that sort of thing; tingling lips could be a sign. And just being a bit wobbly – I can remember when I was first diagnosed and would go into the canteen for a snack, and on some occasions just couldn't move my legs in the ways that I wanted, and people would speak to me and I wasn't able to respond.
>
> Whereas now I seem to be quite able to chat to people on the phone or in person at 2.2mmol/l, so I've lost all those signs that other people might pick up on.

Paul, who was diagnosed at the age of six, says he has never been aware of falling into a coma (although he is reminded by Natasha, his partner, that he was once unconscious for about four hours), because generally he keeps functioning and is not a 'collapsing diabetic':

> My brain shuts down and just says keep walking, get something to eat and that's what I do; it's happened at work in different places, but I just keep going.

Charmaz (1995) delineates the rigours and exacting demands of diabetes, its incessant clamour for attention to prevent loss of body, mind, and spirit. Determination, patience, and skill seem essential to performing the ongoing tasks inherent in this highly complex illness. Accurately weighing and measuring food intake, withdrawing exact amounts of insulin for injections, and gauging alterations in blood glucose levels resulting from stress, exercise, or health issues, can have strong impact on day-to-day living, and a 'hypo' can affect planned activities detrimentally.

Paul explains how weather changes can affect his blood sugar levels:

> I try to keep my bloods up so when I'm on a walk, they're rising as I walk and so it stays level and when I get back, I'm not too bad. But different weather conditions have an impact so today, although it's quite blustery which means it's harder to walk, I was warm on the walk and so burned off more. In summer, you strip off to a pair of shorts and a T-shirt so actually you're cool on the walk.

Mol's observations of the 'miniaturized blood sugar measurement machines' as diagnostic devices (2000: 19) draw attention to how an individual may learn to be independent from medical professionals as he or she become expert in self-regulation. But, if they are hypo-unaware, they may not recognise when testing and the reading of numerical results should take place, and therefore still risk potential hypo episodes unless they test very frequently; in which case the device may become an unwanted but necessary intervention instead of a valued assistive technology.

Mol allows that use of the diagnostic device may be 'a practical nuisance', an irritant that can ruin plans and 'spoil the day' (2000: 20) despite its significance to an autonomous lifestyle. Being diagnosed with Type 1 diabetes brings hard work and complex procedures; managing its effects to lead the best possible independent life incorporates obligatory management of the tiresome but beneficial blood glucose monitor. But if there is no recognisable symptom of a forthcoming hypo, many are compelled to rely on guesswork and repetitive success or failure of the optional test.

In this situation, the scenting ability of a hypo-alert assistance dog is influential. A partner or friend may insist on the frequent need to do a blood sugar test which can lead to ructions in relationships and refusal to oblige, but the DAD will continue to perform an alert regardless of the individual's mood or language; will provide good practices of care despite argument and tension; and, being animate, warm, and friendly, is likely to gain acceptance of the alert and the need to follow it with a blood test, reducing friction and the need to nag.

Canine 'alert' communication

Natasha comments on the mental and physical agility used by Nero to communicate an alert when Paul is sleeping too deeply to be roused by the dog's usual nudging and staring:

> Nero gets up, he goes shake, shake, shake (*she demonstrates his head swinging from side to side so his ears fly up and down*), you hear his collar going and his ears flapping, and that's what wakes me up . . . but it doesn't wake Paul so Nero'll come padding round the bed and I'll just watch his behaviour while I'm pretending to be asleep in the hope that he'll go round that side, but . . . he launches over him, actually on him because he can't get to my side of the bed, but Paul still doesn't wake up; Nero clambers all over him and he still doesn't wake up.

Sara describes Apple's similar nighttime alerting method:

> Before he jumps up on the bed, he does a lot of walking about at night. He'll get up, shake and you hear his tags jingling, and he paces around the room, sniffs the air and stands next to the bed, and he tends to wake you up then and you realise. If you don't, he'll jump up on the bed, but it does give you a chance to wake up gently – normally I think it's my husband who'll say to me 'the dog's up' and I'll look.

76 *'Doing' diabetes Type 1*

Blood and pollution

Janet Carsten (2013: 132) writes of the management of blood in laboratories where blood is extracted and screened, examined, and analysed, before results are entered into information systems where data can be retrieved and referred to by medical practitioners. 'The processes of extraction, analysis, storage, disposal, and data-recording are at the heart of what goes on in the labs', she asserts; and perhaps not surprisingly, similar procedures are performed in every residence that is home to someone with Type 1 diabetes.

Carsten shows interest in the need for social engagement to make things happen, for example, 'interactions between medical lab technologists and patients, between working colleagues, and between the staff of the labs and the samples they analyse as well as with the equipment they use' (2013: 132). This research is focused on social engagement and the resultant interactions between medical assistance dogs and their diabetic human companions, between the participants in this research and members of their families and health care teams, and between themselves, the dogs, and the insentient blood glucose meters, insulin pumps, and test strips, the contents of their treatment toolkits.

Blood, pumping its circulatory route along arteries and veins, transports gases, nutrients, and whatever is needed by internal organs to maintain and safeguard life. But blood has further function externally, whether in the form of transfusion, blood-letting or clotting, and in this instance, in providing internal information on blood glucose levels to the external observing eyes of its human 'container', who, being hypo-unaware, cannot comprehend or manage without measurements and statistics being presented visibly or audibly. Those who have lost hypo-awareness are impeded by the loss of perceptive abilities that recognise warning signs of hypos and instead rely on the vital drops of blood that are so constantly and determinedly extracted and monitored manually.

Considering here that our skin is the external porous and elastic casing of the body that contains among other essentials to life, the blood flow system, Carsten's (2013: 4) alternative proposal of 'the literal uncontainability of blood – its capacity to move between domains', coincides with Mol's concept of corporeal 'leaking' and the skin's porosity. 'Blood can secure life, but also be a source of danger through its lack of boundaries', Carsten suggests (2013: 5). For the most part, the body acts as an efficient receptacle for organs, bones, arteries, and veins and is equally efficient at enabling the circulatory system to function optimally in pumping blood for life.

Sally comments on the difficulty of testing blood sugar levels when away from home where a hygienic and private environment may be hard to find:

> Toilets aren't the cleanest places . . . and doing the test through clothing isn't ideal, so people usually go for the quick and easy way and that's in your tummy or arm.

During my observation sessions, none of the participants ever wore latex or any other form of material glove to prevent molecules of dirt or dust combining with their blood on the test strip or attaching to their pumps, cartridges, or glucose

'Doing' diabetes Type 1   77

monitors. However, they all took care to test in environments that were hygienic, and always at home before and after exercise, shopping trips, or any public venture. Having the dog close at hand generally ensured that an alert would give sufficient time to find a safe and clean area in which to test blood glucose levels.

Mary Douglas's well-cited observation of dirt as being 'matter out place' therefore seems not to require bold emphasis here (2002: 44). Blood is not dried, spilled, or considered 'dirty' in this arena in the same way that it might become dirty and out of place as the result of a nosebleed or cut from broken glass or fall on a tarred road. However, to avoid contamination of the blood drop that is placed on the test strip, and any possibly incorrect blood sugar level readings resulting from that, advice on the Diabetes.co.uk website does suggest that test strips 'that have been in contact with dirt, crumbs, food or liquids' should not be used; on the test strip, those items would always be identified as 'matter out of place'.

Injecting insulin

As Richard exemplifies, not everyone with Type 1 diabetes is automatically given an insulin pump. His treatment in the early 1990s involved 'one of those huge syringes' which injected a set amount of insulin every day. Sally has shown me one of these during a visit to MDD head office, and it is indeed 'huge' and heavy and shoots the insulin almost with a thump into the chosen anatomical area – I wonder at the strength of character and pain threshold exhibited by those insulin-needy 'patients' of former years.

However, when he moved into a new residential area, Richard's doctor informed him that the way he was injecting was 'very old-fashioned' and he would find it easier with a 'pen'. At the kitchen table, Richard opens what looks like an optician's spectacle case, takes out a 'pen' and demonstrates how it works:

> You just dial up the number and there's a plunger which moves up every time you release a little insulin, so you've got a visual of how much insulin is left before you need to replenish the pen. I keep one in the fridge at work, one at home and one on me.
>
> However, the ready-mixed insulin first recommended didn't work at all because I don't have the same amount to eat at the same time every day. It didn't give me any freedom and, if you're working and socialising and such like, you can't live your life to such a tight regime. I was having lots and lots of hypos with it, so it wasn't helping.

He now has long-acting insulin in the morning and evening and can top-up with short-acting insulin during the day, depending on the variables likely to extend his blood sugar levels. It is about an hour since he had breakfast when his levels dropped from 16 to 12 and then to 6.7mmol/l:

> It's okay at the moment, I think (*but he tests anyway*); it generally stays high after a meal for about an hour, but then it's keeping it right between meals. Oh, it's still quite high, it's jumped back up to 16.4. I can take a correcting

78 *'Doing' diabetes Type 1*

dose – you put in the time, followed by the blood sugar level and it tells me I only need one unit to bring it down which is about 3mmol/l.

As he works at this seemingly non-stop balancing act, this continual 'doing' of diabetes care, he explains:

In reality, I'd be inclined to take more than one unit, but it's all dependent on exercise. If I was going for a long walk, then one unit or none might be more appropriate.

The insulin pump

Patients are encouraged to attend explanatory courses such as the DAFNE, or Dose Adjustment for Normal Eating, in order to gain skills and knowledge that help in understanding and maintaining the effective use of insulin pump therapy and that enable those attending to share tips that may make life management easier for one another.

Several participants revealed significant personal experiences from incorporating a pump to attain more accurate insulin dosage. Janet sighs and relates that she used to swim a lot as a child but, although enthused by the pump's improvement to her blood sugar monitoring, she has not been swimming for some time because 'you can only have the maximum of an hour of it being off and then you have to do the extra insulin to compensate for what you've not had'.

Paul, recently accustomed to wearing an insulin pump which has been 'a godsend; it's so much better, not perfect, not brilliant, but so much better, I wouldn't be without it', also regrets the curtailed pleasure and comfort gained from relaxing for a long time in a hot bath because of the pump-free time limitation.

Like other informants, Sally has no hypo-awareness so her diabetic alert dog, Maggie, a sturdy and inquisitive chocolate Labrador, informs her when she should check outside the regular testing times. Sally has an insulin pump which reduces the likelihood of severe hypos but does not prevent them all. Although she has the 'latest' pump which will turn off the insulin when the blood sugar level is too low, Sally explains the ever-present need to know that the sensor's reading is accurate. She emphasises that 'we're relying on so many bits of technology to work, it can be quite scary'. But that is where the assistance dog's keen sensitivity can reassure and there seems to be comfort and relief in knowing that the canine alert is accurate in predicting 'hypers' and 'hypos'.

I enquire how the pump is attached to her, and while disentangling a flexible line from beneath her clothing, she explains that

You've got a little cannula which is hollow so the insulin will go down that line into the part that's just under the skin (*the cannula is a small tube inserted into the body to allow fluid to enter or escape*). It's a bit like an injection every two or three days, instead of five or ten times a day. Because the insulin

'Doing' diabetes Type 1   79

is short-acting, the tube that's now inside, has to stay open so you have to make sure it's not blocked or kinking and therefore have to check your blood sugars to make sure it's always open. Air getting in isn't a huge worry as we only deal with very small amounts of insulin.

But even with this latest technology, there isn't any less hassle; you've still got to be on it. If the line came off at 3 a.m. and my blood sugars were going up, I'd have to change it at 3 a.m. – I can't wait until morning to do it.

I remark, as I find myself doing frequently, that I am astounded at the amount of work and time employed in maintaining a 'normal' existence. Sally agrees and says people suffer from 'diabetes burn-out'.

You go to the clinic and they say your blood sugars aren't good enough, try harder, so you go back and again they're not good enough . . . it's difficult for teenagers. Whatever you do, will affect your health, and hormones can affect your blood sugar levels as well. With most conditions, you can have a day off without meds, but with diabetes, you can't.

Paul is seated at a table set against one wall of the sitting-room when diabetes alert dog, Nero, announces my arrival with a low-key bark and a fast-wagging tail. Natasha – who is a partner, carer, and an executive who has organised the administration of her business so that she can conduct it principally from their home – invites me in. Paul explains that he is putting in a new cannula:

It goes in every three days or thereabouts, it depends on the person. Because I'm still quite insulin-sensitive despite everything, I don't have as much difficulty as others with the sites. When you're injecting a lot of insulin, it tends to get sore. You can get a residue, a lump under the skin. You can see the little marks when I pull it off.

(There are small red discolorations of the skin above his right and left hipbones.)

On another occasion, I ask Richard if he has received the insulin pump that he was hoping for 18 months earlier. He says that he was found to be eligible and has completed the DAFNE training course which is undertaken to ensure users fully understand the pump's requirements and practices:

The idea is to give you a much tighter control so you can adjust your dose according to the number of grams of carbohydrate you're eating. It's been a real success, the course, because I keep control that much tighter which avoids the longer-term complications like sight loss.

Richard is aware of the 'wild swings from highs to lows' in his blood glucose levels, so he has 'phoned again in the hoping of speeding up the pump's arrival.

80 *'Doing' diabetes Type 1*

Janet hesitates before admitting the pump has made her life 'better' in that she can manipulate the settings to aid control, for example, 'if you're going to have a fatty meal which takes longer to absorb, you can set the pump to split the insulin so you have X amount straightaway and the rest over the next hour-and-a-half'.

I note her hesitation and ask what she considers to be the pump's disadvantages. She laughs:

> Having to wear it; especially for me, I have to wear it on my arms because, where I've injected in my tummy for 20-odd years, I've got lots of scar tissue so absorption there is horrendous. The pump's a lot better for people who haven't got that because it's completely hidden. But I don't have that luxury so it's quite obvious; but you know, I'm used to it and I think the benefits of it far outweigh the fact that I get a bit self-conscious.

The test strips

Paul, still seated at the table, continues to talk as he removes a narrow plastic test strip from a vial that, unopened, would usually contain 25 or 50 strips. So that I can later understand what his recorded words relate to, Paul lets me take photographs as he opens and closes boxes, bottles, and the zipped blood glucose meter pack that are required items.

> You take the strip out of the bottle and insert it into the monitor. It stays like that until you put your blood onto the strip (*he pricks his finger and puts a drop of blood onto the narrow white test strip*). That's that and you wait for the result . . . that's lovely, perfect for me, 7.5 on the screen. Then you enter information denoting whether the test is pre-meal, post-meal, bedtime or other. Obviously if you want a snack, you put in your planned carbohydrates and it tells you how much insulin you need for the blood sugar – for the moment, I don't need anything, so we turn it off and that's that.

The diabetes test strips, despite their insignificant appearance, provide an important function in monitoring blood sugar levels. According to information appearing on the Diabetes.co.uk website:

> When blood is placed onto the test strip, it reacts with a chemical called glucose oxidase producing gluconic acid from the glucose in the blood. At the other end of the test strip, the meter transfers a current to the test strip. The test strip has electric terminals which allow the meter to measure the current between the terminals. The current between the terminals changes depending on the level of gluconic acid that has been produced. The blood glucose meter then uses an algorithm to work out the blood glucose level based upon the difference in current.

Cannula and pump

Paul continues his explanatory demonstration:

> Now the fun bit. Everyone does it differently, this is the infusion and it goes
> in there (tell me if you want me to slow down or stop or anything?) and that's
> then what flies into you. (*He pushes a gadget with a spring mechanism that
> has a stapler effect attaching a small pad to his skin.*) You take the safety off
> and throw that away. (*He drops the lancet, a short fine needle, into a yellow
> hard-plastic, lidded Sharps bin, so-named for its usage as a secure container
> for used needles and other sharp waste that might injure or carry infection.*)

Paul shows me how he removes any air bubbles from the cannula, fills up the vial
and the reserve and starts up the pump again.

> Now you take this one; I stop the pump and you can see there's an air bubble,
> so I need to get rid of that. I go onto the infusion set timing, it tells you three
> seconds (*he taps to move the bubble using a similar action as if moving an
> air bubble from a filled syringe*), if there were vials that just fitted, then there
> wouldn't be any air. I've got to watch it all the way down through the cannula
> and when it's gone out, which it has, I now hook up and that has just filled the
> reserve – there's a little vial that needs filling up before it goes into you. You
> need to fill it up before getting insulin. Then you re-start the pump.

He changes the cannula every three days and 'the entire kit, changing the vial
and everything, is every six days':

> I've got to have all the kit ready. You have to draw one of them up so now
> I do them (*the insulin vials*) in blocks of five. I have four in the fridge and
> one out, because you get fewer air bubbles if they're warm. The vials come
> in a box so you take one out, then get the pack of insulin and take out one
> of your insulins – they can be out of the fridge for about a month. Everyone
> thinks that if you're going on holiday, you must keep them in the fridge – no,
> although once they've been out of the fridge, you can't put them back again.

Nutrition

The longer I spend with participants, the more I realise how much of their lives are
entangled in the always-moving, ever-grabbing tentacles of Type 1 diabetes. I ask
Paul how he caters for the varied needs of his embodied illness and how he deals
with the very time-consuming weighing, estimating, and balancing of ingredients
for every meal.

> It was never that accurate with the jabs. The pump is much more accurate so
> it tends to be that much harder to get it spot-on; you have to work a little bit

82 *'Doing' diabetes Type 1*

more, you have to weigh food more, and guessing has more or less gone out of the window. If you get chips out of the freezer, you've got to weigh them, so if you're cooking for two, it becomes harder.

I ask if he takes a scale when they go out for a meal, but he shakes his head and says:

No, it's just years and years of learning and guesswork . . . going out for a meal is hardest. I might order something with a bit of sauce on it; it doesn't taste sweet, but it might be. Then if you jab for that, it might not be correct, so you do tend to run one way or the other if you go out for a meal. I run high generally because I go for a dessert as well and of course you've got no idea with desserts.

Nero nearly always alerts when we go out to eat. If I'm just peaking and then going to start dropping, he doesn't bother. A number of times I've checked and seen I've gone really high, so I have a jab and then he suddenly alerts, so I think 'what now?' and test again, and I've dropped because I was just peaking when I first checked.

Natasha remarks on the need to 'know your carbs, your complex and your simple carbs' and recalls that in the past week Paul's blood sugars have been running high 'for no reason':

He hasn't been doing anything differently, still been injecting the same, no air bubbles in his feed, he's on the insulin all the time, he even swapped the vials because he thought the insulin might be dodgy.

Paul interjects, saying that that he develops a resistance 'to pretty much anything over a period of time':

Lucozade will work for a few weeks and then stop; same with sugar in tea; dextrose will work for a while and then take longer to work. Even different flavours or just changing the flavour, has an impact. Some days I can eat what the pump dictates, like 28 grams of carbs, for example, so you have 28 grams of fast-acting carbohydrate to bring you back up to roundabout the 7 mark which is what my pump is set at for a good result. I do that and 20 minutes later when I check, I'll still be low so then it says eat XYZ. I do that, wait another 20 minutes and check again; I'll just be coming over so it says eat a little bit to bring you above. Well, two hours later, I'll be as high as anything because all that I've eaten has now taken effect – but at the time, it hadn't.

It's a guessing game a lot of the time . . . an educated guess, but still a guess.

His narrative paragraphs are neither edited nor shortened in order to allow a reader without Type 1 diabetes to comprehend the issues involved in what should be the

'Doing' diabetes Type 1   83

simple act of eating when hungry. Natasha values frozen food 'like jacket potatoes; much as I'd rather have fresh when I cook, it's just so much easier because the carb count's on the packet; someone's already done it for you'.

Paul says that 'bread's a nightmare' because of the many different varieties available and Natasha explains that they've currently got a brand of bread that isn't mentioned in the 'carbs and cals' book. 'There's no label on it to tell you so you don't know how thick to slice it – and that'll have a different impact on your blood sugar levels'.

Sara concurs with the complexities of eating to keep blood sugar levels within an acceptable range. When asked whether anger plays an emotional role in the time-consuming food preparation and digestion, she admits that she does get annoyed when 'you end up having to eat when you're not hungry':

> You might have breakfast and an hour or so later, you'll have a hypo because you need to eat something, toast or anything – and nobody, nobody wants to put on weight . . . you look at something and might as well apply the cake to your thighs as opposed to eating it!
>
> I'd do the housework one afternoon for an hour and a half, we'd sit down and eat a massive spaghetti Bolognese, then the dog would be going alerting mad, I'd test and my husband would say but you've just had that massive meal and then it would really start to plummet me down; twice during that evening I'd have a bowl of cereal, then a bit of toast – on top of the spaghetti for dinner – and you're like I really don't want to be eating all these calories because my trousers are feeling a bit tight. . . . I've given up on the weight but I do the carb count thing because I have to work out my insulin.

Mel increases my knowledge of nutrition in balancing blood glucose. Her family share their home with Gemma, a spaniel of boundless enthusiasm who took up residence as the young children's companion before showing altered behaviour patterns prior to a hypoglycaemic episode occurring in one of them. Gemma's outgoing attitude and scenting ability enabled her to be trained more fully in hypo scent detection and accurate alerting by the charity's instructors. Mel relates an example of how nutrition, or lack thereof, affected her son in the years before he was given an insulin pump:

> We went to my parents for Christmas and they decided to have a break between dinner and pudding. I'd given the injection for everything in the middle of his meal so I said: 'you can't do that because he's had all the insulin and needs to eat the pudding now'. It took a long time, but I thought we might get away with it. My dad likes to go for a walk first, but I said no, no. Mark was lying in the middle of their living-room floor, screaming, and my mother wanted to tell him to stop – but he can't.

In the days when children were invited to share their 'packed' school lunches, there was less knowledge of allergies or illness contagion through germ transmission.

84 *'Doing' diabetes Type 1*

However, Mel tells me that, to offset the chance of this happening in a contemporary situation, the primary school attended by her children does not allow any learners to offer or receive items from 'others'' lunchboxes.

Janet is pregnant when we first meet. She was diagnosed with Type 1 diabetes when aged four:

> I've never known anything different; you just find diabetes is always there – before you eat, you have to carb count, figure out what insulin you need and whether you're going to be doing any activity – you just find your mind is always thinking about diabetes . . . (*she sighs and then laughs*) yeah, pre-empting all the time.

'Not fit for purpose . . .'

Complications arising from Type 1 diabetes can cause renal failure, partial or total loss of sight, limb amputation, neuropathy (a degenerative disease or disorder of the nervous system), cardiovascular disease including heart attack or stroke, as well as possible sexual dysfunction and depression (Diabetes in the UK, 2010). Adult participants talk matter-of-factly about different illnesses – such as asthma, depression, or the consequences of neuropathy – that are known to emerge on occasion before, after, or alongside the diagnosis of Type 1 diabetes. There may be a need to ask for help from human and non-human members of the family, or from visiting friends or healthcare professionals, if severe neuropathy prevents maintaining a secure grip on hot pans, or visual impairment prevents accurate reading of recipe ingredients or oven temperatures.

Excerpts from participant narratives show how differently they are affected:

> . . . With diabetes, your blood goes into every cell so the smaller the cell, the harder it is for the blood with that much sugar, to get to the tips of your fingers, which is why quite often you end up with neuropathy in your fingers, why you have hearing problems, eye problems, because all of these have really fine veins so the blood can't get through; so it shuts down the blood supply which causes more problems.
>
> . . . Went to see a specialist about erectile dysfunction.
>
> . . . I've got peripheral neuropathy – zingy hands and feet sometimes – so I couldn't hold things for long. I was always dropping things out of the oven and getting very frustrated.
>
> . . . They diagnosed me with bladder neuropathy. I failed a job interview and got depression. We had to give up the flat.
>
> . . . You suffer lots of complications. One of them is hearing. The nerve-endings to your ears and blood vessels clam up and don't work so well. On top of that, I've got tinnitus; my eyes have problems so I'm having laser treatment.

Vision difficulties

Paul comments on his own failing eyesight when we have safely negotiated an uneven pavement leading from home to a park where Nero can run unleashed:

> Most of the time, I'm so used to my eye being the way it is that I don't realise how bad it is. When someone says 'oh, you're partially sighted', I'm like, well, no, because I can see. I'm so used to it that I've adapted so that it isn't so much of a problem. Obviously walking the dog with not much vision becomes more of a problem . . . (*he hesitates for a few seconds*) . . . and it takes concentration.
>
> I can see the edge of the pavement if I'm looking but I've got very little vision this side; I've got a bit of peripheral vision but not enough for me to see clearly. I know I've got my hand there and I can see my hand there, because that's what I'm expecting to see. If the pavement changes, it's just grey . . . but if a colour changes or it's moving, I can see things easier – you know when you look through Perspex and it's all scratched, that's kind of what's going on in that eye. I've got a lot of what they call scarring where I've had laser treatment, the relics of that, and where I've had bleeds and they haven't cleared, you've got this kind of . . . spider's web.
>
> It was that bad at one point that I was literally two feet in front of the TV just to see people and you know, I couldn't work out what was going on.

He is silent for a moment and then says, considerately: 'Erm, mostly, you're kind of, erm, facially I couldn't distinguish you from somebody else . . . when something's new, it's a little bit harder'. I realise then that he can walk across a field with Nero and around the village because the routes are familiar to both himself and his companion, and that he can distinguish certain things if they are vivid in shape and colour. Paul stresses that

> If you see me walking around, you wouldn't know, because I tend to know my environment. It's the same when I go shopping; they move stuff around in the shops but generally I know what's where – and people are objects, you can see people, you can see cars. I can see enough, distinguish enough at least to get out of the way. But if I've turned my head and am looking the other way, then I'll walk into people.
>
> I don't see myself as partially sighted . . . because I'm so used to it now, I've adapted for that. People say: 'can you sign there, by the cross?' and the cross is that faint, or the colour isn't strong enough so that I'm looking and thinking, I can't even see the cross.

Natasha describes Paul's vision impairments in relation to Nero's placement when they are walking together along pavements:

> Nero walks on his right because that's where Paul's got his sight . . . he's really only got this half-good eye because this (*other*) eye doesn't really see

86 *'Doing' diabetes Type 1*

anything at all. We asked if it was okay for Nero to walk that little bit ahead of him. (*Guide Dogs are encouraged to maintain a light tension in the leash as they 'lead' their partners, whereas medical detection dogs are asked to walk on a loose leash next to their companions. This attached 'way of going' is described as having a leash with a smile, or a 'U', in it, perhaps to remove any connotation of binding together with forceful restriction.*)

Paul volunteers that he is partially sighted, wears glasses, and is able to write, but he finds that 'it's a lot of effort for me; my spelling's atrocious and I'm slightly dyslexic'.

I question Sara about any visual difficulties she has noticed, and she hesitates before responding:

> I'm getting a few problems; my eyes go blurry and I've got a big black blob of a floater; you want to wipe it away. You try to look round it but of course you can't because when you move your eyeball, it moves and then it goes blurry.

This is something about which I can empathise – reading to the end of a line and expecting to start the next one immediately, but finding it necessary to wait for the floater to catch up before continuing; or trying to sweep away a fly dancing in front of your eyes, only to discover it's a floater and cannot be so easily removed – a tiny painless irritant, but a creator of frustration, distraction, and slowed reading. Sara continues:

> A top consultant at the eye clinic said . . . when your blood sugars go up, your body dehydrates so all the water in your body that's left goes to the vital organs that need it, so the first thing to dry out is your skin which doesn't need to be supple and smooth and doesn't need water to keep you living whereas your heart, kidneys etc all do need the water. Well, your eyes are made up of 70% water, I think, and if the water goes from your eyes, they shrink, the bit at the back of the retina shrinks, and that's why you get that blurred vision with diabetes.
>
> She said glasses wouldn't really help; because you get different levels of blurriness, your prescription could be six different things on six days of the week so you can't get glasses for when your eyes are bad because it's not like long- or short-sightedness. Good blood glucose control prevents this – that's what they say, isn't it?

On a visit to talk to Richard and Higgins, I ask Richard about his visual acumen in relation to a hypoglycaemic episode:

> I think when I go low to the point of collapse, that's when my vision goes funny and it's almost too late to take corrective action. I just see light shining

'Doing' diabetes Type 1   87

very intensely. I get a different perception of light – but Higgins now doesn't let me go that low – it's very foggy when you come round and you're not quite sure where you are or what you're doing, but in the run-up to a hypo, I can remember trying to get the right sort of sugar, like jelly babies or the little jars of clear honey that are easy to carry and not too difficult to get the lids off.

Driving and transport

Freedom to drive whenever and wherever allows choice and independence. Only one of those participating in this research is now able to maintain a driving licence and chooses to drive for short distances because of fluctuating blood sugar levels, preferring to use public transport to travel further afield. Others are compelled to rely on buses and trains or on available family members or friends to transport themselves and their canine assistants. This significant alteration to the habitual way of life has brought about changes in employment, reduction in mobility, and loss of self-confidence and self-regard. Janet had worked independently and successfully in the field of health care despite her Type 1 diabetes diagnosis. However, when she could no longer recognise symptoms of hypoglycaemia, she was informed abruptly of her shrinking and insecure 'reality bubble'; that is, her personal *umwelt* (Von Uexküll, 2010 [1934]):

> My job included driving patients in my car so when I lost my hypo-awareness, I was told I wasn't safe . . . they deemed me not fit for purpose and my driving licence was taken away.

Sara was also compelled to change methods of transport and household management:

> I had my driving licence taken away because of my hypo-unawareness, so I walk everywhere, to public transport, to the bus, I walk for everything, walk the dog – we reckon I must do about 15 miles of walking a week. But I think if I did anything more cardiovascular, for instance if I was to mop the three hard floors downstairs, I'd have to sit down half an hour later because I'd have a hypo, but then again, it can get you two hours after that.

Tina says that during her first train journey on her own, Harley had to alert her three times:

> And then it used to be that I'd come down on the train and people would give me money for the charity because, you know, they were so touched by how good he was. And then you sort of forget about your past and look and move forward – I can't believe how far I've come.

88 *'Doing' diabetes Type 1*

Paul rarely collapses. However, other side effects have thrown powerful obstacles across his life course. When he had to stop driving about 15 years ago, his world was shaken violently:

> Not riding the bike was the worst one because I did enjoy the freedom. It gave me my space, it gave me a calm, you know, used to go out on that, buzz around, loved it to bits . . . yeah, I do miss the bike.
>
> I used to have motorbikes, cars, used to drive a JCB at work and a dumper truck, a forklift – I was in and out of all these different vehicles all the time with no problem – and then suddenly I can't, I'm not allowed to . . . the fact that I no longer have that piece of paper saying I can . . . that was hard.
>
> (*Silence*) . . . Erm, giving up work, you suddenly feel like, well, what am I good for? And that for me, was a big, big issue which took me a long time (*he labours over each word and his voice drops*) . . . and I'm still not over it now (*his speech is slow and hesitant as he ponders his current situation*).

School

For children and adolescents, having Type 1 diabetes can offer opportunity for unwanted prominence in the classroom (although, according to several parents interviewed, current improvement in health education of staff has produced a greater understanding of the difficulties and needs of a school-going child with Type 1 diabetes). Difficulties and emotional outbursts were remembered by those already diagnosed with Type 1 diabetes when first attending school:

> . . . I was the only one (with Type 1 diabetes) at primary school and I'd quite often collapse in class. I did have one fit while I was at that school so I used to get called a diabetic spastic . . . so I isolated myself quite a bit because there just wasn't the understanding. Secondary school was a lot better and the teachers let me go and do blood tests without questioning it. Then at college everyone was very understanding because there were more diabetics.
>
> . . . My friends couldn't understand. Initially they were understanding but soon got quite frustrated with me because I was so nervous about doing things, always worrying about something happening and having to deal with it. This did knock my confidence way off.

Losing hypo-awareness

Alfie lies on the sofa behind Janet, nose resting on his neatly folded front legs and his eyes closed; the occasional twitching of a velvety ear reveals that he is paying attention to the nuances of our conversation but there is no sign of flaring nostrils, suggesting that his detection of steep changes in Janet's blood sugar levels.

'Doing' diabetes Type 1   89

When in hospital after collapsing several years ago, Janet tested her blood and found she was hypo despite not feeling any symptoms. She spoke to a nurse who explained that, since Janet had had diabetes for more than 20 years, her body had lost the ability to give recognisable advance warning signs and because she had been hypo for so long, her body now accepted a hypo as the 'norm' and any alarm signals had 'worn out'. Janet states bleakly that that explanation completely changed her life.

I ask if she could describe her body's former 'warning signs' of an impending hypo; her rate of speaking increases and she clumps words together so that the sentences become abrupt and stilted. As she ploughs through explanation, fear seems to stalk her words and activates speech in both the present and past tenses, even though her hypo-awareness disappeared several years before:

> . . . Blurred vision, I get very shaky, go very pale, get quite panicky and jittery; erm, everyone always said I go really pale around the eyes; I wouldn't be able to talk very well, probably wouldn't be able to get my words out how I wanted.

Not having all those signals was quite disorientating, she recalls, and I wonder aloud if it felt strange and perhaps a bit frightening. Janet sighs:

> Yes, definitely. You become dependent on those warning signs, otherwise you become anxious because you don't know what's going on all the time and so I started blood-testing obsessively.

A few weeks later, I visit Sara and over coffee in her kitchen, we talk about losing hypo-awareness. Apple, her diabetes alert dog, lies silently on his bed next to her chair throughout. Sara was diagnosed with Type 1 diabetes at the age of 31 but maintained hypo-awareness for the following six or seven years.

She then contracted shingles after which any sign heralding a hypo vanished and no awareness has ever returned. She volunteers a comprehensive description of the incidents and lifestyle alterations that then took place.

> About three weeks after the shingles had gone, I'd find my blood sugar levels had dropped as low as 2, but I didn't feel like I was 2. I'd suddenly be really low without even feeling it and that resulted in collapsing a couple of times. The doctor said I was still having hypos but my nerve-endings had been suppressed by the shingles, so I was to give it time and the feeling would come back gradually. I waited a while and collapsed a couple of times a week. I'd stand and have a conversation and, boom, I'm on the floor, or I'd be teaching and the next minute I'm on the classroom floor.

Sara broke her arm falling down a flight of stairs at the school where she teaches and continued to be hypo-unaware, failing to recognise any signs that might give her warning of a forthcoming hypoglycaemic episode. Medical professionals

90 *'Doing' diabetes Type 1*

suggested she keep an eye out for different signs such as an odd taste, or experience of an aura or unusual smell.

> I read somewhere that coffee stimulates part of the brain that can make you more sensitive to hypos, so I thought I'd drink a couple of extra cups of coffee a day to see if that helped – it didn't. But while I was searching online for hypo-awareness information, I came across hypo-detection dogs and found the website for Medical Detection Dogs.
>
> We hadn't ever had a dog because we both work and didn't think it fair to leave a dog on its own all day, but I was in danger of losing my job because of the number of Accident and Emergency admissions I'd had and the frequent falls. If I lost my job, I'd be at home alone all day and if I collapsed, there'd be nobody here. At least if you collapse at school, there are people around to call an ambulance.

Natasha is used to Paul and Nero going out for their daily walk, but she recalls a recent incident when they planned to be gone for only 20 minutes, but were out for over an hour. 'He came in in a hypo state as he'd had a hypo on the walk'.

Paul recalls being aware of his blood glucose levels being at about 4.2mmol/l and having something to eat. Then he played ball on the field with Nero. He stood there, thinking it would give the levels a chance to drop a little: 'I was walking on and he alerted again, and I tested again and found I'd dropped, so I had something else to eat and then on the way back, . . . ' Natasha says he doesn't remember how he got back, but Paul claims he can remember bits of it, although not the entire trip.

> In the end, I grabbed hold of the lead, pulled it right up tight against his collar and followed him home, so he actually walked me back. He didn't cross the road, he waited till I'd come round a bit and all of a sudden this woman turned up – I don't know where she'd come from . . . I was that fixated on getting home which is how my brain tends to work when I'm having a hypo. I've got no mental capacity, I've just got to get to something, so my feet will walk, my brain is focussed on my feet walking, nothing else exists. All I was doing was literally holding onto the lead and the dog was walking and he got me home.

The impact of mood swings

The complications of chronic illness can lead to other mental and physical issues which may directly affect individuals working or living in proximity to the person with Type 1 diabetes. Paul comments that:

> Diabetes is horrible because you snap at people, you know you're doing it and you're not doing it purposefully, it's not like you want to lash out at people and sometimes you don't know you've done it . . . well, in a hypo state, you're not all there, you know. So occasionally you can be a bit snappy, sometimes you can completely blank things out without realising.

'Doing' diabetes Type 1   91

I remember Sally's 'fight or flight' comment in which she explained her lack of control in a hypo state and this emotional side-effect is recognised and related to by several participants. The impact of Sara's diabetes took its toll on her family relationships. Before Apple joined the household, Sara recalls her husband's irritation at driving home from work during office hours because she hadn't answered his telephone call. She says she often missed the sound of the phone ringing when she was outside, or because of the noises made by the washing machine or vacuum cleaner.

> He'd be cross to find me having a cup of tea, having driven across town for 20 minutes because he'd thought 'she's out cold on the floor; I've got to get there. . . .' It would cause arguments because the family would quite rightly be worried – but then I'd say I didn't ask you to, and I couldn't help not hearing the phone.

Paul and Natasha recollect incidents resulting from 'mood swings'. Natasha tells of a 'spat' they had had one morning just before I arrived at their home for a follow-up interview:

> Today I snapped back . . . but 95% of the time I take it with a pinch of salt . . . today he caught me unawares . . . it's the things that he's said to me before and I've gone out of my way to fix . . . occasionally I have to vent too.

Paul explains the reasoning behind his 'outbursts':

> What you've got to remember from my point of view is that I used to work on buildings, I used to be very active, very mobile, I used to ride bikes, drive a motor and all that. That was my release. Well, now I'm kind of, everything's been taken so sometimes you just can't cope.

On another occasion, I ask if walking Nero across the fields helps to provide some form of release and Paul responds:

> What he's done for me is amazing, he's got me out of my shell, he, I was suffering depression . . . I mean there are days when my bloods aren't right and whatever, you know, take me out the back and shoot me, put me down, that kind of thing, but . . . (*he hesitates*) . . . we go out for walks and I always calm down on a walk, relax . . . If I'm wound up before I go on a walk, when I come back, I'm a lot better; not perfect but a lot better'.

Natasha paints a different picture:

> Then on the contrary, he can go out in a good mood and the dog can really annoy him on the walk and he'll come back saying 'bloody dog' because Nero's eaten cat faeces and Paul's now got to do his teeth!

92 *'Doing' diabetes Type 1*

But it is obvious how much they care for Nero; he's washed and dried carefully if he's played in stagnant water or rolled in mud or manure, his teeth and gums are brushed and monitored, his weight kept in check, and anything out of the ordinary is recorded and the charity and veterinarian informed.

Paul continues to explain his earlier 'venting':

> In my view, it's because I'm annoyed at things I can't do. You're so annoyed you can't do this, you can't do that, you just end up lashing out 'look at that, can't you do that. . .' and really it's nothing to do with that, it's to do with the fact that there are things I need to do and I just can't. I'm comfortable enough to know that I've upset you, but it lets me vent and then it's okay, well, I've calmed down.

Natasha says that she succeeds in 'washing it off in the shower' but then relates the effect of their 'spat' on Nero:

> The poor dog, caught up in the middle of it, is going 'oh no, they're shouting at each other', so I go over to him and tell him it's alright and 'it's not your fault, mummy still loves you'. Oh, he's so sensitive.

Despite the earlier human disagreement, Nero seems in high spirits during my visit: he squeaks his ball and throws, catches and pounces on his 'cuddly' animal toy. He collects the mail from the front door and drops a packet decisively at Paul's feet. However, Natasha urges Paul to check his blood sugar levels because Nero has reignited an old habit of getting all his toys out of the box as an alert, rather than performing in his usual manner. She has also noticed him go up to Paul and give him a nudge and that he's 'fidgety' and not settling.

That they volunteer details of the stresses and strains caused by illness complications is to be appreciated. It cannot be easy to live within the constraints imposed by chronic illness and it takes courage to admit difficult issues and how they are or are not resolved to a relative stranger. However, it also provides depth and intensity to this observation of interspecies coexistence.

Mortality and improving control

Tina's fear of being found dead in bed, mentioned earlier, is not without medical foundation. 'Dead in bed (DIB) syndrome' is a phrase used when a person with insulin-dependent diabetes, usually under 40 years old, has gone to bed apparently well but is then found lifeless 'in an undisturbed bed' (Diabetes.co.uk, 8 January, 2017). People with Type 1 diabetes are advised to avoid nocturnal hypoglycaemia by attaining blood glucose levels within a 6.5 to 8.0 mmol/l range before they go to bed and between 5.5 and 7.5 mmol/l when first awake.

It has been noted that DIB has occurred more often since the introduction of synthetic insulin in the 1980s. Research by Teuscher and Berger (1987: 382) among others, found that a change from beef or porcine-derived insulin to human-made

'Doing' diabetes Type 1   93

insulin was observed to cause less pronounced 'sympathoadrenal symptoms (tremor, sweating, &c)' in insulin-dependent diabetic patients, thereby reducing possible prediction of hypos in humans, compared to the years when nonhuman animal insulin was utilised.

A 2008 study by Rock and Babinec highlights biomedical research into the historical employment of nonhuman animals as models for diabetes exploration, and draws attention to the fact that insulin required by humans, affected by diabetes between the 1920s and 1980s, was taken from bovine and porcine 'donors':

> All people with type 1 diabetes, who had lost the capacity to produce insulin and therefore required regular insulin injections for survival, thus became dependent on industrial slaughter facilities.
>
> (2008: 326)

Cattle and pigs became involved in insulin 'donation', or were until the 1980s, joining cats, dogs, and humans in an anthropocentric giving–receiving multispecies relationship, in becoming object/subject organisms with 'flexible personhood' (Shir-Vertesh, 2012). Bird-David (2006: 47) talks of the 'sharing relations' in animist ontology which collect different types of 'persons' into

> A pluralist community as "we, the relatives," "we, the family." A we-ness is stressed that absorbs the differences. Sharing and caring are expected, even of perspectives.

Shir-Vertesh (2012: 428) concurs, suggesting 'animals can be included in families and homes as "flexible persons", but their nonhumanness sanctions the possibility of exclusion at any juncture'.

Keeping 'high' and life expectancy

The following paragraph is intended to inform, rather than concern or confuse, and is included to highlight the immediate need for further research into, and increasing development of, medical treatment technologies and to indicate the significance of medical alert assistance dogs as animate instruments of prevention, enabling human blood sugar levels to be kept within safe boundaries.

According to key statistics published by Diabetes UK, life expectancy for people with Type 1 diabetes is reduced, on average, by more than 20 years. A systematic review and meta-analysis, conducted 'to provide reliable estimates of any sex differences in the effect of Type 1 diabetes on risk of all-cause mortality and cause-specific outcomes', has been published online in the Lancet with interpretation suggesting women with Type 1 diabetes have an approximate '40% greater excess risk of all-cause mortality, and twice the excess risk of fatal and nonfatal vascular events, compared to men with Type 1 diabetes' (Huxley et al., 2015).

Complications deriving from Type 1 diabetes can be limited by tight glycaemic control, but the idea of keeping blood sugar levels consistently high to avoid

94 *'Doing' diabetes Type 1*

'hypos' can cause further severe medical complications such as cardiovascular disease or renal failure. Terry says that high blood sugars are what you look at for organ or nerve damage, and Nick adds:

> With diabetes, you've got restriction of blood flowing to extremities so, like one gentleman we know, he's had diabetes, he knows he's got diabetes, he's terrified of passing out to a low, so he's always kept his blood sugars high. We can't say specifically, but he's lost part of one of his legs below the knee and his other one looks like it's going that way as well. You often see people with diabetes where the skin on the lower leg is reddened, almost beetroot-colour; the skin's flaking.

Terry suggests it looks as if he sat too close to a fire for too long:

> If you're losing nerve feeling at extremities, hands, on your skin, then there's pressure sores as well . . . very quickly you know there's a lot of damage that can be done from high blood sugars. Low blood sugars will kill quickly, but high blood sugars will kill you slowly.

There is no cure for diabetes Type 1, nor is there any way to prevent it from developing in the first place (JDRF). The need for children to have regular tests, of what the National Institute for Health and Care Excellence (NICE) identify as seven key measures, is essential to ensure diabetes can be controlled as far as possible by medical treatment and appropriate lifestyle management. The measures suggested include weight, cholesterol, and blood pressure checks as well as diabetes risk assessments (NICE, 2014 [2004]). Paul remembers:

> I got diagnosed when I was six and to have control and live by the regime is very hard to do. (*He is silent for a minute and I feel I have dragged the following sentences out of him.*) It's not until you get older and you get all the problems, you want to be free, you want to live.
>
> When I first got diagnosed, it was like the chances are, you know, he's not going to have much of a life, he's not going to live beyond xyz, that's pretty much how it was, sort of 40s, 50s, with problems, you probably won't make it, so you've got that barrier . . . well, if I'm only going to live to that age, I'm going to enjoy it.

Fortunately, mechanical and medical methods, such as the insulin pump, do exist to enable successful management of this chronic illness, despite the likely initial anxiety, possible depression, and frustration immediately after diagnosis.

Type 1 diabetes and pregnancy

Janet was relieved at no longer having to 'set alarms throughout the night' when Alfie took on 'night watchman' duties. She goes on to explain the dog's

'Doing' diabetes Type 1   95

newly-acquired method of alerting: 'It's quite funny now because he's had to change his alert since I've been pregnant. Because I seem to be sleeping a lot heavier, he now growls to wake me up.' But he doesn't touch her and has not jumped on the bed in the night since her pregnancy.

I ask Janet how Alfie normally alerts her to a possible hypo and she says, in the daytime, he paws at her and is very focused on her. But when her blood sugar levels are high and she is tending to show early symptoms of hyperglycaemia, 'he does this funny walking backwards and crying . . . so he does two sort-of different alerts.'

Since Alfie has changed his methods of alerting during Janet's pregnancy, I ask if he has altered any other of his usual behaviours. In her first trimester, Janet relates she had more than 80 blood sugar readings below 3.8, and felt she was hypoing so much that Alfie struggled to keep up. She became more tired and he had to wake her up continually so 'I got quite emotional because I thought if he wasn't there, I would have gone into fits and nobody'd know':

> My confidence is just transformed . . . anxiety levels have dropped because I'm not constantly having to blood test . . . we've just got an incredible bond. He lies outside the bathroom door and he's even alerted when I've been in the bath; he'll cry outside the door.

Measuring and recording

The charity Medical Detection Dogs only came into being in 2008, so it was very much an infant organisation when Richard applied for a medical alert assistance dog. His doctor and hospital consultant endorsed his application and the charity then asked him for a continuous record of his blood sugar levels for a week. The hospital provided him with the results in the form of 'a series of little graphs showing when my levels were dropping and rising, when I'd had insulin, and the carb content I was eating'.

The MDD charity requires clients with assistance dogs to record two to three months of blood testing annually. Included on the computer forms to be completed by them, are questions relating to times when the dog has alerted, what the individual was doing at the time, and the blood sugar levels captured. Terry relates that Jim has 95–100% accuracy in alerting. The recordings sent to MDD enable an image of the dog's alerting success rate, whether there are particular times or reasons why alerting has not occurred or may be inaccurate, whether training has been maintained regularly, even a picture of exercise taken, travel and transport methods to events, to work or to holiday destinations.

This information, although time-consuming to collect and enter into the form, has wide-reaching consequences, in that clients are aware of the charity's interest in both their lives and the lives of the alert dogs and therefore must attend consistently to the ups and downs of their shared existence. At the same time, both client and charity gain evidence of the efficacy of the dogs' work and the success of canine scent detection. The charity can offer human assistance to visit client

96 'Doing' diabetes Type 1

homes to help with solving problems if test results appear unusually erratic and communication between the species looks to be blurred on occasion. The oscillating behaviours of human client and assistant dog are 'umpired' by the charity to ensure the mutual well-being of both.

Paul, Natasha, and Nero are soon to visit the MDD training centre for a 'refresher'. Natasha relates that she spoke to the trainer and heard that

> It will be a sort of social day; there's three or four other partnerships going from what I can gather, and I think, because we got him in May, our annual assessment will be in May, so we'll get a letter saying we need to give six weeks of bloods, with the highs and lows, and when Nero alerts, when he doesn't alert and so on.

Paul refers to Nero's alerting abilities:

> Some days he's brilliant and he can go for weeks being absolutely brilliant and catch 95–100% of everything, and then other days, it's like he's just completely lost the plot and he either misses them or keeps doing false ones – but I'm still convinced that it's the . . . (*Paul's additional chronic illness*) because the dog smells something's not right, different; and I think we've said to you before, like when Natasha has a headache or a nosebleed, or whatever, his behaviour will change.

Paul talks of the pump's effect on Nero:

> All of a sudden I smell slightly different, or that's what I put it down to, because I've got insulin running through me all the time.

They continue talking about Nero's personality but I am sharply reminded of the wayward behaviour of my son's dog during the former's cancer treatment and wonder whether the strong chemical odours, from both the cancer itself and the chemotherapy drugs, upset and confused her so that she barked incessantly and occasionally nipped; behaviours that failed to accord with her natural way of being. What beneficial canine olfactory actions do we fail to attend and react to because of our own ignorance of nonhuman animals' perceptive abilities?

5 Dogs as biomedical resources and health technologies

Our connection with another species may rest on categorisation: whether the member of the other species is purchased as a commodity to be eaten or investigated in a laboratory, whether traded to become a domesticated and owned 'pet', or whether trained and donated as a working animal for the betterment of human life. Tenuous threads may bind one species to the other in the early stages of the latter category, but the result is Coulter's (2016a) anticipated 'interspecies solidarity' of an ethically permissible kind. Participants see the working dogs as respected practitioners of healthcare and equally as good friends and recognisable as family members.

This chapter explores the issue of dogs becoming working equipment in much the same way that they are employed as sentient colleagues and companions, calling for broader discussion and analysis of the canine and human interactive participants. Coulter (2016a: 11), looking through 'the lens of animal work', notes that 'animal workers adapt to human demands and needs, and that animals shape multispecies worksites'.

Savalois, Lescureux and Brunois (2013: 88), referring to the human participants they observed who were all male 'trainer-users' of herding dogs, conclude that:

> A trainer–dog association leads the former to enrich his knowledge, improve his competencies in understanding animal behaviours, and find satisfaction in the resulting quality of their relationships . . . More than a work tool, the dog appears to be an assistant, working in the establishment and maintenance of an optimal inter-relational distance between human, dog, and livestock.

After observing over time how the participants in this research interact with one another and within the situations in which they are placed, a feeling emerges of not merely a multispecies camaraderie but also of a human learning and appreciation of what 'be(com)ing' dog might be like (Maurstad, Davis and Cowles, 2013). Human participants actively, through training and experience, and by a seemingly subconscious picking-up of signals, learn to anticipate the dogs' ways of being in the shared world of chronic illness; to know what might happen in a given situation, whether surrounded by travellers on the 'Underground' or on planes and buses; and to recognise the most favoured reward item, where their canine

98 *Dogs as biomedical resources and health technologies*

companions most enjoy free running, and even which locally resident dogs or humans they prefer to avoid.

As companions in chronic illness, the dogs in turn evidence a 'be(com)ing human' in that a level of intersubjectivity is necessary for them to succeed in their situated roles. Earlier discussion related how these scent-detecting dogs act as 'stand ins' for the loss of human-embodied sensation (hypo-awareness). In this instance, as Hurn (2012: 125) contends, animal 'objects' standing in for humans, 'can also become active subjects with the capacity to impact on the relationships between the humans involved'.

When talking of the dogs as equipment or mobile devices, there is no suggestion of superiority; it is more an acceptance that they should be respected for what they 'do', as family members, as autonomous medical assistants, and as mobile devices. Although I cannot record the alert dog's verbal opinion, both species offer tolerance and appear content with the benefits obtained from shared residence which enable successful symbiotic practices of care and lengthened, more secure lives for both, notwithstanding Srinivasan's 'anthropogenic norms' mentioned later (2013: 114). Budiansky's (1997) reasoning as to why animals 'chose domestication' impinges on contemporary coexistences among species. He notes, by way of historic and current human-dog relationships, that the survival of dogs has 'nothing to do with being rewarded for their utility to man. It has to do rather with their superb adaptation to human society' (1997: 36). Examining coevolutionary development, Budiansky observes how 'one species' behaviour can influence the evolution of another's. The environment that a species inhabits often includes the behaviors of other species, which thus become a force in determining its evolution' (1997: 52).

Physical and imagined boundaries and behaviours are variously constructed: the garden fence and the front door contain and protect both species; the dog is expected to eat given food and expects to be given food. An identifying jacket and lead removed from a wall hook may induce visible excitement in the dog at the prospect of 'going out' while simultaneously bringing about an imminent human restriction of canine 'freedom' through the length and tension of the lead between them (whether U-shaped when relaxed or flattened when taut), as well as decision on the route to be taken.

Srinivasan (2013: 114) clarifies subjectification in nonhuman animals:

> The lives of animals are shaped by humans either by selective breeding and/or disciplinary techniques to such an extent that they are arguably unaware of alternative ways of being, and therefore govern themselves according to anthropogenic norms. This would explain a caged bird that does not fly away when released or a horse that does not throw off its rider.

There is no consciously exhibited imposition of human norms besetting the human-partnered assistance dog; as a participating observer, however, it is necessary to view with some caution how human influence does affect the life management and activities of the working nonhuman.

Dogs as biomedical resources and health technologies   99

Thousands of years of adaptation, domestication, reward, and appreciation enable the caring and empathic dyads studied here, to permit and accept 'other' behaviours. Routines and habitual responses, to and by each member of the dyad, support a comfortable accordance with sometimes unanticipated norms that may be introduced from necessity by independent or cooperative decision-making and by the coembodiment of complexities arising from living with chronic illness. Srinivasan's (2013: 117) 'Note 10' has significance:

> Knowing what animals want is complicated because humans and animals do not share an unambiguous mode of communication. This inability to know with certainty makes it all the more important to constantly query what is done in the name of animal wellbeing . . . by 'paying attention to what the dogs [and other animals] are telling [me]' (Haraway, 2003: 48) and by deploying 'somatic sensibilities' (Greenhough and Roe, 2011), I use my embodied encounters with animals and wider reading on animal sentience (Dawkins, 2006) to arrive at always tentative understandings about animal/ dog wellbeing.

The human 'doing' of Type 1 diabetes has been narrated in an earlier chapter, so investigation now turns toward what the diabetes alert dog is seen to do within the symbiotic relationship that embodies this chronic illness. Nonhuman animal exploitation by human-created procedures is then considered before exploring canine usefulness in the field of biomedicine and human illness, and the concept of an assistance dog becoming an animate instrument, a sentient piece of equipment adapted to work within human health concerns; empowered to make decisions autonomously but under human-manipulated norms.

Control of diet, exercise, and lifestyle management are at the forefront of the diabetic individual's successful daily existence and this is echoed in the personal sentiments of Joseph Cevetello whose chapter in *Evocative Objects* (Turkle, 2007) suggests diabetes is all about the control of blood sugars, timing of meals, what food should be eaten, exercise planning, and the balancing of insulin intake to food. Interactions between himself and his glucometer define who he is, his sense of identity:

> My meter maintains my image of myself as a man able to take care of himself. It also defines me as a diseased person, one who needs the aid of objects to sustain my life. The meter . . . communicates to others that I am different, somehow incomplete.
>
> (2007: 67)

'A diseased person, one who needs *the aid of objects*' to survive, a claim by which Cevetello gives a true assessment of his situation, but the inanimate phrase falls heavily. How much more encouraging would be *the aid of sentient others* in helping to sustain his life, and perhaps communicating a lesser difference? (My emphasis in italics.)

100 *Dogs as biomedical resources and health technologies*

Cevetello (2007: 67) continues:

> My interactions and dependency on my meter have made me realise that relationships between people and medical machinery are evolving.

Annemarie Mol (2000) examines the blood sugar measurement device which, like other diagnostic devices such as the diabetes alert dog, is an active intervention employed in specific situations. The blood glucose monitor is intended to maintain levels, as far as is possible, within the individual's normal range. Those who 'do their bit' in treating a person with diabetes – 'the doctor, the diabetes nurse, the patient, friends and relatives, the note book, the food habits, and so on' – are links in the 'great chain of beings', among which the blood sugar monitor is a 'crucial link' (2000: 14). Mol notes that with self-measurement, an individual with diabetes has greater freedom, fewer regulations restricting life and 'it becomes possible to lead an irregular life' (2000: 19).

Cevetello considers that his glucometer and self interactions may foreshadow 'the nascent stages of a cyborgean relationship' (2007: 68), which notion follows Haraway's (1991: 291) cyborg or cybernetic organism, 'a creature of social reality as well as a creature of fiction', and the enhanced technohuman that Bostrom (2005) and Wolbring (2006) envisage.

For some diabetic individuals, for whom the continuous glucose monitor (CGM) remains unattainable, a welcome development is the personal insulin pump which assists in the regulation of insulin into the bloodstream on a continuing basis so that high and low blood glucose levels fluctuate less extravagantly, and an improved quality of life is obtained and maintained. On the one hand, this is advantageous, but on the other, the small pump may be considered an unwelcome corporeal intrusion.

The continuous glucose monitor has become a beneficial addition to self-caring practices for some, and transhumanist concepts of cyborgean relationships seem irrelevant to participants concerned with the visible advantages gained from the invasive inanimate piece of equipment. Paul is hopeful that he will soon be able to add a CGM to his medical toolkit:

> The pump is going very well but I would like to change it for a CGM. It connects to the insulin pump so, like when your blood glucose levels drop down to 4.5mmol/l, it shuts the pump off. On a walk I often go out quite quickly, I burn up a lot of sugar and then if I stop, the pump comes back on because the initial push has dropped me, so having something like the CGM which constantly monitors your blood sugar, would benefit me considerably.

Research is under way to develop an artificial pancreas which could release insulin into the body according to changes in blood glucose levels and would unite insulin pump technology with a continuous glucose monitor (Diabetes.co.uk, 2015). A closed-loop insulin delivery system, developed by Cambridge University and consisting of an external insulin pump that communicates wirelessly to

Dogs as biomedical resources and health technologies   101

a CGM worn as a patch on the skin, is already being tested on human research participants, according to Diabetes.co.uk.

Also reported online by Diabetes.co.uk (February 2015) is an announcement that De Montfort University is in the process of creating an implantable insulin delivery device which makes use of a bioresponsive gel that enables insulin to be released faster in the body when blood sugar levels are high and slower when blood glucose levels are low. This small device could be implanted surgically and would release insulin into the peritoneum, allowing insulin to be delivered into the bloodstream more quickly than if delivered into the fat layer directly beneath the skin.

Transhumanism

Transhumanism, according to Bostrom (2005: 1), promotes an 'interdisciplinary approach to understanding and evaluating the opportunities', such as those mentioned above, 'for enhancing the human condition and the human organism, opened up by the advancement of technology'.

Bostrom suggests (2005: 2) that there is 'no reason to think that the human mode of being is any more free of limitations imposed by our biological nature than are those of other animals' and continues:

> In much the same way as Chimpanzees lack the cognitive wherewithal to understand what it is like to be human – the ambitions we humans have, our philosophies, the complexities of human society, or the subtleties of our relationships with one another, so we humans may lack the capacity to form a realistic intuitive understanding of what it would be like to be a radically enhanced human (a 'posthuman') and of the thoughts, concerns, aspirations, and social relations that such humans may have.

Remarking underdeveloped human sensory modalities, Bostrom highlights the contrasting keen sense of smell, magnetic orientation, and sharper eyesight of some animals and suggests that a range of possible sensory modalities may exist beyond the animal world. Macrosmia in many animals is a prime example of what the weaker human sense of smell cannot achieve. The keen olfactory sensitivity of creatures at home in the air, in water, or on land, is now opening new vistas for increasing the biomedical armamentarium for all species and not just for human conflict advantage.

Supporting the basic tenets and values of transhumanism, Bostrom (2005) discusses the beneficial feasibility of a radical extension of the human lifespan; eradication of disease; elimination of unnecessary suffering; and augmentation of human intellectual, physical, and emotional capacities: all goals that merit striving for achievement and in which the olfactory sensitivity of the dog and other macrosmatic species can play an important 'technological' role.

Max More (2013) similarly expresses the view that becoming posthuman removes the sufferings of disease, aging, and inevitable death (notwithstanding,

102 *Dogs as biomedical resources and health technologies*

admittedly, the likelihood of different challenges emerging over time), and enhances physical ability and individually suited cognitive and emotional qualities. He contends that interest in philosophy and neuroscience among transhumanists shows acceptance of the Cartesian concept of the mind as a single entity to be no longer supportable.

More (2013: 13) suggests that

> Transhumanists typically adopt a universal standard based not on membership in the human species, but on the qualities of each being. Creatures with similar levels of sapience, sentience, and personhood are accorded similar status no matter whether they are humans, animals, cyborgs, machine intelligences, or aliens.

Anticipation of good things to come, despite risk and danger, seems to pervade the concept of transhumanism. Not necessarily a 'throw caution to the wind' yearning for advancement, but, for some believers of its vision, a determinedly focused, cautious push for continual progress (refer to More's extropian principles [1990] in which it is stated that transhumanists appreciate the never-ending pursuit of knowledge and understanding).

Perhaps the above offers a comforting prospect and an approach in some ways consistent with this interdisciplinary, interspecies investigation into improving quality of life for those with chronic illness. However, as well as employing nanotechnology, prostheses, or artificial intelligence as progressive technologies, the human condition is also currently being enhanced positively through canine olfactory perception: an inexpensive, noninvasive but nonetheless effective use of a pre-existing biological 'tool' that detects, identifies, and differentiates odours through the sense of smell and therefore prevents the life-threatening effects of hyper- or hypo-glycaemia on people with Type 1 diabetes.

Gregor Wolbring (2006: 32) reflects on the transhumanist model of health and disease, which

> Sees every human being as defective and in need of improvement (above species-typical boundaries) leading to the transhumanist model of disability/ impairment where every unenhanced human being is, by definition 'disabled' in the impairment/patient sense. The only way out of the impairment/patient label is to enhance oneself beyond the species-typical boundaries.
>
> (2006: 34)

Those who cannot afford bodily enhancement will be marked impaired, becoming Wolbring's 'new techno-poor disabled' (2006: 33).

In the case of chronically ill humans who suffer inequality in life and lack means of social integration, the assistance of a medical alert dog seems to provide an economically viable, noninvasive and nonmechanical form of bodily enhancement that enables comfort in the community as well as in the self.

Dogs as biomedical resources and health technologies 103

Coembodied within the world of chronic illness, the diabetes alert dog may become an extension of the human self (Belk, 1988, 1996; Sanders, 2003). Where Sherry Turkle writes that Cevetello's glucometer becomes 'more than companion: the glucometer "has become me" '(2007: 325) and he waits for it to tell him 'what to do' (Cevetello, 2007: 68), Belk (1996), in describing 'pets as part of self', explains that 'the investment of time, money and energy on our pets' enables intense attachment to them and a perception that they may also become 'extensions of ourselves' (1996: 129). This extension of self, endorsing expressions of human identity, also allows the 'pets' to be 'appendages' (Belk, 1996: 131), whose pain may be felt by the human and whose empathy may be reciprocated.

Although Belk's 'pet' dogs are not considered in the category of assistance dogs, his observations reflect similar human–canine encounters in which the dog, acting as part of a human extended self, represents 'a divided self that is both civilised and tame, well-behaved and animalistic, controlled and chaotic . . . as a mixed metaphor, it reflects the way we view ourselves in the contemporary world' (1996: 140).

In contrasting the environmental backdrops of wolf and dog, Mark Rowlands (2008: 30) inverts the notion of the dog as extension of the human self or mind:

> The dog has been forced to rely on us. More than that it has developed the ability to solve its various problems, cognitive and otherwise. For dogs, we are useful information-processing devices. We humans are part of the dog's extended mind.

Often a diagnosis of diabetes conjures immediate negativity – in the individual, among family members, friends and work colleagues. The person with diabetes takes on the label of 'poor so-and-so', whether or not achievements are later gained in the contexts of sport or exercise, home, college, or work. However, the effort to take and maintain control of food and other lifestyle behaviours beyond that required by more healthy individuals deserves to engender personal sentiments of pride and accomplishment, and a conscious awareness of managing life well, enabling feelings of satisfaction to reverberate through the individual's *umwelt* (Von Uexküll, 2010).

Cevetello asserts his need for objects to assist the sustenance of his life. Technoscience plays an important role but is thus far insentient, despite the advances in social robotics (Turkle, 2007; Miklósi and Gacsi, 2012) and Haraway's 'genetically engineered mice' (1997: 53). Assistance objects, such as the insulin pump (which gives current blood glucose readings that can be acted upon), are not prescient and have to be manoeuvred to benefit the user.

It is the ability to prevent medical emergencies through sensory warning that has pushed the work of the companion nonhuman animal assistant into the forefront of Wolbring's once 'techno-poor' (2006: 33), now *en*abled, group of chronically ill humans. Unlike the inanimate insulin pump, a medical alert assistance dog may be considered an animate instrument.

Animate instruments

For many years, well-loved dogs, whose human carers were unable to look after them for days, weeks, or even months at a time, came to share those periods with our family. Some dogs visited because they were known to become ill during car journeys and therefore disliked travelling, some because their human companion was hospitalised or had died, and a few because they had caused serious injury to members of their own or other species. The majority, however, came to stay, often bringing suitcases brim-full of personal items, because their families were travelling abroad on business or holiday; this was in South Africa, from where dogs could not travel far without long-term quarantine regulations coming into play. We endeavoured to replicate the meals they were given at home; to play with them and keep them safe, warm, and clean; and as far as was humanly possible, to situate them in a friendly, companionable environment.

Many returned year after year, rushing out of the family car to stand in front of the same kennel they had occupied previously. They recognised staff members and knew the daily routines; their memories proved outstandingly accurate, perhaps prodded effectively by their exceptional sense of smell which, as in human animals and as mentioned in the earlier section on olfaction, encourages reminiscences of the previously familiar.

Occasionally a client request necessitated driving a dog to their veterinarian for euthanasia and this would evoke discomforting internal questioning of a daily occupation which was principally to care for members of another species in the absence of their usual companions – could such a journey ever be viewed as morally acceptable, even compassionate? Reflexivity can induce alarming mental disquiet so that, fearing Coetzee's incisive writing would scratch open scars of past and present ethical concerns, it has taken many years to read *Disgrace* (1999) and the unwelcome descriptions of dogs being kennelled and euthanized.

However, it is *because* of Coetzee's critical observations of human–dog interactions and cognitive–behavioural intersections that the following citation may be flagged up to illustrate his perception of this complex, often conflicting multispecies relationship. 'They are part of the furniture, part of the alarm system. They do us the honour of treating us like gods, and we respond by treating them like things' (Coetzee, 1999: 78).

The medical alert dog is judged to be a companion, friend, help-mate, and assistant, a facilitator of safer living and a guard against the perfidies of chronic illness. However, he or she may also, sometimes simultaneously, be considered an animate instrument – 'having life' (Pearsall and Trumble, OERD, 1995: 52), 'a thing used in performing an action' (Pearsall and Trumble, OERD, 1995: 730). The action here is the olfactory sniffing and subsequent warning performed by the alerting dog to prevent hypoglycaemia affecting the human companion with Type 1 diabetes.

Unlikely to be thought of as 'furniture' – more likely to be appreciated as medical equipment (refer Paul and Terry commenting that they partially view their dogs as equipment), and certainly considered 'part of the alarm system' that is required for

Dogs as biomedical resources and health technologies 105

day-to-day living when chronically ill – the diabetes alert dog is, however, much more than a 'thing' to the unwell human carer or to the observing public. Budiansky comments in relation to farmers, hunters, and 'the few others in our modern world whose daily work brings them into contact with animals' (1997: 12), 'they know that animals are not people, but they are not things, either' (1997: 13).

None of the human participants, caring for their canine companions under the auspices of the provisioning charity, have evidenced unkind or irresponsible behaviour towards their well-respected partners (within my observation periods). But Coetzee's phraseology continues to agitate emotions of guilt and shame at the way nonhuman animal neighbours are generally taken for granted without moral consideration, at how they are shaped mentally and physically as commodities to convenience our own interests while theirs may never be sufficiently accommodated and are, sometimes knowingly, ignored.

Hurn (2012: 104) suggests that:

> In a capitalist market the value of social relations is influenced by the perceived value of commodities, but this value often rests on the symbolic qualities that 'things' are thought to possess.

She adds that 'pets might also be regarded as commodities when they generate social profit for their owners' (Hurn, 2012: 105). Although the diabetes alert dog may be considered a working companion rather than commodity or pet, there is no doubt that 'social profit' is gained by a human partner, previously prevented from enjoying full social integration by the effects of illness.

Igor Kopytoff (1986: 64) examining 'commoditization as process' in economic terms and the concept of commodities as material things, begins by approaching 'the notion of commodity' in terms of slavery. The slave, he avers, is captured or put up for sale or both, loses social identity and 'becomes a non-person (1986: 65)'; but is then acquired by an individual or group, gains new status and identity, but may continue to be a commodity, a property of another.

Whether working herd dogs, guard dogs, or hearth-loving companion canines, dogs in the UK are still considered to be the possessions of their human keepers, as set out in the Animal Welfare Act of 2006. 'By contrast, in India, the law recognises the independent status of ownerless street dogs and so these animals are not confronted with the stark injunction to live well or die' (Srinivasan, 2013: 106). The Code of Practice applicable to all dogs in the UK provides guidance to help dog-keepers comply with provisions of Section 9 of the Animal Welfare Act of 2006; it is emphasised in the introduction that 'you are always responsible for your dog's needs' and should be aware that 'dog ownership is a major responsibility' (DEFRA, December 2009). Although changes in international animal welfare laws over time have led to the occasional or partial prohibition of cruelty and suffering to animals for the benefit of human entertainment or consumption – the contested lives of caged dogs in meat markets come to mind here – there remains an ongoing human compulsion to exploit and hurt other species in the name of science or entertainment.

106 *Dogs as biomedical resources and health technologies*

What is legally allowed, but appears 'morally impermissible' (Nobis, 2016: 26) in ethical thinking about the use of animal others, does not always benefit them when they are selected for a human-designed function. The transbiopolitics concept introduced by Blue and Rock (2011: 354) is significant in relation to 'animal and human bodies [that] not only coexist but are instrumental in constituting one another, at many different scales and across multiple spatial and temporal dimensions'. Human provisioning of 'care' for the racing dog, and canine provisioning of funds that enable that care, produce a cycle of interspecies complexity. If, for example, greyhounds are well fed and 'housed', given opportunity for regular exercise, welfare checks, and companionship, competing in the greyhound Grand National or the Oaks may be legally permissible. However, in terms of moral 'rights', caging and releasing greyhounds to race after a speeding mechanical lure, an artificial hare, seems unkind and abusive in the same way that pheasants and partridges are bred, caged, fed, released, and shot for so-called 'sport'. These sentient creatures are the animate instruments of British tradition, legally permitted to be treated as such, but moral acceptance of these traditions and adherent instruments poses an increasing challenge.

Exploitation

Exploitation signifies taking advantage of another for benefit, whether it involves slavery, circus entertainment, laboratory experimentation, or the often inhumanely and repetitively produced gain from factory-farming or puppy-milling. Exploitation reflects more than shadows of human depravity and such moral corruption can rarely be deemed a force for good. Yet advantage of sentient nonhuman beings for human financial profit continues to be taken and observed in the fortunes made (or lost) by breeding and betting on animals compelled to participate in activities such as dog-fighting or greyhound- and horse-racing.

A further exploitation of other animals is undertaken for apparent social advancement when they are used as human status symbols (handbag or teacup primates and pigs, or supposedly fearsome dogs adorned in heavy metal-studded collars). Referring to consumer items designed to be thrown away after a brief life in order to satisfy trends of 'new and even-better' consumption, Hurn (2012: 103–104) contends that in current consumer thinking, companion animals may similarly be commodified and exploited as 'potentially disposable material accessories in much the same way as cars, jewellery or clothing' – a form of 'planned obsolescence'.

Puppy-milling and dog-fighting, factory-farming, or bear-bile extraction do not play roles in this research because of the current inhumane use of animals as technologies solely for human gain. This is not to say that every human individual employed to work with animals in science and industry has no heart; many of them demonstrate concern and emotion at inhumane human–nonhuman animal practices in agriculture, for example. The writing of John Law (2010) relating to the anguish of farmers and veterinarians compelled by government authority to euthanize healthy animals in order to contain foot-and-mouth disease on farms

Dogs as biomedical resources and health technologies   107

in Britain, and that of Kim Baker (2013) examining the developing relationships between pigmen and pigs in industrial farming, both offer balance to my condemnation of human cruelty to nonhuman creatures in agriculture. However, the likelihood that a proportion of canine and human research participants currently consume products manufactured from other animals, who did not choose martyrdom based on a utilitarian maxim, may seem to undermine a non-speciesist ethic supporting the kindly, nonexploitative use of assistance animals.

The use of multispecies biomedical technology is in the frame to illustrate how the well-domesticated dog and the chronically unwell human become colleagues coembodying good care practices and finding a single identity to guide them together through the uncertainties and complexities of chronic illness. Apart from the mutual care expressed in the symbiotic relationships between assistance dogs and their variously-impaired human companions, other positive human–canine collaborations, based on sensory perceptions and concomitant training methods and co-operations, exist beyond the boundaries of health; for example, the often-exemplary care demonstrated by homeless people to their close animal friends (Irvine, 2013).

Cooperative enterprise is described in the works of former Royal Marine, Pen Farthing (2014), founder of the Nowzad Dogs charity rescuing the commonly abused stray dogs battling to survive in Afghanistan warzones, and finding them safe and caring homes in other countries. Media communications and personal anecdotes frequently highlight the advantages of multispecies' shared enterprise, for example, when members of police or defence force teams return home from service abroad, bringing their canine instruments of war with them. These may be drug-, body-, or explosive-detection animals who have become emotionally attached to their human partners and together have created bonds, often deepened as the result of fear and heroism.

But exploitation rears up here too, since war and destruction may heap pain, exhaustion, neglect and abandonment on the nonhuman creatures enlisted to work in war zones (Allon and Barrett, 2015), who may suffer from mental 'shellshock' as well as physical injury, and who may not 'go home' with their human keepers. Do they suffer from symptoms of post-traumatic stress disorder (PTSD) that may haunt human witnesses of fatal vehicle accidents, murder, or other violent death? Although media coverage of the recently recognised diagnosis of canine PTSD is beginning to spread in the 'West', there is sparse research literature available (for example, Mark Bekoff, 2011; Coulter, 2016a: 80–81) to examine the psychological effects of traumatic events on animals in war zones; or indeed that explores treatment interventions which might assist mentally affected nonhuman creatures who suffer from the conscious contribution of an animal to a dystopian world of human manufacture.

Ryan Hediger (2013: 55) contrasts the 'superior sensory abilities' of dogs used by the US military in the Vietnam wars, with their abandonment as 'mere machinery' when the US forces withdrew. Bearing the status of canine heroes when used in warfare, 'most of the 4,000 or so dogs used in conflict were abandoned in the war zone when the United States withdrew, leaving many of the dogs to become meat, to be eaten by the Vietnamese' (2013: 55).

108 *Dogs as biomedical resources and health technologies*

More recently, Allon and Barrett (2015) have written of the Dobermann dogs co-opted into marine service in the Pacific wars, some of whom suffered 'shellshock' and were destroyed.

Dodman (2016), a veterinarian accustomed to treating canine cases of PTSD, and Alger and Alger (2013), have also noted how trauma affects dogs well after they witness violence or crisis. PTSD is only diagnosed in humans when 'the full symptom picture is present for more than one month (Criterion E: DSM-IV-TR®) after exposure to an extreme traumatic stressor' (American Psychiatric Association, 2000: 463).

Ignoring this scarcity of research into PTSD in companion animals, use and exploitation of domesticated animals continue to be practiced at each end of the elastic commodity continuum. The domesticated canine may be considered a highly valued companion but may also be shaped into a commodity to be fashioned and used as an instrument, one that can be selected from the ranks of health tools contained in the biomedical armamentarium.

Use and exploitation

Kendra Coulter (2016b: 146) reminds us that 'what we condemn and condone' are affected by our knowledge and understanding of those alternatives. Observing animals 'as working, and even as workers, may increase their immediate value in particular ways', she avers, and then highlights how 'becoming "useful" can change how individuals and/or species are seen and treated'. She offers an example, pertinent to those with macrosmatic scenting ability, of the rats employed by the Belgian APOPO organisation (Anti-Persoonsmijnen Ontmijnende Product Ontwikkeling, which translates into English as 'Anti-Personnel Landmines Removal Product Development') to sniff out both concealed landmines and symptoms of tuberculosis. From being generally considered a destructive, dirty creature who carries disease, the African Giant Pouched Rat (*Cricetomys ansorgei*) has gained status through 'usage' and is now at least recognised anthropocentrically as a life-saving individual worthy of human gratitude.

Moving away from animals used in war zones to those working in the field of health and illness, Tzachi Zamir (2006: 179–199) differentiates between use and exploitation in the field of animal-assisted therapy (AAT). He posits the liberationist stance that places value on the animal's life and the quality of that life and suggests exploitation harms the exploited but is beneficial to the individual whereas, in AAT for example, 'service dogs are used, though not exploited, since their welfare is promoted by the relationship' (189).

However, Serpell et al. (2010: 497) contend that 'the use of animals in animal-assisted activities and therapy imposes a unique set of stresses and strains' and recommend a set of guidelines for their care and supervision during such usage, the issue being 'how to balance the needs of human clients with respect for the needs of the animal' (2010: 502). The provisions offer 'basic ethics principles for the use of the therapy animal', 'procedures for ethical decision-making regarding therapy animals' and 'implications for ethical decision-making regarding therapy animals'.

Dogs as biomedical resources and health technologies 109

MDD maintains responsibility for the rescued or donated animals who they train in biodetection. Clients do not purchase diabetes alert dogs and the charity covers the costs of veterinary care, canine insurance, medical needs, toys, equipment, training, and food. Only after dogs have taken up residence with human partners do those clients take over the expenses. The charity issues clients with guidelines, similar to those proposed by Serpell et al. (2010), directing essential but ethically-based humane care and treatment of the diabetes alert assistance dogs, and time is taken to ensure both human and nonhuman are well suited and likely to form deep and long-lasting bonds.

Terry considers the charity's current 'matching process' asks questions and expects answers that 'push you to the limit'. Because working with a dog at the centre takes place on individual days over several months, prospective clients need to show genuine commitment to wanting a diabetes alert dog and be prepared to travel for ongoing visits to the MDD centre. He adds that those who say they're coming down to the charity for a day and want to take a dog home with them will be unlikely to succeed, since they show no sign of moral commitment to ongoing consideration of the working dog's 'rights' to a harm-free and cared-for future.

If either dog or human present signs of discomfort or a lack of interest in the other, then the dog will not become that individual's companion and further discussion will take place before a different dog may be introduced. Paul, for example, emphasising that Nero is 'the right dog for me', says he was offered a different dog by the charity before Nero, but 'there was just no connection'. Similarly, Janet recalls how deflated she felt at the lack of interest in her shown by the first dog introduced by the charity:

> We went for a walk in the park, did a bit of 'recall'; he was very good, obedient in the shops and everything was perfect but you could just tell he wasn't interested, and the trainers felt that as well, so they said they had a dog who was a bit hyperactive to show me in the afternoon.

Janet and her mother had two elderly cats in their twenties at home and were thinking 'this might not work' when Alfie came 'bounding in, full of energy'.

> As soon as I spoke to him, he responded straightaway . . . he kept looking up at me and when we took him to the park and did some recall, he came galloping back all excited which was lovely. My mum even noticed that he was mimicking my walk and so of course. . .

Human participants affirm the need to 'click' with the canine working assistant, this 'click' being an emotional feeling within human cognition that is thought to signify mutual liking and a possible future bond of friendship. Among many studies into the effects of interaction between companion humans and dogs on their oxytocin levels, are those of Odendaal and Meintjes (2003) and Miller et al. (2009). Swedish researchers, Handlin et al. (2011), examined heart rate and levels of oxytocin, cortisol, and insulin in 10 male Labrador dogs and their female

110 *Dogs as biomedical resources and health technologies*

human companions, in response to an interaction during which the 'owner stroked, petted, and talked with her dog during the first 3 minutes', after which blood samples were taken from both species. The researchers found the dogs' oxytocin levels were 'significantly increased 3 minutes after the start of the interaction (p = 0.027)' while the 'owners' oxytocin levels peaked between 1 and 5 minutes after interaction (p = 0.026). No such effect was seen in the controls' (Handlin et al., 2011: 301). Similar experiments might provide instrumentation which the MDD charity could adopt as means to quantify the interspecies bonding 'click' necessary for successful processing of their partnerships.

Anxiety: fear of failure

There is little certainty for members of the canine or human species sharing life together with chronic Type 1 diabetes. The daily turmoil of fluctuating blood sugar levels ensures intervals for relaxation may be brief for either partner. The dog cannot be switched off for a nap, nor are he or she always able to rouse the deeply sleeping or comatose diabetic. If a timely reward is not given for correct alerting because the human partner is slow to react or fails to notice an alert, how can the dog's uncertainties be resolved?

Coppinger, Coppinger, and Skillings (1998: 133) observed that the most common working dogs in the 21st century could be those who assist people with tasks that they are unable to manage as individuals. According to ADUK (personal communication, April 2017), 7,000 dogs are now qualified to work within the ADUK accreditation system, so it appears Coppinger, Coppinger, and Skillings (1998) may have forecast the situation correctly. Their paper relates particularly to dogs pulling wheelchairs or opening doors for people in wheelchairs, indicating the possibilities of the dogs becoming injured or failing to achieve the expected goal. Relevant here is their conclusion that not everyone instructs their assistance dogs correctly so it becomes important that those matched with assistance dogs acquire the training and experience necessary to comprehend the quantity of possible complications and how they can best resolve them.

Birke and Hockenhull (2015) discuss horse–human miscommunication and failing cooperation that appear remedied over time and proximity as each gains trust and knowledge of the other. The horses 'are not animals simply plodding around at the behest of a human, but they are mindful of how to read the human from moment to moment – mindful in moving and being moved' (2015: 97). Birke and Hockenhull continue:

> Sadly, we humans all too often misread what animals are trying to tell us, often with dire consequences for the animals. We may never know for sure how they themselves experience the relationship but knowing how they behave within it does tell us something. A better understanding of how togetherness and partnership are built, by humans *and by companion animals*, would surely benefit us all.
>
> (emphasis in text, 2015: 97)

Dogs as biomedical resources and health technologies 111

Coppinger, Coppinger, and Skillings (1998) suggested that inability to perform a wanted task was less to do with the inadequacy of the dog but more relative to the difficulty of the required tasks, 'the inadequacy of much of the equipment they are required to perform with' (1998: 143), and the instinctive behaviour of the dogs themselves.

Terry relates to the 'difficulty of required tasks' when attempting to manoeuvre himself, his wheelchair and assistance dog, Jim, safely in and out of lifts in multistorey buildings:

> If I'm approaching a lift in the wheelchair, I've got to make sure my dog is safe going in and out because it's incredibly dangerous going into a lift with a dog whereas you wouldn't care if the chair hit the lift door.
>
> Once you've learned to handle the wheelchair, you have to be aware of ground surfaces because a pothole can throw you right out of it; but working with a dog keeps your mind more active which has to be a good thing.

The possibility of diabetes alert assistance dogs suffering anxiety at the collapse into unconsciousness of their human companions is itself cause for concern and rigorous investigation; for example, whether the frequency of such episodes may cause the dog to develop learned helplessness or deepen the possibility of depression at failure to succeed in assisting the human partner – or at least from a repetitive failure to receive anticipated rewards for active alerting. Public observation of Harley's anxiety and concern when Tina became 'hypo' and collapsed serves as an appropriate example here. However, Harley's naturally, at least outwardly, cheerful temperament appears to have prevented symptoms of depression overly affecting his personality, and his alerting ability to warn of both hyper- and hypoglycaemia remains at a high level of accuracy, according to the charity staff members and his diabetic companion who regularly observe his emotions and behaviours.

A lack of reaction to an alert, particularly by those who live without other human company, draws attention to stresses that may occur in the assistance dog's life; no reaction to a given alert may signify failure, no alternative option, and no reward. Clara Mancini and colleagues, who work in the Animal–Computer Interaction laboratory at the UK's Open University and at times in conjunction with MDD staff, clients, and their diabetes alert dogs, are investigating methods and developing means to lessen the types of anxiety likely to affect working assistance dogs in situations such as that facing Harley, and to find outlets for the dogs' anxiety if their alerting efforts fail to be acknowledged by the unwell human.

Researchers in the animal–computer interaction field consider nonhuman animals to be active participants in investigations. They believe that nonhuman animals need to be involved comprehensively in the design and development of multispecies user-friendly, interactive technology which should relate beneficially to the users' personalities and idiosyncratic traits. Such interactive technology should be framed in welfare-centred ethics which relates to aspects of the nature of the work to be undertaken, the context in which the activities will be situated, and how the species will be empowered by such technology (Mancini, 2016).

112 *Dogs as biomedical resources and health technologies*

Investigating the development of technologies that could empower diabetes alert assistance dogs, Robinson et al. (2014) presented a paper at the Intelligent Systems for Animal Welfare (ISAWEL) conference, which contended that a lack of predictability and control of their environment could cause stress and possible depression in dogs. Such consideration, which draws on the real and imagined points of view of both human and dog partners living in homes affected by chronic illness, could build or restore certainty in what might sometimes be a difficult-to-balance mutualistic relationship.

The ISAWEL 2014 conference paper (Robinson et al., 2014: np) 'explores the intersection of assistance dog welfare and intelligent systems with a technological intervention . . . an emergency canine alert system'. The authors suggest the possibility of a diabetes alert dog becoming distressed when their partner becomes unconscious due to a hypo, perhaps because of temporary separation during which they cannot estimate when their human partner will regain their normal behaviour patterns, and they therefore cannot practice their usual methods of keeping control. These researchers explore the idea of a canine emergency alert system by which the dog could, for example, pull on a wall-mounted rope tug-toy and trigger a software system that would set off an alarm request to external sources, perhaps from the human's health and social network. This could benefit the welfare of both dog and human user, the dog empowered to act positively and receive an appropriate feedback signal, and the human to receive medical assistance more swiftly. Just as knowledge and awareness of multispecies interactions are expanding, discussed above in relation to human and horse co-operations (Birke and Hockenhull, 2015), so too is technology increasing to aid safety and security for both assistant dogs and unwell humans.

Tina explains Harley's focused alerting:

> He's sharp, he's very sharp you know. But even if I go into a coma, when I come round, he's sat there with the medical kit in his mouth. And you know that he's tried everything, so, yes, he's good . . . but they're [MDD] making me a pulley at home. It will actually go through to home care that'll send help out. If I go into a coma – you know I'm out for anything up to five hours – well, in that time Harley will pull the rope and when they don't get a voice, they know to come straight away.
>
> Before that I was given a thing for my bed because when you go into your comas, you actually faint, but that was forever going off, and I thought 'I can't live with that', so I'd much rather have Harley so that if I'm out, he can pull the rope.

Canine life enrichment is a priority if the 'instrument' is to maintain effective levels of alerting. Balanced nutrition, fresh water, and outdoor exercise that enables interspecies social contact and improves circulation, muscle strength, and heart rate, together with problem-solving games that invigorate brain activity, all contribute to the dog's well-being and enjoyment of life in a human home. The economic as well as physiological status of the human with variously-impaired

Dogs as biomedical resources and health technologies   113

abilities is likely to play a role in evaluating the degree to which enrichment, nourishment, security, exercise and play, interspecies and same-species social interactions, grooming and welfare needs are sufficiently supplied to maintain a healthy and satisfactory personal lifestyle for the assistance dog sharing the home.

Paul contends that his care of Nero is the same as he would give to any dog:

> The fact that he's an alert dog makes no difference. If he was just a pet, he would still get the same care . . . he gets a good brush, he gets his teeth done; normally about two or three times a week he gets a dental stick . . . I do look after him. He sleeps on the bed now because it's easier for me to have him on the bed than to have him padding around every hour and a half to two hours.

Parasitism: a selfish harvesting

The notion of the assistance dog being a useful item of sentient equipment may appear contra the thinking of Randy Malamud (2013) who suggests human inadequacies cause inferiority and produce a sense of entitlement to 'harvest' and 'co-opt' nonhuman animal abilities. He further posits that we should rather think of ourselves as 'service animals' and what we can offer to nonhuman animals in return for what we glean. Lynda Birke's direct question 'what's in it for the animals?' (2009: 1) resonates here, and emphatically invites us to take responsibility, even though we may have no knowledge of their 'points of view', when engaging with those whose abilities we 'harvest' so often without regard for their consciousness, their feelings and their thinking.

The concept of a kindly interspecies reciprocity is agreeable and, provided there is mutualism in such shared coexistences, it may be possible to accept an invitation to become less vehemently disapproving of the usage and usefulness of long-domesticated and carefully trained assistance animals. Trained diabetes alert dogs do receive health and welfare benefits and become recognised and socially distinguished partners in symbiotic relationships – partnerships that enable one member to provide nonjudgemental companionship and exceptional olfactory ability in safeguarding human health, and the other to give security, shelter, and nutrition, and even the prospect of a collaborative friendship. Seemingly, these donated behaviours are considered forms of provision and gratitude rather than entitlement and succeed in highlighting an empathic multispecies interaction that *does* endorse Malamud's thinking. Extracts from interviews with research participants illustrate this instrument–companion oscillation.

Cassidy (2002) contends that racehorses change from subject to object dependent on how they are perceived and by whom, for example, by their jockeys, owners, grooms or the betting spectators. Shir-Vertesh (2012) suggests that a dynamic range of factors can influence how people perceive and act towards their pets, for example, the flexible status of a companion animal obtained and treated as a child substitute whose position is later pre-empted on the arrival of a human baby. When Richard refers to Higgins making the olfactory transition over time from alerting to a scent pot to alerting to himself as 'the real thing', he may sense

114 *Dogs as biomedical resources and health technologies*

Higgins as equipment prior to the dog becoming companion: 'he's not something that you just switch on and off'.

There is increasing need to study the expanding biomedical situations inhabited by human and nonhuman animals. The apparently beneficial use of both humans and dogs for multispecies health improvement should not always be decried – *provided*, of course, that good care is the paramount concern and any use does not become exploitation that causes suffering to any sentient creature whether through mental or physical abuse or cruelty and resultant anguish. Responsible and sensitive research (Birke, 2009) should also not harm nonhuman subjects, nor reduce any forms of life enrichment they may be able to access, so that their good health and welfare are always to be maintained at the highest level. And if that is the case, making use of the cared-for biomedical animate resource should promote a greater wellness in the user. Rock and Degeling (2015), in their research into One Health and public health ethics, 'conceptualise solidarity to encompass not only practices intended to assist other people, but also practices intended to assist nonhuman others including animals, plants or places' (2015: 61). Their conception is supported in Coulter's 'Anifesto', in which she also calls for recognition of the role played by economic oppression 'in perpetuating both people's and animals' suffering' (2016a: 163).

Recognition

These canine biomedical collaborators reciprocate the care and attention given by their human counterparts in the field of chronic illness, so it seems that a plastic symbiotic coexistence emerges in which each species depends on the other to an extraordinary degree for survival. Hurn (2012) illustrates the swings and roundabouts of symbiosis in domestication with examples of the human–nonhuman relationships between the Welsh breeders and exhibitors of 'indigenous equines' (2012: 66); human and nonhuman animals who are interdependent and who 'live off' each other, unlike promoters of factory farming who are sole beneficiaries of nonhuman animal products and therefore engage in a more parasitic relationship.

Leung and Poulin (2008: 107) unravel the complex categories of parasitism, commensalism, and mutualism which oscillate variously along an elastic continuum of symbiotic interactions. Although Coppinger and Coppinger (2016: 133) refer to commensalism or 'eating at the same table' as an ecologist-favoured term for the human–canine symbiotic relationship that evolved from dogs' need to 'feed in the presence of humans', it is mutualism – in which neither member of the relationship harms the other in a mutually beneficial sharing of life – that seems to identify most nearly with the symbiotic partnership of the coexisting unwell human and assistance dog.

The intertwined lives of dog and human see the former become a resource in the creation of an animate instrument able to assist in navigating through the culture of chronic illness performances and care practices. In this activity, some benefit for the dog comes from a work ethic that suggests the provision of enrichment

Dogs as biomedical resources and health technologies 115

opportunity and occupation may reduce the prospect of boredom or frustration in a confined space.

A lack of occupation is a common cause of inappropriate behavioural problems occurring in companion animals (Horowitz, 2009: 216–217; Serpell et al., 2010: 481–503). Therefore, having this useful occupation of animate, active biomedical resource not only situates the medical alert assistance dog as a valued and knowledgeable cosmopolitan, instrumental in both chronic illness treatment and in social environs, but also, and perhaps more importantly from the dog's perspective, allows some degree of agency and opportunity for empowerment and enrichment.

Mental and physical stimulation are enabled in the work of an assistance dog, but choice of when, where and how play should be conducted, is reliant on human decision. Research into working dog welfare by Rooney, Gaines, and Hiby (2009) provides guidelines for practitioners caring for kennelled working dogs, which the working DADs are not.

Referring to the psychiatric service dog (PSD), Tedeschi, Fine, and Helgeson (2010: 421) suggest certain 'obvious' benefits to human recipients of a PSD, for example 'increased social interaction [and] reduced feelings of avoidance and stigmatization'. But they are concerned by the new demands now made on service animals and cite Burrows, Adams, and Millman (2008) who identified 'lack of rest, recovery time, and opportunity for recreation, lack of structure in a daily schedule, and unintentional maltreatment as the primary concerns for the welfare of service dogs working with autistic children' (Tedeschi, Fine, and Helgeson, 2010: 433). Their Table 20.2 (2010: 434) lists exclusion criteria for potential PSD handlers (life circumstances, individual characteristics and patient's clinical status).

Although the above pertains specifically to PSDs, the impact of 'service' on a medical alert assistance dog also requires continuous monitoring. Tedeschi et al. emphasise dogs' sensitivity to emotional and mental status changes in humans and suggest thorough and accurate screening of clients can determine 'requisite stability and readiness of the handler or recipient' (2010: 436). Screening of MDD clients is maintained throughout their coexistences with diabetic alert dogs to ensure both gain maximum benefit from the partnerships.

The medical alert assistance dog may be trained to alert to specific odours and be rewarded when successfully performing the warning, but there is choice here in that failure to alert will not be punished (other than loss of potential reward). Although some of the diabetic alert dogs give an accurate alert 95–100% of the time, there are those of both species who may be resistant to alert training once situated in a client's home.

Paul comments on Nero's 'headstrong' character which had originally made him difficult to work with, causing his return to the centre for further training. He says the charity had to put in a lot of work leading up to Nero's accreditation as a medical alert assistance dog:

> You have to bear in mind that I'm not a well person so what looks easy to a healthy person, you know, and when you're adjusting the dog, and checking the dog, and doing all the things you need to do to get him to qualify, it's hard

116 *Dogs as biomedical resources and health technologies*

work for me. And they always say it's not the dog, it's the owner, you're giving cues and this and that.

There are occasions in every family when expected synchrony fails and a misunderstanding of voiced or silent communication causes conflict, but there is perhaps a greater effort to comprehend and resolve such issues immediately between the dog and human who work in chronic illness and need their interdependence for bettered existence. Time and timing may be significant in interspecies activity within Type 1 diabetes. It may not be possible to extend argument when conflict vies with necessity for an immediate alert and medical treatment.

Natasha is relieved that Paul and Nero did bond again: 'well, had we had another three months like that, we would have divorced each other, I think'. They both laugh but the situation appears to have had serious implications. She continues:

> You know you want to know how the dog affects the family unit? I'm not kidding you, we, I mean Paul and I don't fall out, we very, very rarely argue, but then we really were, it was not good; it gets me emotional just thinking about it. He wanted Nero to go and I wanted him to stay.

Paul interjects: 'You say I wanted him to go, but I didn't, I just couldn't cope with what was happening'.

This 'headstrong' behaviour by Nero draws recollection of remarks by Terry about Jim's 'playing without stopping'. Terry describes Jim's method of alerting to high blood sugar levels or hyperglycaemia, as 'frenetic'. He wonders how many dogs are being re-homed because of that behaviour, caused by people's blood sugars rising to a high level when they have not been diagnosed as diabetic.

> How many people have planned to re-home their dogs because they think they can't control them when in fact, the dogs are doing their best to alert to high blood sugars? If my sugars go high you cannot stop it (*Jim's playing*), and yet as soon as I get the test kit out and I've done the test, he'll go and lie down.

This conjures an immediate image of West Highland terrier, Becky, hurtling wildly round and round my 12-year-old friend Jane as she stood in the garden. 'We call them her mad-dog episodes; she's always doing it' – both Jane and her father had Type 1 diabetes, so it is likely Becky's days were often interrupted if intense play is indeed a form of hyper-alerting. Whether she and Jim were merely trying to use up excess energy by having fun or were attempting instead to draw urgent attention to their human companions' erratic blood sugar levels, is for further contemplation.

An 'alliance of friendship'?

The lion may be anthropocentrically heralded 'king of the beasts', and the horse as 'man's [sic] noblest creation' (Cassidy, 2002: 137), but those are titles that, while

Dogs as biomedical resources and health technologies 117

calling for admiration of aristocratic breeding, create distance from the iconic creatures so labelled. In terming the dog 'man's [sic] best friend', the anthropocentric intention seems to be a plaudit for the 'other', an appreciation of the goodness and a tribute to the best in companion animalship; and perhaps an attempted classless bringing-in to the human 'fold'. There seems to be an increasing and to-be-welcomed human desire, illustrated at least in contemporary social science literature (for example, Birke and Hockenhull, 2015; Braidotti, 2009; Hurn, 2012; Irvine, 2012), to eradicate ideals of our superiority over nonhuman animals and reduce differentiation between human and other-than-human beings.

Is this kindly best-friending a genuine wish to share a common status? Adam Miklósi (2009) is among those who consider that the human-dog relationship could be an alliance of friendship, and referring to Silk (2002), he contends that this form of friendship could engage 'a social dimension for mutual trade without the need of immediate reciprocation, having a propensity for sharing things and the possibility of offering social support (and thus enhancing mental and physical health) and engaging in cooperative actions' (Miklósi, 2009: 165). In the case of a diabetes alert dog and human 'alliance', sharing, supporting and cooperating are definite facets of the friendship, but there is, however, a need for immediate reciprocation in mutual trade, since as soon as the dog gives an alert, the human needs to test blood sugar levels and reward the dog for an accurate assessment straightaway. As commented on by Richard, a few seconds of delay in offering a reward for appropriate alerting can seriously offset alert training since dogs benefit from association with the action and reward in order to bolster memory for future alerting:

> I think I was a bit disorganised in terms of alerting when he first arrived and didn't recognise an alert quickly enough. The charity said I had to 'treat' him more quickly but I'm slow at checking my blood sugar levels.

Certainly Hurn's (2012) contention that friendship may be an appropriate way to think about the human-companion animal bond, seems viable and easy to accept, provided there is mutual desire for such bonding and resultant friendship regardless of the usefulness of each to the other. The 'spark of mutual attraction, or a recognition of personhood across the species barrier' (2012: 109) invites trust and co-responsibility to deepen new bonds of friendship.

Perhaps by now we have been sufficiently encouraged to move away from Cartesian dualism (the separation of mind from body) and are ready to recommend a contemporary mutualism to fuzz those divisive boundaries that separate 'man and his dog'.

Dogs are not the sole sentient instruments of detection and identification. As discussed in the section on olfaction, academic research, anecdote and media articles have all reported the scenting abilities of rats and elephants, land, avian, and marine creatures. Serpell (1996: 19) contends that pigs are 'no less intelligent than dogs or cats; they are sociable and clean and, when tamed, make amiable pets', despite the general belief that they are unclean creatures. The pig is also

118 *Dogs as biomedical resources and health technologies*

an efficient and accurate olfactory sensor in the detection of drugs, for which employment there is reward; and, in a very different industry, the pig, as shown later, is proving to be a key factor in contemporary scientific experimentation to improve human health.

Xenotransplantation and animal models for human treatment

Here is undoubted controversy, where head and heart collide, and advocacy for equal status among species and a symbiotic code of ethics vents vociferous protest above laboratory experimentation on nonhuman others. Xenotransplantation is no longer an imaginary construct, and the 'pigs might fly' adynaton – that is, an exaggeration beyond the possible – may not always be so, as stem cell technology and gene editing are fast altering definition of what it is to be pig, bird, or human.

Pierson et al. (2009: 263) suggest xenotransplantation, the use of nonhuman animals in organ donation or transplant surgery, may reduce or close the gap between insufficient human cells, tissues, or organs, and the needs of numerous people with diabetes who may require pancreatic islet 'allotransplantation'. Allotransplantation transfers cells, organs or tissues from one individual to another of the same species with a different genotype, whereas in xenotransplantation, the transfer takes place between different species, for example, pigs and humans.

A study in *Cell Stem Cell* examines 'tolerance induction and reversal of diabetes in mice transplanted with human embryonic stem cell-derived pancreatic endoderm (hESC-PE)' (Szot et. al., 2015: 148). Results 'support the clinical development of hESC-derived therapy, combined with tolerogenic treatments, as a sustainable alternative strategy for patients with Type 1 diabetes' (2015: 148).

More recently, Yamaguchi et al. (2017) injected mouse pluripotent stem cells (PSCs) into rat blastocysts deficient in Pdx-1 (pancreatic and duodenal homeobox [*Homo sapiens* (human)])-, generating rat-sized pancreata composed of mouse PSC–derived cells. Islets from these pancreata were transplanted into mice with streptozotocin-induced diabetes where they 'normalized and maintained host blood glucose levels for over 370 days' (Yamaguchi et al., 25 January, 2017). The researchers suggest their data provide proof-of-principle evidence for the therapeutic potential of 'PSC-derived islets generated by blastocyst complementation in a xenogeneic host' (25 January, 2017).

Complex and progressive as this experimentation would appear, use of the pig (and rats, mice and others) as a laboratory model and 'future xenograft donor' (Hansen, Dahl, and Sørensen, 2002: 45) invites concern over the 'transgression of species boundaries' (Birke and Michael, 1998: 245).

Recent advances in animal biotechnology and deepening discussion of the field of bioethics are highlighted by Richard Twine (2015); Donna Haraway's 'genetically engineered lab critter, patented under the name OncoMouse', is creeping into broader public knowledge (2008: 76). This 'transgenic animal' was created to act as a model for breast cancer investigation, but other transgenic mice have been used 'to study the expression of AIDS in the human immune deficiency system'

Dogs as biomedical resources and health technologies 119

(Salvi, 2001: 16) and, as mentioned later, continue to provide vast numbers of living models for ongoing global experimental studies into human health and illness.

Gail Davies questions 'what might it mean to become with an inbred mouse'? (2013: 130). Talking of 'managing mutation in mouse models of human disease', she examines the increasingly useful role of mouse models to understand human biology and disease which has resulted in a human–mouse biomedical entanglement and inbred mice who become globally commercial and in Haraway's words (1997: 7) scientific instruments 'for sale like many other laboratory devices'.

Looking at directions for future research, authors of the JDRF Type 1 Diabetes Research Roadmap suggest that new animal models in the field of diabetes complications need to be created since, they opine, there are relatively few robust current models and, 'although the progression to disease is compressed into approximately six months compared to the decades of progression in humans, molecules accessed from industry could be rapidly tested and moved into new trials where appropriate' (2013b: 24). Support here perhaps for Cohen's (1986) contention that animals should increasingly be used in biomedical research.

Different options may evolve from the ongoing research into beta cell replacement, regeneration, and transplantation (JDRF, 2013b) that involves mice as laboratory 'models'. Animal models, for example nonobese diabetic mice, are commonly used for research into Type 1 diabetes, but do not always display identical modelling to that evidenced in human Type 1 diabetes. A JDRF (2013b: 17) article points out that these mice may 'spontaneously develop insulin-dependent diabetes as a result of insulitis, an inflammatory autoimmune reaction within the islet cells', which can cause divergence from human Type 1 diabetes.

However, although this developing research conveys breakthrough options for the future, there is no doubt that the ability to participate safely and confidently in daily social activities remains the current major objective of those already diagnosed with Type 1 diabetes, whether living alone, or with family members, friends and colleagues.

Morrison and Morgan (1999: 10) examine models as 'autonomous agents' and detail how they function as 'instruments of investigation'. Models, they suggest, may function as tools or instruments and are 'independent of, but mediate between things; and like tools, can often be used for many different tasks' (1999: 11). That the authors refer to models as 'one of the critical instruments of modern science', does not preclude the concept of the medical alert assistance dog working autonomously as an instrument of varied function. The dogs provide effective alerting to fast-falling blood sugar levels but also, in representing and coembodying chronic illness, bring knowledge to the individual companion and to a diabetes-unaware public (refer Sarah's comment earlier on the invisibility of diabetes).

Tim Ingold (2000: 294) views the use of tools as 'an instance of skilled practice' in contrast with the use of them as 'the operation of a technology'. He suggests 'tools of coercion, such as the whip or spur' (2000: 307) were and still are used by the 'human master to control the skilled tool-using performance of his charges' under conditions of human or animal slavery. In the training of medical alert assistance dogs, the whip is more likely made of a strongly flavoured edible item of

120 *Dogs as biomedical resources and health technologies*

reward, and all requests are asked in positive terms and the wanted responses are similarly recognised. But there remains the issue of the animate instrument.

The significance of this sentient means of improvement in healthcare is well illustrated by Paul who portrays his canine companion Nero, in terms of both equipment and 'pet' animal:

> I see him first as an aid like a blood monitor, in other words, he's just another tool that helps me. Bearing that in mind, I obviously also see him as a pet, he gets me out, he gets me doing things. . . . I mean I'm walking again and I'm exercising which I wasn't doing, he's keeping me fit, he gives me a better value of life – so he's just another tool on top of being a companion; he's just another tool that adds to the list of things that will help – in a really cut-throat kind of way, he's serving a purpose. I see him in that role – and then I see him as a pet, but the pet is the last thing.

Natasha takes an opposing view, observing that Nero is a member of her family and she considers him 'first and foremost to be a pet who just happens to have a very cool, clever, life-saving ability'.

I note that Terry talks of his well-mannered DAD, Jim, as a companion but, like Paul, he also perceives the dog as an instrument. He compares his reading of Jim's signals to reading the signals of a faulty vehicle:

> You know when there's something wrong with your car and you take it to a mechanic if it's not driving right or the brakes are a bit sloppy – you know, you just know. And in that way, I treat the dog like a piece of equipment because I'm reading the signs that this piece of equipment gives me.

But, as Paul has explained his varying views of the tool–pet, inanimate–animate dichotomy, Terry also observes that

> The dog's not a robot, not a piece of machinery; you've got to allow the dog to be a dog and do what a dog needs to do. You've always got to think they're animals, not like robots or a wheelchair. You can't park him up in a corner, put the brake on him and say that's it – I'm not using you for the next eight hours.
>
> Of course, he can be a bit naughty; he's a dog, not a robot, that's the sort of difference. My wheelchair won't misbehave.

This brings a dry 'unless it breaks down' from Nick, and Terry mutters wryly, 'I don't have to feed the wheelchair', but it is abundantly clear that Jim holds high status and they are aware of his needs as much as their own:

> With an animate tool like the assistance dog, you have to think of another individual. If you're going along a busy road, how will your dog react to something like a 10-ton truck going past – you may have to change sides,

Dogs as biomedical resources and health technologies 121

putting the dog on the inside (*instead of between Terry in the wheelchair and the traffic*) for his own safety.

Among a wide-range of complex situations they face every day, they recall Christmastime ventures into town with Jim and the wheelchair:

> It's busy and people are carrying big bags and they don't think . . . you get clobbered, never mind the dog. They step straight out of a shop and because you're below their eye-level, they don't see you.

Continuing with the theme of the living, active dog and the 'static piece of equipment that just sits there', Nick relates comment about a well-known sports personality who has embodied wheelchair living for most of her life:

> To start with, she believed you've got to walk, you must wear leg callipers, you must walk because walking's good for you; but she found it such hard work and was so tired. However, in a wheelchair, she said she's got life, she can go off and do things, play with other children and 'run away' – things she couldn't do in callipers, so to her the wheelchair was an enabler whereas to others, 'it's the end of my life'. You've got two completely different attitudes to the wheelchair – it's turning more towards thinking of it as a life-enhancing piece of equipment – but so is an assistance dog.

Referring to disability studies (for example, Bury, 1991, 2001; Charmaz, 1995, 2006; Nettleton, 2013; Shakespeare, 2014; Taylor, 2014), in which stigma and disenfranchisement are highlighted and result in a negative slant towards individuals lacking certain abilities, such research also envisages treating disability equipment as means to make an individual feel unique and to have a life worth living – raising personal status to an achievable and desirable standard. Tom Shakespeare (2014: 97) investigates people with impairments who are socially identified as disabled but may be reluctant to identify with what has become a stigmatising label.

Janet, for example, feared that the co-presence of DAD, Alfie, would draw attention to her illness and cause her increased social isolation. However, others such as Terry, whose capabilities are hampered by physical impairment and the need for specialised equipment, identify themselves as 'normal' and not disabled in the first place.

Wearing status

In public, the dog wears a jacket identifying a link to the charity training and matching the diabetic alert canines to their human partners; a collar and lead are similarly labelled means of identity, bringing attention to the dyad and an elevated status to the working dog. This scarlet, labelled jacket designating the dog's prowess in biomedical achievement, echoes Rebecca Cassidy's depiction

122   *Dogs as biomedical resources and health technologies*

of the importance and power assigned by racehorse clothing. 'Perhaps the most significant horse clothing of all is the rug presented to the winners of big races; usually brightly coloured and bearing the name of the race and its sponsor, the horse carries its status on its back' (Cassidy, 2002: 27). The alert assistance dogs may not be race winners, but the jacket identifies the significance of their work and broadcasts the high status earned by each of them.

Terry remarks on their visibility in public:

> It's not just the fact you've got an assistance dog; you're an ambassador for the charity. People see the name of the charity (*on the dog's jacket*) so they're expecting a certain level of behaviour from you and from the dog. People will approach you and want to know what the charity's about.

Rod Michalko (1999) offers alternative reasoning for clothing designating prestige to the wearer. He suggests that his guiding dog, Smokie's harness presents a cue to the social observer that symbolises 'work and blindness'. Similarly, the DAD's jacket and leash therefore represent work and diabetes, drawing attention to the usually-hidden complexities of this illness. To an observing member of society, this is likely to indicate that a dog in an identifying jacket is a well-trained, working assistance dog.

However, online columnist Helen Dolphin is among those who are 'concerned that growing numbers of untrained and badly behaved fakes could compromise the credibility of the real thing' (Disability Now, 4 January 2016). Terry and Nick mention they know of three 'fake assistance dogs cropping up' in their region. People buy or make dog jackets in order to convey the impression that their dog is a well-trained assistance dog, permitted to enter buildings or organisations into which a dog would not normally be allowed access. If an untrained dog then misbehaves while wearing an 'internet'-purchased 'fake' assistance dog jacket in public, Terry believes that accredited assistance dogs may 'get a bad name'. On the other hand, as seen in the many online responses to Dolphin's concern, there are long waiting lists for qualified assistance dogs and some people with mobility issues find it necessary to train their own dogs as best they can in order to have any sort of social contact.

So that we can see Gemma 'working' in public, Mel and her family drive one of the charity's instructors and myself to a shopping mall and we park on the roof of a multistorey car park. Gemma wears her red DAD jacket and I am struck by an apparent change in her bearing compared to her unjacketed self when on a 'free run' earlier in the day.

On our walk in the countryside, I listen to the conversation between Mel and the instructor and watch Gemma and her young companion, Mark, zigzagging ahead. Gemma is off the leash but continually looks back at him. She jumps over tussocks and bushes, racing through long grass and saplings, ears flapping like soft wings. Every time Mark calls to her, she rushes back to him. However, there is a single hiatus when the smell of decomposing rabbit proves too much to ignore, when she could be said to demonstrate individual agency in activating her inner

Dogs as biomedical resources and health technologies 123

'dogness' to enjoy the fruits of her macrosmatic sense of smell: she parades the corpse. However, she returns to Mel immediately when called and allows her to retrieve the rabbit and dispose of it without argument. She then continues to explore her chosen pathways.

Wearing her jacket in town later in the day, Gemma appears to hold her head higher, her stance is more erect and her gait is shortened, more precise, neat and purposeful – her identity seems to take on the persona of an authoritative assistant, yet retains that of a happy, well-loved family member.

But then, other participants say they see no change at all in their dogs' demeanours, jackets on or off. Paul and Natasha believe that Nero portrays the other side of the coin. Anthropomorphically, they consider him to be 'a man of his own mind' and put human words into his mouth so that his imagined emotions may be verbalised:

> It's a bit like when we used to give a talk and get all dressed up in the MDD-logo clothes – you could see him sitting on the stairs going 'oh god, I'm going to get patted on the head all afternoon. Will I get a run at the end of it or. . .?' But he's so affable, he'll do anything you ask him to do. . . . He's not a cuddly dog and as far as putting the jacket on, he's a man of his own mind and I don't think it makes any difference, I don't think he's more proud, he doesn't do a 'ooh look I've got my jacket on'.

I wonder if I, too, am imagining, anthropomorphising, incorporating what others have told me that, when their dogs wear their labelled jackets, they seem to be aware that they are professionals and have a sense of pride in their work. 'A sense of pride?' That is inference and not knowledge so I must be attributing certain human personality traits to these dogs, allowing them some form of emotional awareness and abstract thinking, even the cognitive ability to possess 'theory of mind', and to attribute mental states to themselves and to others.

This is a topic well investigated by Bekoff (2002, 2004), de Waal (2010), Panksepp (2005, 2011), Von Uexküll (1934 [2010]), Weil (2012) and others who have considered that bonobos, chimpanzees, elephants, and dolphins, as well as more domesticated species, for example, dogs and humans, are able to share in the perceptions, emotions and environments of other familiar beings. However, despite increasing neuroscientific investigation (Panksepp, 2011), definition of nonhuman animal consciousness shifts over time and remains unclear, perhaps because of the impossibility of accurately 'reading' another's mind or of absorbing aspects of their subjective *umwelt*.

Miklósi and Topál (2013) write of developmental social competence, 'an individual's ability to generate social skills that conform to the expectations of others and the social rules of the group' and this reminds again of Srinivasan's 'anthropogenic norms' and conjures further guidelines for my human imagining that dogs have degrees of 'awareness' – although having a sense of pride in their occupation may not yet be recognised evidence of canine competence and cognition.

124   *Dogs as biomedical resources and health technologies*

Gemma's altered presence in my imagination from that of playmate to professional may perhaps be compared to horses entering a show-ring or dressage arena. 'She's such a diva' is a frequent comment but it's not a censure, rather an acclaim, an admiration of the horse's altered self-carriage and 'presence' before spectators, and a further example of attributing human-created values to a nonhuman other. Similar attributions of 'presence', 'stamp', and 'type' are spoken by spectators and breeders observing prized Welsh Cobs entering a show ring with their 'handlers' (Hurn, 2008a, 2008b: 32 and 41n13).

However, it seems likely that the diabetic human's status would be perceived as of higher import if the dog were unidentifiable (un-jacketed) beyond the rank of companion animal. In contrast, the rider would be 'just a rider' without the horse demonstrating his or her prowess. Hurn (2011: 109) contends that 'the act of clothing animals' is a means of control over their 'animality', whereas the 'removal of clothing and material paraphernalia' (for example, the DAD's jacket, collar, and leash) could instead signify respect and recognition of nonhuman animal personhood. But then again, if the alert dog was *not* wearing identification when the dyad is viewed by a public eye, their combined access into many institutions and organisations could be barred.

Disabling identity

What has been noticed by participants is that the add-on items of our material culture, the labelled jacket and harness, also highlight the human inability to perform many of the functions achieved by more able members of their communities. Even though being diagnosed with diabetes does not strap an identifying jacket onto the human self, an imagined discriminatory label is felt to have been metaphorically attached to the individual walking with the jacketed assistance dog. This may lead to unwanted isolation and social disenfranchisement, the result of a public designation or at least inference of the possibility that the human partner has failed to live appropriately within the generally accepted norms of society and its local cultural patterns.

Clinton Sanders has examined the impact of guide dogs on their visually impaired human companions, noting how 'the stereotypic expectations of the sighted public' affected feelings of self-worth and accorded diminished identities to the unsighted or partially sighted humans (2000: 136). In this way, assistance dogs draw negative attention to the human disability and, as a result, are objectified by the disabled person as well as by a wider society.

Sanders affirms that others follow this way of thinking, suggesting that some people with visual impairments see their assistance dogs as 'mobility devices'. The diabetes alert canines may equally be considered 'diagnostic devices' leading to social isolation. For the chronically ill individuals depicted here, the medical alert assistance dog may be a sign that visibly highlights their *in*abilities to society, a symbolism from which they may fervently wish to disentangle themselves. However, they may not survive without the ever-present early warning system that accompanies them on the bus to go shopping, who lies close by in the pub or

Dogs as biomedical resources and health technologies   125

restaurant, who nudges an arm at the cinema, or who disturbs their sleep at night so that extreme fluctuations in blood glucose levels can be quickly rectified.

Regarding the DADs as animate equipment, as sentient colleagues, can significantly change how people with chronic illness regard themselves and their social interactions. Self-esteem is boosted by cooperative endeavours and enables the previously mentioned Michalko-merger of the two-into-one for those with vision difficulties, into a shared identity, the 'two-in-one', for those with complex Type 1 diabetes.

The dogs become intricate, even contradictory symbols (semiotically speaking) which can impact on the way their humans perceive them. This leads to the notion of 'flexible personhood' introduced by Shir-Vertesh (2012: 420) to 'describe the Israeli cultural reasoning in the treatment of pets that encourages people to react adaptively and opportunistically to changing ways of life and social conditions' (2012: 421). Within the observed multispecies relationships, she discovers an oscillating momentum that alters boundaries and practices, activity that is similarly reflected later in Janet's changing perspective. Shir-Vertesh proposes a theoretical approach which 'goes beyond the treatment of animals as commodities or symbols that are treated irresolutely in their service to humans' (2012: 429). This perspective, she concludes, enables investigation into the 'intimacy created' with companion animals as a 'flexible, yet structured, space with its own objectives and meanings' (2012: 429).

Prior to Alfie's arrival, anticipation of an always-in-attendance medical assistance dog provoked Janet to consider whether she might be labelled 'disabled' *because* of the dog's constant proximity. Having put forward this suggestion, she then kept silent for several minutes before admitting that:

> For a while I had a bit of a thing where I didn't want people to think that because I had an assistance dog, I was disabled, and I had a real thing in my head that that was how I was going to be seen.

But the advantages obtained by sharing life with the assistance dog appear to outweigh the disadvantages, and she added that her fear of the disabled label

> . . . didn't last too long. I think once our bond properly started and he was alerting effectively, that just went out of the window. It became – that's what he does and it's far more important than how I feel or am being perceived.

The bond established between Alfie and Janet, and the efficacy of the working dog's alerts, banished her fears of public identification as disabled, and therefore considered incapable, because of the dog's presence.

Animals as health technologies

Considering early Anthropocen(tr)ic management of and collaboration with nonhuman animals to be the tinder sparking forever-after domestic 'use of other

126 *Dogs as biomedical resources and health technologies*

animals as technologies' (Twine, 2015: 14), and recalling the previous domestication perspectives observed by Budiansky (1997), Clutton-Brock (1995) and Miklósi (2009), regarding historical canine domestication, Silverstone, Hirsch, and Morley's (1992) theory of domestication is now employed to expand the concept of using domestic animals as instruments to improve health. The four tenets of this perspective – appropriation, objectification, incorporation, conversion – enable exploration as to how the diabetes alert dog might be considered an everyday health technology. Haddon (2007: 26) reminds that the metaphor of 'domestication' evolves from 'the taming of wild animals' but was applied by Silverstone to describe procedures mobilised in the domestication of information and communication technologies.

The difference suggested here between consideration of diabetes alert dogs as animate instruments or as health technologies or both may rest partially on degrees of activity or passivity; whether they function as domesticated, obedient tools available for selection among those in the human's medical bag or as domesticated but agentic and autonomous enablers of human health improvement.

Morrison and Morgan have articulated the concept of models as mediating instruments, an example which can be effectively reflected in the DAD's performance as equipment and companion:

> Models have to be used before they will give up their secrets. In this sense, they have the quality of a technology – the power of the model only becomes apparent in the context of its use.
>
> (1999: 12)

It is only this century that has seen 'the power' of the dog's olfactory sensitivity and its use in rendering an individual with Type 1 diabetes free from social isolation and the fear of a hypoglycaemic coma.

Peter Soppelsa (2015: 252) examines the question of animals as technology, following Ann Norton Greene's (2008) contention that horses were 'a crucial power source' behind the rise of American industrialisation. Coulter supports this by suggesting that 'horses do work of various kinds for people, and people garner material, social, or personal gain from that work' (2016a: 6) and adds that this statement 'can be extended to aptly characterize animals' work more broadly' (2016a: 6).

'Our technologies both shape and express who we are', claims Soppelsa (2015: 253) and this is evident in the coembodied interspecies partnerships which become single entities in the public understanding of multispecies performances. Two necessarily entangled beings with one identity, discovered by sociologist Rod Michalko with his guide dog, Smokie (1999), and the becoming of Goffman's (1959) presentation of 'our self', the two in one in blindness or in chronic illness. The alerting assistance dog and the human with Type 1 diabetes take on a shared persona, becoming a carefully choreographed but independently active instrument of biotechnology performing the complex dance that is exacted by chronic illness.

As living organisms trained as, guided by, and ultimately 'doing' medical technology, these human–nonhuman products of interspecies cooperation and

Dogs as biomedical resources and health technologies   127

collaboration accept the challenges of chronic illness, navigate its unpredictable oscillations, and foretell the vagaries of lives that would be lost without insulin.

Soppelsa (2015: 255) suggests Greene's book demonstrates how 'socially desirable animals also serve to reshape the society' in which we reside. Horses defined the economy: used as a technology to 'drive' industry, pulling fire engines and canal barges, hauling gun-carriages and ploughs, extending human abilities through their actions. Ingold (2000: 308) hammers home the unedifying point that 'perhaps in no other employment has an animal come closer to being converted into a pure machine, functioning simply as a prime-mover'. What did these bred ever-larger, ever-stronger, horses gain from this evolutionary determinism?

Repeating Lynda Birke's (2009) question that refers to researcher accountability to their nonhuman participants, what is in it for the animals? Avoidance of harm, perhaps, but did the 'mechanical' horses of industry become more successfully empowered to improve their own welfare? As soon as insentient technology was developed, for example, in the form of steam engines and armoured tanks, the heavy horses devolved into showpieces at agricultural shows or were brought out of redundancy for ceremonial occasions, and are now rarely considered desirable shapers of society, regardless of their historical industrial worth.

Seen as 'socially desirable', perhaps achieving a greater reward and avoidance of harm in comparison to the harnessed horses of the pre-Industrial era, the working medical alert assistance dog has had a more recent impact on the reshaping of our society. Used as instruments of biomedical technology to rearrange and improve management of life with chronic illness, dogs' olfactory skills stretch and hone human capabilities; when compared to many cold inanimate diagnostic or remedial devices, their warm practices of care sculpt socially acceptable multispecies niches.

Contemporary canine domestication

If the Latin word, '*domus*', is translated into 'house' or 'home', it is simple to understand 'domicile' as a place of settled residence. Yet, if the noun's meaning changes when it is adapted to become 'domestic', a servant of others in the home, it is also altered further in significance when the word becomes 'domesticate/d' or 'tame/d', inviting visions of servitude and connotation of human domination and control over a 'wild' nonhuman being (Ingold, 2000; Malamud, 2013).

In this instance, there is a softer side to domestication whereby the human offers to share a trusting coexistence (Armstrong Oma, 2010; Palmer, 1997) and to shepherd a fear-free and curious dog into a human-made protective fold; an invitation that can result in an emergence of symbiotic health care practices within the bounds of an already-domesticated unwell individual and a collective social '*domus*'; an acceptable multispecies niche.

Historical canine domestication and the engagement of an 'other' in care practices have been previously mentioned, with focus on the diabetes alert dog's ability to assist an unwell human with coping skills for survival management; so more contemporary approaches to multispecies domestication are now explored.

128 *Dogs as biomedical resources and health technologies*

Donna Haraway (2008: 207) highlights the collaborative world of humans and dogs who work together in sports agility competition and remarks in that context:

> Training together puts the participants inside the complexities of instrumental relations and structures of power. How can dogs and people in this kind of relationship be means and ends for each other in ways that call for reshaping our ideas about, and practices of, domestication?

Haraway recalls Despret's (2004) concept of 'anthropo-zoo-genetic practice' in her redefinition of domestication where people and animals become more available, more interesting, more open to each other and gain new identities.

In using this approach to domestication in support of a routinely used health technology, motivation was informed by the writings of Haraway and Despret; by research into the role of communication and information technologies in the home and in society (Silverstone, Hirsch and Morley, 1992), by Jeannette Pols' (2012) research into care and technology, and by a study (Carter, Green and Thorogood, 2013) examining the domestication of an everyday health technology, the electric toothbrush.

However, instead of the inanimate electric toothbrush which requires manipulation via electric current and human dexterity, under focus here is the domestication of a sentient 'everyday health technology': an entirely animate and long-domesticated canine, the working diabetes alert assistance dog. Consideration is given to whether this canine creation may be perceived as an everyday viable health technology mobilising improvement in the diabetic individual's way of living.

Tim Dant (2007) suggests that daily interactions with material objects depend on the way individuals make sense of their significance and how they may be altered to fit current needs. He writes of design and consumption in respect of car repair and furniture construction, but here dogs come already designed (macrosmatic scenting ability) and constructed (trained), and consumption of their scenting prowess relies on interactions between the human and nonhuman in order to achieve required goals.

Miller's concluding request in *Stuff* calls for 'a consideration of things commensurate with the place they evidently have in our lives' (2010: 156) and, as items of material culture who hold ongoing significance in, and for, the lives they share, diabetes alert dogs deserve consideration and approbation as living beings 'in our lives'; as creatures whose status seems often to rank of equal significance to that of the human with whom they coexist.

The electric toothbrush is an efficient health technology for oral hygiene as is the well-marketed insulin pump's usefulness as a health technology in Type 1 diabetes, to balance insulin intake against carbohydrate ingestion and exercise. However, both material items have inanimate dispositions and lack the ability to function without human intervention.

The guide dog has been recognised as a material source of health and social improvement for sight-impaired people for more than a century, but the notion of canine scenting ability being sufficiently accurate to change the boundaries and relationships inherent in human chronic illness, and in other life-altering diseases, has only recently become reality. The concept of a dog's sense of smell actively leading to the detection of cancers is becoming more widely accepted (Guest, 2013; Lippi and Cervellin, 2012) while the canine olfactory prevention of human hypoglycaemic collapse is now prominent in media presentations, well supported by research evidence and viewed as a positive health intervention by the general public.

However, a hypoglycaemic collapse that requires emergency health care, often brings shame and embarrassment to the individual in social situations. Once consciousness is regained, the no-longer comatose person is likely to feel stigmatised and that any form of social inclusion is denied to them. This is in direct contrast to the positive effect of an attending hypo-detection dog who acts as a preventative technology, a constantly on-hand biomedical and biosocial resource that adds to positive identity rather than detracting from it, as shown, for example, in the significant impact on onlookers made by Harley when Tina collapses in public.

A theory of domestication

The four phases of appropriation, objectification, incorporation, and conversion, proposed by Silverstone, Hirsch, and Morley (1992: 18) as 'elements of the transactional system in which the moral economy of the household is expressed', may themselves be 'appropriated' conveniently to allow the alert dog to be seen as a commodity in a 'transactional system', and as a functional health technology within, and beyond the household defines.

Domestication theory in this context involves cultural, social and technological networks of household daily life. Haddon (2007: 26) suggests the metaphor of 'domestication' came from the taming of wild animals, but contends that Silverstone, Hirsch, and Morley (1992) intended it to 'describe processes involved in "domesticating Information and Communication Technologies" when bringing them into the home'. The meanings and significance of all media and information products depend on the participation of the user, according to Silverstone (1996), and this suggestion can reflect how much meaningful use is made of the autonomous working assistance dog by a chronically ill person.

The first phrase employed to describe the concept of domestication as envisaged by Silverstone et al. (1992: 18–23), is:

> *Appropriation*: when a technology leaves the world of commodity, that is 'at point of sale', it is appropriated. Then it can be 'taken possession of by an individual or household and *owned*'. Appropriation permits artefacts to become 'authentic (commodities become objects) and achieve significance'.
> (1992: 19)

When a medical alert assistance dog is trained as a health-improving technology and is 'matched' to a human individual with Type 1 diabetes, the label of sentient

130 *Dogs as biomedical resources and health technologies*

biomedical resource is necessarily altered. The dog is brought into another species' living space as a commodity which, in the UK, may then be 'owned' (cf. Kopytoff, 1986), the joint purposes being assistance and companionship. The dog crosses the boundary from formally trained commodity to a seemingly well cared-for sentient possession situated in the domain of health care and improvement.

But does the dog remain a commodity, and not a possession, when adopting the clothing of a biomedical assistant? This question may be related to Shir-Vertesh's concept of flexible personhood and the notion of a DAD becoming an emotional commodity when considering the moral appropriation of the assistance dog. In the public's general gaze, the dog becomes an ethically-cared-for individual and is seen to be ethically consumed for human health benefit. Participants are, however, contracted to give optimal care to the dogs who share their homes, under the observation and supervision of the charity's staff. Acts of appropriation, the passage of artefacts from commodity to object possessed, enable 'self-creation', a way of defining and distinguishing themselves from, and allying themselves to, each other. Such appropriation allows for new identities to appear and be clarified; and reciprocal practices of care and service to be engaged.

Objectification is expressed in the use and in the physical situating of objects in the home's 'spatial environment' and in the 'construction of that environment'. Silverstone, Hirsch, and Morley aver that:

> All technologies have the potential to be appropriated into an aesthetic environment [. . .] Many are purchased as much for their appearance and their compatibility with the dominant aesthetic rationality of the home as for their functional significance'.
>
> (1992: 20)

As 'objects that appear and are displayed in an already constructed (and always reconstructible) meaningful spatial environment' (1992: 20), working alert dogs may add to the aesthetics of the human home, thereby seeming to boost the homeowner's status, through coat-colour coordination with room furnishings or because of their natural grace and elegance. However, it is for their functional as well as aesthetic significance that they are objectified here (*refer to Harley's image reflecting on Tina*). The pungent smell of wet dog, the cacophony of welcoming or defensive barks, clumps of shed hair on floor and furniture, or half-eaten 'chews' left in doorways may not invite an aesthetic sensory appreciation of the environment from a human visitor to the canine home. But the interspecies dyads of this study bond chiefly through need and 'likeability'. The beauty of the beast might be obvious but is not considered of high import compared to the good practices he or she make available.

Incorporation: Silverstone, Hirsch, and Morley (1992) draw attention to the ways in which objects, especially technologies, are used, suggesting that 'technologies are functional. They may be bought with other features in mind and indeed serve other cultural purposes in appropriation' (1992: 21). In order to become functional, the researchers contend that a technology has to 'find a place within

Dogs as biomedical resources and health technologies 131

the moral economy of the household, specifically in terms of its incorporation into the routines of daily life' (1992: 21).

Incorporation, as they claim above, may facilitate 'control' of time and this is highly relevant to chronic illness where time plays a prominent role in measuring and eating, blood testing and insulin preparation, rest and exercise. 'Where a technology is located and when and how it is used (and of course by whom) become crucial elements in the moral economy of the household as a whole' (1992: 22). While Silverstone, Hirsch, and Morley refer to control and use of television remotes and computers, such 'usage' of a diabetes alert dog by a chronically ill individual in their home, can become a routine health technology.

But, once trained, the alert dog functions autonomously in working to maintain the safe and prolonged existence of the human partner, and at the same time coembodies a shared way of living life within societal and medical contexts. As a technology, the DAD helps maintain the choreography and chronology involved in the day-in and day-out dances of diabetes.

Conversion: as with appropriation, Silverstone et al. suggest conversion 'defines the relationship between the household and the outside world' (1992: 22). It may happen that 'artefacts and meanings, texts and technologies' pass through boundaries, as the household 'defines and claims for itself and its members a status in neighbourhood, work and peer groups in the "wider society" (1992: 22). The behaviour of the jacketed and therefore purpose-identified dog, with a human partner – for example, Gemma and Mark or Terry and Jim – achieve conversion from two single beings to a conjoined dyad and gain a status that seems to earn greater levels of respect than either would have achieved alone.

An example of a technology 'passing through boundaries' might include insulin travelling from the vial via the pump and cannula to the bloodstream; but may also be seen in the conversion of council legislation to allow assistance dogs and their human partners to enter institutions and societies formerly forbidden to them as single minorities.

The domestication of 'wild' animals and the history of human–canine companionship are topics covered earlier, but here, the dog is already domesticated and has now become a household commodity – we too have been 'tamed' into domesticity (Budiansky, 1997) and want things to ornament our homes, to assist in improving our existence. The animate technologies, bolstering health practices in the home, are trained to convert their best care practices and perform them equally in the streets and buildings of 'wider society'.

Tools and devices

I write of dogs and, concomitant with this species as companions to human animals, is the frequent endeavour by the latter to tame, train, and 'make behave' so that a connecting 'leash' between the two species itself becomes an object of domestication and a device of obedience; perhaps one of Ingold's 'tools of coercion' (2000: 307) and not always the 'smiling', U-shaped link encouraged by MDD trainers. Training of the diabetes alert dog involves use of the leash, but

132 *Dogs as biomedical resources and health technologies*

the goal is that, after consistent practice, a smile should develop in the material allowing the dog to walk next to his or her partner without tension in the device being felt by either of them.

Domestication theory, writes Jeannette Pols (2012: 18), 'grants humans more agency: animals, plants and technologies do not determine our lives but come to live with us, in our homes, and on our terms', not always in the ways and uses for which they were 'designed'.

Telling of heuristic 'activities that "unleash" and "tame" individuals and devices', and that precede the 'domestication of a species or their living together – or apart – happily ever after' (2012: 18), Pols speaks of new technology being 'let out of its box' so that 'individual devices are unleashed into the daily life practices to which they come to belong' (2012: 18).

Here, both the diabetic alert dog and the leash become individual devices working together in the daily practices devised by their human partners, the one being animate, the other, inanimate (although the latter, if constructed from leather, may have been constructed from a deceased once-animate being).

Referring to the unpredictability of the unleashed device and its unexpected activities contra the design formulation, Pols (2012: 18) takes the 'domesticated telephone' as an example, whereby the intention was to 'transmit the business conversations of American men', but it instead became a widely used instrument of social discourse for American women. 'The history of technology shows again and again that devices will behave differently to what their designers intended' (Pols, 2012: 18). Indeed, no one would have predicted that dogs bred for herding or guarding would become adept at sniffing for explosives or disease.

Pols' second activity 'in the process of mutual adaptation involves taming the devices' so that they become practical and fit for purpose, even if not all the available attributes are needed or used (2012: 19). Here again, the medical alert dog, as a technological device, is already domesticated and tamed, and through contemporary positive training methods is enabled to match the requirements of the chronically-ill individual; to nudge or 'scrabble' (Higgins) rather than bark or to bring the medical kit autonomously (Gemma/Harley). But the dog could easily be trained to switch on lights, press doorbells, pick up dropped laundry, collect mail posted through the letterbox, and so on. Taming here is 'according to requirement', to make 'fit for purpose'. Terry explains that it took five minutes to teach Jim to turn the light off.

> He'd come and cuddle at night and, because all my light switches are low down, I got him used to working with the laser pointer. I pointed it at the light switch and said 'touch', which was the first bit. He touched the light from the pointer with his nose and it flicked the switch, so he got lots of praise for that and now he knows.

'We taught him "fetch help" that way too,' and Nick moves into the kitchen and faces away from where Terry and Jim are sitting. Terry directs the laser pointer so that the red dot is visible on the back of Nick's shirt and says 'look, look'. Jim runs

Dogs as biomedical resources and health technologies   133

to the kitchen and jumps up, placing both paws on Nick's back. 'That's the only time he's allowed to jump up – good boy' and Terry gives him a treat, 'so that's how all this training's been done'.

Terry's previous canine 'device' only alerted to low blood sugar readings. As soon as the pen drawing up the blood sample 'clicked', the dog would lie down. Dogs, accepted as beings with agency, are unpredictable in temperament and behaviour no matter how similar in colour, size or pedigree. Jim, unlike Terry's previous assistance dog, is a more attentive and perhaps a more conscientious individual who waits for the 'beep' to show the meter reading is ready. Terry describes Jim's behaviour and, like other participants, enables the dog to have linguistic ability, in this case to explain his conscious decision to 'lie down' only when his work is complete:

> You do the click of the pen, draw the blood, put it on the strip, wait for the machine to diagnose the level and it goes beep when it's got the result. He goes 'you've got the result there, I'll go and lie down, I've done the job'. Sometimes, if he knows your blood sugar has gone quite low, he'll sit there and make sure you've eaten a biscuit or had something – then, he'll watch you for another ten minutes or more, then slowly relax and lie down.

There are seemingly different rates of metabolism and conscientiousness in dogs, just as exhibited by human individuals. Despite advancement in genetic engineering, the animal consciousness has not yet been cloned and dogs remain similar enough to fit with specified breed appearance, but not in terms of motivation, temperament, personality, or conscientious endeavour. They may assent, adapt and comply with questions asked to become adequately 'tamed' devices but users need to take inventive action to achieve a progressive and accurate 'goodness of fit', a measure of temperament in psychosocial functioning, for example.

Pols' third heuristic 'for analysing domestication processes looks at how devices unleash the imagination and creativity of their users who promptly invent new applications' (2012: 19). The founders of the canine biomedical resource under focus might never have expected crossbred and pedigreed dogs to adapt, tolerate and collaborate with humans to the extent that they become highly sensitive medical detectives, regardless of birth and social education. The dogs' keen scenting ability to detect VOCs in cancer cells has been acknowledged and expanded creatively so that medical detection dogs now assist humans with diabetes, allergies, potentially early stage malaria and other illnesses, while acting as their proverbial 'good companions' in social contexts.

Budiansky's concept of nonhuman animals domesticating humans and the need for 'cooperative associations' for survival (1997: 16), in this instance supports Pols' fourth heuristic which observes how devices dance a *volte face*, a turn-around intended to tame the humans, 'by allowing for, or even forcing, some activities while hindering others' (Pols, 2012: 19). Manipulation of the human by the diabetes alert dog is a visible and accepted construct in their cooperative domestication. It is essential that an individual with Type 1 diabetes follows a set

134 *Dogs as biomedical resources and health technologies*

procedure that is insisted on by the dog's warning behaviour. The dogs are unable to relax and 'chill' until their human companions have performed a blood test – and acted upon it, by topping up insulin or ingesting fast-acting carbohydrate. Jim and Harley have illustrated this avoidance of lying down and sleeping until Terry and Tina have conducted the necessary procedures. A further example occurred when a performance of care practice by the dog, which was not included in the training, 'empowered' him to do more, to act autonomously: to decide how to fulfil an action deemed necessary, for example, by 'blocking' the stairs to prevent his human partner's imminent fall because of 'blackout'.

Pols' four approaches to unleashing and taming enable a practice in which humans and 'devices' have 'established their particular relations':

> Their identities and functions are interdependent. Unleashing and taming processes may lead to a fit between individual devices and users and, eventually, to a form of domestication, implying more or less established practices of cooperation, such as those of the telephone.
>
> (2012: 19)

Such processes may also 'lead to a fit' between the diabetes alert dog as device, and the Type 1 diabetic as user, and to 'a form of domestication' in which their practices of cooperation invite harmonious coexistence. The biomedical interspecies' oscillation that swings from canine olfactory sensitivity to the human monitoring of blood sugar levels and a resultant usually chewable reward for both, contrives a pendulum of activity by which force and hindrance act as gravitational weights.

The urgent nudging to encourage swift testing or the abovementioned physical 'blocking' of the stairs to prevent fall and injury are examples of how the human is appropriately tamed and manipulated by the dog. This perspective of mutual taming amplifies how medical alert assistance dogs act as biomedical resources empowering human self-care practices, at the same time empowering themselves as agents (Mullin, 2002; Coulter, 2016a).

Mills and De Keuster (2009: 322) remark the need to 'appreciate how much dogs are genuinely an integral part of our society' so that we become 'more prepared and willing to seek out solutions of mutual benefit to both species'.

Engaging the 'other' in care practices requires investigation of 'care' with all its complex energies and intensities of meaning. If we care, we involve the consciousness of ourselves and others. Narcissistically, we may care 'selfishly' for ourselves and our own well being, but generally care incorporates the presence of another being – in this case, principally and reciprocally, a dog who cares for, and is cared for, by a human.

6 Symbiotic practices of care

Meanings of care

Thom van Dooren (2014) is affected by the need for caring in conservation and the amendment of daily practices performed in captive breeding. He draws on Haraway's 'unsettling obligation of curiosity' (2008: 36) and stands with Kendra Coulter (2016b: 199) in supporting De la Bellacasa's 'thinking care as inseparably a vital affective state, an ethical obligation and a practical labour' (2012: 197). Caring about and caring for someone or something involve both concern and that notion of the 'unsettling obligation of curiosity' (Haraway, 2008: 36), but where caring about indicates interest and decision whether something may be correct, moral, appropriate, it also permits distance and a broader concern. It is possible to care, on varying levels of conscious curiosity, about the -isms of discrimination, about today's weather pattern, or about the future welfare of refugees and earthquake victims.

But it is also possible to care physically for the welfare of those who are bonded particularly closely, human kindred and nonhuman multispecies animal companions. Those who are well-known to the carer and who may rely on that care for their welfare. Health workers, medical practitioners and veterinary staff care for their own relatives, colleagues and companion animals in the same way, but with an additional, professional focus centred on caring about the comfort and welfare of 'stranger' others in their personal responsibility agenda. This can develop into an empathic relationship between the carer and the cared-about and -for which, in the words of Jeannette Pols (2010: 143), enables care to be about 'sensitivity and concern, about being-there for those in need'.

It cannot be said that the medical alert dogs have choice in being there for those in need, beyond opportunity to exhibit obvious dislike or acceptance or tolerance of a potential human companion. They *are* there, carefully matched and placed with a chronically unwell human partner, and they act autonomously to assist those in need. But, no matter the pleasurable reward gained for correct alerting, no dog will exert him or herself to serve 'those in need' unless they care or at least have some concern about the others, unless they feel the mutual attraction of a bond and are conscious of their companions' altered states of being when blood sugar levels drop dangerously low – and that something needs to be done. As Janet related, 'the dog has to want to do it for you' and in that, there is choice.

136 *Symbiotic practices of care*

Coulter's (2016b: 200) 'multispecies analysis of care work' notes the expansion of interest in 'engaging animals in the provisioning of care work for people' while nonhuman animals' personal ways of caring for others are scarcely perceived as care work of any shape or form. Coulter divides the work performed by nonhuman animals into the three categories of subsistence work, voluntary work, and work mandated by humans. Although training of dog and human are mandatory obligations before matching procedures can be performed, aspects of Coulter's 'voluntary' category relate to this study since she considers voluntary work to be that commonly provided in homes where domesticated animals reside alongside humans, and may be both 'recipients and beneficiaries of humans' care work . . . and may also perform different kinds of voluntary labour' (2016b: 203).

Although emotional support and comfort given by companion animals to human family members often is not considered work or even recognised consciously as caring by another species, Coulter (2016b: 204) suggests this can provide 'interactive care work that is especially important for seniors, marginalized, or vulnerable people, and women who are confronting domestic violence, are homeless, or are precariously housed' (see also Irvine, 2013).

Although Coulter does not mention the significant work of diabetes alert dogs in detecting possible hypoglycaemic episodes, she does draw attention to the engagement of 'animals' abilities to guide, assist, comfort, calm, and detect physical challenges like seizures before they happen' (Coulter, 2016b: 204). In the same way that the human participants in this research perceive their canine companions, Coulter suggests 'people often identify the animals and their contributions as life-saving, transformative, and essential' (2016b: 204).

Understanding nonhuman animal work

Coulter contends that such care involves skill in communication and may induce challenging situations for the other-than-human animal partners who are compelled to ignore how they might naturally respond and disregard all distractions outside the care work on which they are expected to focus. There is therefore the need to acknowledge animal intersubjectivity (Hurn, 2012) without which such communication could not occur. Hurn suggests that by 'standing in' for humans, animals who were formerly considered 'objects' may become active 'subjects' with influence on human relationships (2012: 125). She draws attention to Cassidy's notion of 'intersubjectivity between the thoroughbred and its human attendants' (2002: 9), which depended on the status of the racehorse in the actions or eyes of the human beholders. 'When horses were recognized as active subjects, situated along a continuum which also included humans, then some form of inter-subjective relationship could result' (Hurn: 2012: 127).

In proposing a 'continuum of suffering and enjoyment as a concept and framework for seeking to understand animals' work from their perspectives, across contexts', Coulter (2016b: 205) suggests that their work would fit on the continuum, dependent on 'the occupation and labour required, the coworkers or employers, the species, social relations and interactions, and individual animals' own personalities, moods, health, preferences, and agency, among other factors'.

By incorporating broad context and becoming open-minded to offered nonhuman animal communication, this proposed continuum seems a positive way to develop improved human comprehension of, for example, the working medical alert assistance dog's perspective of life as a care worker. In this way, it becomes possible to achieve more 'accurate, effective, and ethical multispecies standards' (Coulter, 2016b: 209; Serpell et al., 2010: 502–503) for the care programmes in which the dogs participate.

My observations and perceptions of the diabetes alert dogs working with the chronically ill individuals of this study are encapsulated in Coulter's belief (see also Zamir, 2006: 184) that 'some animals can justifiably be engaged' in providing care in the abovementioned ways if interspecies relationships and routine care practices embody "respect and reciprocity"' (Coulter, 2016b: 209). She offers the attractive prospect of interspecies solidarity as means to involve ethical commitment, empathy, and compassion, in multispecies care work: 'others should not have to be like us for us to care about their wellbeing' (Coulter, 2016b: 212). Here again, Milton's depiction of egomorphism (that we understand animals because we perceive them as being 'like us' rather than 'human-like' (2005: 261), is useful in explaining how our perceptions, and therefore understanding, impact nonhuman others, and their influence on us:

> Personal experience, rather than human-ness, is the basis for understanding others, and that understanding is achieved by *perceiving* characteristics *in* things rather than, as anthropomorphism implies, *attributing* characteristics *to* things.
>
> (Milton, 2005: 260, *italics in text*)

Coulter's concept of interspecies solidarity is intended to stress the values of empathy, dignity, and reciprocity, in understanding routine work procedures and political relationships, and in enabling a view of care 'as not only a practice or type of work, but also as the lifeblood of society and of this earth' (2016b: 213). The importance of mutual tolerance and trust could well be added to the above values. If this interspecies solidarity results from a refracted sense of responsibility, we may perceive the necessity of care and take actions to effect its practice through multiple reflections.

Coulter's conclusion reminds us emphatically that other animals 'have minds, bodies, personalities, feelings, desires, and relationships that matter . . . animals deserve to receive care and provide care' (2016b: 215). In the field of medical alert assistance dogs, empathic recognition of the human–canine working relationship and its essential mutualism, also incorporates the significance of an overarching symbiotic ethics of care in guiding approaches and performances to make the intersections of both species and care work, work.

138 *Symbiotic practices of care*

Morally acceptable?

Taschi Zamir's (2006: 179) liberationist discussion of the 'moral basis of animal-assisted therapy', distinguishes between 'use' and 'exploitation', asking the essential question:

> Can such uses of nonhuman animals [*e.g., in animal-assisted therapy*] be morally justified from a 'liberationist' perspective, a perspective that acknowledges that animals are not merely a resource to be exploited by humans?
>
> (2006: 180)

A liberationist perspective encompasses the value and quality of an animal's life, including whether a lack of liberty can be morally justified. Speaking as a liberationist, Zamir (2006: 181–182) contends that using animals to treat humans may be immoral according to the following points:

Limitations of freedom. Companion animals as 'modified pets' have freedom limited whether they are assistance animals or not. But a difference is exemplified in situations where domesticated creatures (his examples include rabbits, snakes and birds) fail to gain pleasure from human-nonhuman animal interactions in the same way that assistance animals seemingly do – 'unlike alarm or service dogs' (2006: 181), they seem unable to pass their social needs onto humans, thereby becoming severely hampered by the loss of freedom.

Life determination. Zamir suggests that making a 'total decision' to use an animal therapeutically, as a companion animal, racehorse or an occupant of a zoo, is more than a 'limitation-of-freedom', more a determination of their future lives (2006: 181).

Training. To use dogs and other species as human health assistants is likely to involve lengthy training that may violate their well-being, he contends, adding that cats and dogs are more accustomed to contact with humans than other species but there is still loss of kinship and therefore the possibility of social deprivation.

Social disconnection. 'Simians live in packs. By turning them into nursing entities, one disconnects them from whatever it is that they maintain through their social context . . . it is morally safe to make the probable assumption that such disconnection (or bringing up the animal without contact with the animal's kin) is a form of deprivation' (Zamir, 2006: 182)

Injury. Exposure to strangers and over-handling of therapy animals can lead to anxiety and possible injury.

Instrumentalisation. 'Liberationists turn the human-nonhuman model from the thoughtless instrumentalization that is typical of human relations with objects, into forms of interaction that approximate human-human relations' (2006: 182).

Symbiotic practices of care 139

Zamir opines that any of the above violations of the moral status of nonhuman animals could bring liberationist concern as to the moral legitimacy of animal-assisted therapies and therefore possible censorship of such assistance.

However, he contends that the practice of keeping companion animals is not always objectionable, since 'an ideal liberationist world will include petowner relationships, and such relations – at their best – also show us that a paternalistic, yet non-exploitative, human–animal relation is both possible and actual' (2006: 184). 'Service animals' such as guide dogs, claims Zamir, may belong in the pet-owner category since this can be justified 'in principle' but dogs do pay a price for this way of life:

> They are spayed or neutered, trained for long periods . . . and isolated from their kin. But dogs seem able to transfer their social needs onto humans, and some of the prolonged training can arguably be an advantage, providing important (and pleasurable) mental stimulation to these dogs. If humanity were to endorse a hands-off approach with regard to animals, such dogs would appear to lead qualitatively inferior (and probably shorter) lives in the wild – even in the few countries in the world in which the notion of 'the wild' still makes sense.
>
> (2006: 184)

The anticipated brief and 'qualitatively inferior' lives in the wild of Zamir's assistance dogs diverge from Coppinger and Coppinger (2016: 226) who believe adult street and village dogs may also have a short, four-year average life expectancy but that they 'are fine-looking individuals with rich social lives' within their natural environment (2016: 227). With regard to 'village' dogs and a 'hands-off approach' (Zamir, 2006: 184), Coppinger and Coppinger (2016: 227) consider a reduction in size of their home niche to support fewer dogs – rather than mass sterilisation and rehabilitation as companion dogs in first world countries, or mass culling – might be a more acceptable solution and humane way of reducing populations (see also Srinivasan (2013: 106) below regarding the 'independent status of ownerless street dogs' in India and their individual needs for freedom).

Disentangling Cartesian and Kantian, speciesist and utilitarian arguments, Zamir concludes that 'given responsible human owners', the lives of cats and dogs used in AAT are 'qualitatively comfortable and safe', and their social needs are catered for (2006: 195). Much rests on those 'responsible human owners' when working therapy and assistance dogs are separated from their kin and sometimes from other members of their own species in order to provide needed help and social encouragement in a human residence.

In contrast, and in a broad generalisation of species, Zamir suggests 'rodents, birds, monkeys, reptiles, and dolphins gain little by coercing them into AAT and lose a lot' (2006: 189); although, in a notation, he relates that in some AAT therapy sessions, dolphins remain in their natural environment and are not coerced to obtain 'therapeutic objectives' (2006: 198). He indicates that his remarks

140 *Symbiotic practices of care*

regarding dolphins therefore 'do not apply to such programs'. However, in his overview of species, Zamir refers to the notion of 'bringing a particular member of these animals into existence for the purpose of AAT [that] benefits the member' (2006: 192). Allowing that, say, a rodent bred for use in AAT could have a 'comfortable' existence, and not necessarily be abused by the therapist, he contrasts this with the abuse of animal lives in factory farming.

Serpell et al. (2010), identifying sources of animal welfare problems in animal-assisted activities/therapy (AAA/T) and assistance work as 'growing pains' emerging in the 'new field of animal exploitation', volunteer a number of recommendations and 'specific guidelines . . . pertinent to both services provided in large-scale institutionally based programs as well as small clinical practices' (2010: 499). Their suggested 'ethical guidelines' (2010: 502–503) for the care and supervision of animals used in animal-assisted therapies and activities are fully detailed in Fine's *Handbook of Animal-Assisted Therapy* (2010).

Their guidelines appear to have been consciously and conscientiously followed by some animal therapists and assistance dog charities. Examining the training and care of diabetes alert dogs and following the guidance of Serpell et al. (2010), it seems the MDD charity espouses these recommendations which include principles similar to those of the Five Freedoms.

Recommendations and advice for the ethical care of other beings produce valuable suggestions but, essentially, emotion plays a significant and vital role. In this, empathy is the prominent conveyor of interspecies feeling.

Compassion, empathy, sympathy

Walking along a city street, I saw a grey-haired man, mouth downturned and forehead frowning, who might have been deep in thought or perhaps have been commanded 'to take the dog out'. His demeanour was in total contrast to the ignored spaniel with bright eyes and light-footed gait walking obediently at the end of the lead. My eyes were concealed behind dark lenses so eye contact was minimal, but I smiled at the dog as we drew level, about five yards between us – and the man's expression altered as the dog launched into a tail-wagging frenzy towards me.

On another occasion, driving slowly towards a red traffic light, I thoughtlessly smiled at the sight of a Labradoodle firmly taking a human for a walk along the opposite pavement – the dog jumped into the road to reach me, again with enthusiasm that put them both at risk of annihilation by oncoming traffic if the lights had changed. I now take more care of possible risk to the other before offering the smallest overtures of friendship but remain intrigued by the seconds of instant relationship, of a seemingly common understanding that can flow between species despite complete ignorance of the other's existence seconds earlier.

Is this a form of intersubjectivity as discussed by Hurn (2012)? An example of empathic communication as felt by de Waal (2010), Smuts (2001), Gruen (2015), and others? There was no attempt, nor time, to be consciously in the mind of the other, to interpret how that creature was feeling, but there was an emotional interspecies link between us for those brief moments.

Symbiotic practices of care 141

And not just dogs. Horses, cats, rats, and pigs, sheep and cows are among those domesticated animals who volunteer emotions we can feel and reciprocate, should we make any effort to recognise and appreciate them. This is not necessarily practicing Serpell's (2002: 441) anthropomorphic selection and attribution of admired human traits to nonhuman animals. It is, or should be, natural means of relationship-shaping; an instinctive liking of the other and an appreciation for what they do and how they perform in ways we can perhaps both recognise and understand. Following Milton's (2005) concept of egomorphism, opportunity enables provision of warmth, even gladness, as more appropriate reactions to those performances; the 'distancing' device (Alger and Alger, 1999) of anthropomorphism serves less well here and may be better rejected.

However, Hamington (2008: 182) encourages the use of anthropomorphism as an approach to encompass empathy, understanding and care for the unfamiliar; a 'morally beneficial' way of 'humanizing' animals:

> It is praiseworthy to care for families, friends and companion animals but not as morally praiseworthy as caring for those for whom we are less familiar. That extension or reach to empathize with unfamiliar others requires an imaginary leap . . . anthropomorphism often represents an imaginative or playful attempt to understand animals. I claim that, to the extent that anthropomorphism facilitates caring for unknown others, 'humanizing' animals can be morally beneficial. . . . If we can see our way to care for nonhuman creatures, not as property, but as extensions of ourselves, perhaps we can also come to care for and about one another.

These words drive a human perspective that encourages care and empathy for others, but it holds a valuable premise that allows nonhuman animals to be considered 'extensions of ourselves' (also Milton, 2005) as means to 'care for and about one another'. Thinking of them as extensions of ourselves is less likely to bring about conditions of human domination and control of nonhuman others. Hamington intends to bring about mutual care between species for the good of all, so improving care for the 'less familiar' members of society aids a multispecies moral progression.

Curtin (2014: 40) prefers the word 'compassion' to care or empathy, since she avers that compassion is a 'developed moral capability whereas care or empathy are closer to the natural capacities that make compassion possible'. Compassion, she believes, is a 'cultivated aspiration to benefit other beings' (2014: 40) and is more resilient than empathy since it incorporates both reason and feeling. However, Willett (2014) disparages compassion as having similar significance to the way in which I see the concept of sympathy: as a generous bestowal of cognitive kindnesses and compassion that has a more practical, more selfish emphasis.

A sympathetic mien or verbal phrase is theoretically intended to offer kindness and perhaps elements of sorrow that someone else has received injury,

142 *Symbiotic practices of care*

bereavement, loss of employment, or similar. But this perspective seems to come from above, looking down; it carries faint condescension, separateness, and perhaps a concealed sense of relief that the other is suffering and not oneself. As Lori Gruen discerns, 'sympathy for another is felt from the outside, the third person perspective' (2015: 40), adding that 'while we're being sympathetic, we attempt to be disconnected from others'. Empathy, Gruen (2015: 41) suggests, 'recognizes connection with and understanding of the circumstances of the other . . . the goal is to try to take in as much about another's situation and perspective as possible'.

In instances of bereavement, the phrase 'I'm so sorry for your loss' is genuinely meant and every individual's grief experiences are unique to that person – but sympathy in that context doesn't build strength or assist in the other's coping method. Rather, it conveys 'poor you', that you require consolation, comfort and 'sympathetic concern' (De Waal, 2010: 90); all good, but sympathy manages to maintain distance and infers the other's existence on an inferior level. Sympathy is given with kindly intent but may fail to offer more than knowledge of a sorrowful event and does not necessarily discern what feelings may be induced in the 'object' of sympathy. De Waal (2008: 283) cites Eisenberg's (2000: 677) definition of sympathy as 'an affective response that consists of feelings of sorrow or concern for a distressed or needy other (rather than sharing the emotion of the other). Sympathy is believed to involve an other-oriented, altruistic motivation'. But De Waal believes the personal distress aroused in sympathy 'makes the affected party selfishly seek to alleviate its *own* distress, which mimics that of the object' (2008: 283).

Empathy is an essential quality in the development or improvement of human–human relationships, enabling greater understanding of one another's hopes, desires and despairs and the ability to reflect this comprehension appropriately and meaningfully by each attempting to 'walk in the shoes of the other'. It is therefore a salient quality required by a member of the 'helping' professions in psychological counselling practice just as it is a necessary quality in the health and welfare of symbiotic interspecies relationships.

Hoffman (1987: 4) viewed empathy as an 'affective response more appropriate to someone else's situation than to one's own', proposing that (1987: 3):

> To me, empathy is the spark of human concern for others, the glue that makes social life possible. It may be fragile but it has, arguably, endured throughout evolutionary times and may continue as long as humans exist.

Empathy is more inclusive of the speaker and the spoken-to, and perhaps deserves greater societal acclamation and increased attempts to put it into practice. Eminent primatologist Frans de Waal's (2010) seminal work, *The age of empathy: nature's lessons for a kinder society*, invited attention to other species who are able to take and make use of the perspective of another, thereby giving nonhuman examples for the bettered education of human society. He writes of the need for an increase in fellow feeling and social responsibility, for coordination and caring for and by one another, and echoes Hoffman in taking empathy to be the glue that binds communities and societies:

> The way our bodies . . . are influenced by surrounding bodies is one of the mysteries of human existence, but one that provides the glue that holds entire societies together.
>
> (De Waal, 2010: 63)

When it comes to multispecies empathy, true understanding by human observers may be less easy to achieve but De Waal, Smuts and other researchers have established its existence. Panksepp and Panksepp (2013: 489) suggest it 'reflects the capacity of one animal to experience the emotional feelings of another'. Studies relating to interspecies empathy have been conducted among rodents by these researchers, among primates (De Waal, 2001, 2006; Smuts, 2001, 2006), and among elephants (Mark Rowlands, 2012). The latter work highlights how elephants care for their injured relatives, illustrating the ways in which these beings share in others' pain.

De Waal (2010) points to the connection between imitation, synchrony, and mimicry, and bonding or socially connecting. Cross your legs or lean backwards or forwards a little when sitting and conversing with another, and it is likely your actions will be mirrored. Such behaviour conveys mutual and empathic intention, the wish to understand, and to offer respect and trust; it may be a valuable behaviour in counselling sessions and in enabling confidential intimacies to be spoken and heard during data collection for ethnographic analysis.

Additionally, emotional 'feeling' and empathy enable a deeper understanding, a broader knowledge of the impact of chronic illness on an individual's family, friends and work colleagues, and on the assistance dog – an impact that inevitably and constantly changes personal and social behaviours and the practices of life management when compared to the impact of minor or short-term illness on social existence.

Lori Gruen (2015: 70) provides a comprehensive definition of what she terms 'entangled empathy';: a 'process of sharing experiences and perspectives', an explanation that echoes through moral human–nonhuman experiences as much as in human–human relationships:

> A type of caring perception focused on attending to another's experience of wellbeing. An experiential process involving a blend of emotion and cognition in which we recognize we are in relationships by attending to another's needs, interests, desires, vulnerabilities, hopes, and sensitivities.

Suggesting empathy is a 'moral perception' that requires an ability 'to see what is morally relevant or important' and then to make a decision 'to do the right thing' according to what has been perceived (2015: 38), Gruen (2015: 61) adds that, in wanting to empathise with 'very different others', we need to 'understand as best we can what the world senses, feels, smells, and looks like from their situated

144 *Symbiotic practices of care*

position'. In endeavouring to empathise with those others, we should attempt not to engage anthropomorphic tendencies, but rather to accept changes in perception that may produce unexpected understandings of other ways of being.

Although the dogs and humans of this study have sincere and deep bonds of friendship, it is the empathic assistance offered and received by each partner in their mutualistic coexistences that enables life expectancy for both to increase. An empathic researcher observing the situation of assistance dogs and their human companions, may investigate further and delve deeper into their united lives, without abusing shared confidences or destroying the developing triadic relationship. (However, this could become a risk-laden venture if an overuse of applied sensitivity becomes false rhetoric, a pretentious attempt to share similar experiences or emotions that may appear as not genuine and therefore cause a 'bringing down of the curtain' on any future significant disclosures).

When ill health is the focus of a social gathering, the simple question 'how are you?' invites and anticipates a genuine response and is not a nicety of speech. It is noticeable among groups of bereaved people, who accept or try to find meaning in their grief for another's life, and who, as a result, accommodate, tolerate and empathise with, if not always perfectly understand, wide swathes of physical and emotional unsettlement in others. Similar hard-earned knowledge can be put to beneficial and nonjudgemental use in social dialogue with individuals embodying Type 1 diabetes; those who have recently entered a symbiotic partnership with a medical alert assistance dog and are open to offered experiences from long-term, chronically ill group members.

Collective friendship in adversity develops more quickly and simply perhaps because of the compassion and empathy that infiltrate those who have already faced personal disasters of life and now observe lives of others at risk or endangered. It seems taken for granted that members, with chronic illness and an assistance dog, are already seated in the same boat and therefore understand the situation being confronted newly and similarly by others.

Including the value of empathy in interspecies communication and social integration allows the concept of ethics of care theory and practice to become prominent in examining how empathy affects and assists in dependency and interdependency; and furthermore, how respect, responsibility and trust become involved in interspecies care and being cared for. Sunaura Taylor's research (2014, 2017) illuminates many of the conflicts facing 'disabled' and 'nonhuman' minorities.

Ethics of care

Collected ecofeminist writings of 'intersections with animal others and the earth' are introduced by Carol J. Adams and Lori Gruen (2014: 1) who suggest that:

> Ecofeminist theory helps us imagine healthier relationships, stresses the need to attend to context over universal judgements, and argues for the importance of care as well as justice, emotion as well as rationality, in working to undo the logic of domination and its material and practical implications.

Symbiotic practices of care   145

Deane Curtin's examination of compassion and being human contends that an ethic of care is inclusive 'since it values the diverse ways that women and men tend to organise their moral experience' (2014: 39). It does not assume that ethics should be built on a uniquely human feature, that is, human reason: 'it is less anthropocentric'.

Considering that animal advocacy discourse acknowledges humans as 'stewards of animal welfare', Maurice Hamington (2008: 177) proposes the notion that 'quality' human–animal relationships might encourage a moral imagination enabling the care and empathy necessary for ethical social thinking and behaviour. He takes the concept of embodied care as an extension of feminist ethics-of-care and remarks (2008: 179):

> Phenomenologically, the one cared-for and the caregiver engage in a relationship marked by mutuality in terms of attentiveness and responsiveness. In this manner, care is an ethic that cannot be separated from epistemology – we care about that which we know and it is difficult to care for that which we have little or no knowledge of. Although knowing is not a sufficient condition of care, it is a prerequisite.

And this is where Sunaura Taylor's feminist disability ethic-of-care highlights interdependency and mutual respect as significant factors in well-functioning interspecies coexistences. Symbiotic relationships in which caring for and being cared for (despite certain 'stifling' kindnesses) enable trust, reliance, and responsibility leading to 'rights, justice and an accessible society that does not limit or make impossible our involvement and contributions' (Taylor, 2014: 109).

Taylor writes from a position of knowledge in that she herself is compelled to accept care and apply habits and routines of dependency, being both grateful for assistance and repressed by the need for it. Her chapter '*Interdependent animals: a feminist disability ethic-of-care*', in the Adams and Gruen–edited collection (2014), draws attention to issues echoed in the daily activities necessarily performed by the human participants of this research. Tina recalls the simple act of 'putting something in the oven, then having a hypo, and it would be burnt'. She continues:

> So now all of a sudden I'm on ready-made meals and everything's from a box, but when I read the instructions at the back, if it comes into a different line, I can put the kitchen light on but still not see it. It's all muggled together so now I look at the number and hope it's said six minutes, but if I can't work it out, I shove it back in fridge and have it in daytime.

Frustrated in the kitchen by her impaired sight, she is also compelled to ask others for help in the office but is at the same time grateful for their concern which enables her to maintain employment and social purpose.

Remarking the dependency of domesticated animals on human care and responsibility, Taylor suggests (2014: 110) that 'a feminist ethic-of-care

146   *Symbiotic practices of care*

offers a framework of justice that has the potential to complicate conceptions of dependency . . . to understand animals not as dependent beings with no agency, but rather as vital participants and contributors to the world'. Vitality and agency are key properties for the multispecies collaborating individuals involved in doing diabetes on a daily scale and Taylor fittingly recognises 'that to understand another being who does not communicate in ways able-bodied/able-minded humans have historically valued, we must pay attention to individuals – learning from them so that we can recognise their agency and preferences' (2014: 111).

Taylor encourages any discourse relating to the liberation of animals and the less able members of society to concentrate more on 'radical discussions about creating accessible, non-discriminatory space in society in which individuals and their communities can thrive' and focus less on 'suffering and dependency' (2014: 111). What do animals say, want, and contribute, asks Taylor, and what might it be like for them to be cared for?

Taylor asserts that the 'language of dependency is a brilliant rhetorical tool, as it is a way for those who use it to sound concerned, compassionate, and caring while continuing to exploit those who they are supposedly concerned about' (2014: 114). Dependency, she writes, 'is a reasoning that has been used to justify slavery, patriarchy, colonization, and disability oppression' and of course, it gives apparent reason for the human need to kill and eat domesticated animals since, according to Callicott (1989) and others such as Budiansky (1997), if released into the wild, such beings would no longer be able to cope with and survive in a 'natural', unfettered state of existence.

However, Coppinger and Coppinger (2016) provide a different stance when studying the 'village dogs' of this world and their coping mechanisms. Taking note of the reduction in numbers of vultures in India (see also Van Dooren, 2010a, 2010b) that enabled an increase in the range of dogs, they suggest that sterilisation or culling – or ostensibly, killing for food – may not greatly reduce populations as other species, or more of the same species, will move into the vacated 'niches'. They depict an alternative approach to 'dog control' conducted by planned humane methods in which stray or street dogs are captured, neutered, and then transported to 'rich countries to be adopted into family status, where they are made totally dependent and entirely restricted', and where apparent benefit to the dogs, who are highly social by nature, 'is not measured in terms of a better social life for them, but, rather, in terms of longer, healthier lives' (Coppinger and Coppinger, 2016: 227). Srinivasan (2013) emphasises the individual requirement for freedom that is promulgated in India so that street dogs may roam safe from human culling practices.

Coppinger and Coppinger commend 'the village dog' as a 'wondrous animal with a self-tailored lifestyle' and suggest that, instead of the above, the most humane way of reducing their populations is to lessen the size of their 'niche' so that it could only cater for a smaller number of dogs (2016: 228), a similar contention to that put forward by Zamir (2006). But such an evolutionary notion would take more time to effect than a speeding bullet or veterinarian's knife or needle,

Symbiotic practices of care 147

even if the result were of greater multispecies benefit in the long-term. Reordering evolutionary direction may return us to economic battlegrounds rather than moving domesticated species forward to safely interdependent environments and ways of being.

Whether extinction of the domesticated species, who have become dependent on human whimsical, faulty, mercenary, gentle, or harsh notions for their quality of life, is the right, moral and responsible direction to take, leaves, or should leave, an unpalatable sense of guilt and responsibility among the human so-called guardians of nonhuman animals: the unnamed held in abattoirs, laboratory cages, fattening pens, or zoo enclosures, or, indeed, the named and trained autonomous care-workers in health assistance organisations or the loved playmates of myriad human children. Erasure of the domesticated creatures, tamed, altered, and harmed by human endeavour, is surely anathema to moral thinking. Creating extinction of those we developed to better our lives, whether for the purposes of survival, industry, or care performance, must be a reversal of ethical social norms and a fast-track to demolition of what might be good and just in our evolutionary developments.

Where the social contract fails

Taylor refers to Martha Nussbaum's discussion of the social contract's failure to 'address [disability, species membership, and nationality] as it assumes that in a "state of nature" the parties to this contract really are roughly equal in mental and physical power' (2009: 118). This assumption does not account for the likely lack of physical and intellectual balance between disabled and able humans, the well-off or the poverty-stricken, or between humans and nonhumans. Significant here is Nussbaum's contention that the 'social contract tradition's reliance on the idea of mutual advantage falls short when addressing disability and "species membership" as disabled individuals and animals don't necessarily offer mutual advantage per se' (Taylor, 2014: 118) and, in fact, claims Taylor, one may disadvantage or unbalance the other.

She elaborates (2014: 120):

> What disability studies and a feminist ethic-of-care brings to the conversation is a more nuanced understanding of how to define mutual advantage and a much-needed analysis of what it means to be accountable to beings who are in many ways the most vulnerable. A disability studies perspective of interdependence is about recognizing that we are all vulnerable beings, who during our lives go in and out of dependency, who will be giving and receiving care (and more often than not, doing both), and that contribution cannot be understood as a simple calculation of mutual advantage.
>
> Animal ethics also requires a critical engagement with our assumptions about who is valuable and who is exploitable and a reimagining of what it means to contribute to the world.

148 *Symbiotic practices of care*

Why veganism?

Gruen and Weil (2012: 482), in writing '*Animal others – editors' introduction*', ask:

> How can we turn shame into compassion, response into responsible action? To tend to an animal, to respond to her is to change her as it is to be changed by her in return. The 'difficulty of ethical responsibility' is that we must accept it in the face of uncertain changes.

They continue: 'How might we balance conflicts between different sorts of oppression? Should feminist animal studies scholars be vegan?' and my reading is interrupted by this latter question. I have been following Adams and Gruen, Donovan and Taylor, and other feminist writers in their efforts to find 'connections between sex, gender, and the more than human world' (Gruen and Weil, 2012: 485), and to encourage

> development of a praxis built on compassion, care, and empathy, one that includes cognition and affect in ways that cannot be disentangled, and that will lead to richer, more motivating approaches to understanding and improving our relationships with others.
>
> (2012: 479)

I have endeavoured to find a fitting explanation as to why I have not eaten meat for the last two decades. Regrettably, no moral factor swayed the original decision to halt meat consumption. I did not become overly concerned that the meat-filled plate before me might contain part of a murdered nonhuman animal (Gaita, 2004: 198) and thoughts of Jeffrey Dahmer, who seemingly first cooked and ate nonhuman 'roadkill' before moving on to human edibles, did not disturb sleep. Much more mundane, I did not like the smell of meat cooking, I did not like the texture, nor did I much like the taste. I did not want the dogs I cared for to smell their food, the flesh of other species, being cooked long before it would be given to them – not because I was ashamed to be catering for their needs in that way, but more because it seemed unkind to let them salivate and anticipate when the meat was too hot to serve them. Simple reasons that expanded and grew into a firm dislike of any form of meat, and, subsequently, fish and dairy products. I increased intake of fruit, nuts, salads, and legumes and found that vegetarianism had health benefit as well as enjoyment and engaged certain moral as well as nutritional fibre.

I appropriated a 'holier than thou' attitude; I was on trend, and it became easy to adopt the stance of a vegetarian. But then the unethical transport of live, often overheated, injured, unfed, and unwatered abattoir-bound sentient species crashed into my pious carrot-crunching, and action against animal cruelty – whether on individual or industrial levels – overtook the sedentary, passive non-meat-eating route.

Veganism was the more ethical option but was harder to follow, despite the contemporary food-counter alterations in supermarkets to accommodate vegan

Symbiotic practices of care 149

shoppers. Personal food consumption becomes less of a moral issue once the decision to 'become vegan' is made; the problem is in realising what your shoes are made of, the dog's collar, cosmetics, 'the bristles of make-up brushes to the gelatine that encases vitamin supplements' (Irvine, 2009: 1), and glue, as well as with coping with advertisements and labels detailing the contents of soap and soup. This involves harder, more circumspect thinking and more intense, more active caring for others. Using products sourced from lanolin in sheep wool – for example, vitamin D3 added to soy formula for babies – sees acceptance or ignorance of intense pain for the commodified sheep when folds of skin may be removed without anaesthetic after shearing to reduce fly infestation (Emmerman, 2014: 163, 170 [Note 17] with reference to 'cruelty' in wool production [Baur, 2008: 79]).

Tolerance of animal cruelty, or 'unmindedness' of its ongoing performances, allows the wearing of shoes and the carrying of bags created from crocodile and ostrich, buffalo and snake, the purchasing of coats made from the skins of calves and karakul lambs, and the trading of ornament or 'medication' from elephant ivory and rhinoceros horn – it is plain to see who is sacrificed for whom.

In becoming vegan and recognising why, compassion and ethical care for 'others' increasingly occupy the uppermost rungs of a personal moral ladder, ignoring the jaw-snapping consumers of nonhuman animal products urging expansion of factory farming, abattoirs, and tanneries, along with canned lion hunting and puppy milling, residing on the lowest steps. Self-righteous as that sounds, it is concern for the welfare, the doing well of others' lives – human and nonhuman – that has driven study underpinned by feminist and eco-feminist animal studies, ethics of care investigations and individual experiences.

Taking a closer-to-home view of the ethics of care in relation to human rather than animal beings, Mol, Moser and Pols (2010: 13) suggest that 'local solutions to specific problems need to be worked out' and 'fairness, kindness, compassion, generosity' should be considered important norms. 'Care implies a negotiation about how different goods might coexist in the given, specific, local practice'. 'Care seeks to lighten what is heavy, and even if it fails, it keeps on trying' (2010: 14), a phrase which both dogs and humans exemplify in their daily managements of life shadowed by chronic illness.

Highlighted in this text are practices of self care and 'other care', trust and responsibility – by the individuals to benefit their own health, by the individuals for the benefit of their non-human companions, by the medical alert assistance dogs for themselves, and by the MAADs for their chronically ill human companions.

Parental moral views may dictate the hoped-for ethical route to be followed by children but in adolescence and adulthood, environmental nudges may shift thinking about behavioural manners directed towards ourselves and others. Eating meat farmed locally may not continue after viewing televised factory farming, but vegans do live on cattle farms and meat-eating humans are fully able to protest the ill treatment of animals destined for an abattoir. Ethical behaviour and moral belief are intensely individual and highly volatile features of human existence. Co-opting their usage into daily life may be essential for decision-making among

150 *Symbiotic practices of care*

the ideologies of racism, ageism, or speciesism, for determined effort to do the 'right' thing and for protection of self and others against those of differing personal creeds. But their execution can create internal havoc and external upheaval that require informed practices of care for their safe resolution.

Taylor (2017: 217) explains the inherent difficulties of dependency based on leaving domesticated animals to fend for themselves without our moral or immoral interference:

> We are all affecting one another and our environments all the time – all of us depending on one another – sometimes in terrifyingly intimate ways. Perhaps dependency is so uncomfortable precisely because it demands intimacy. With domesticated animals and with many disabled humans, there has to be involvement and interaction; there can be no illusions of independence.

Admitting that such vulnerability could provide 'opportunities for coercion', Taylor (2017: 217) suggests it may also provide 'new ways of being, supporting and communicating – new ways of creating meaning across differences in ability and species'.

Only recently have vegan or vegetarian 'dog food' items been produced for general purchase and the MDD charity currently feeds meat-based kibbles to their canine collaborators. Although dietary requirements vary, and each dog is considered individually, some form of meat product is generally the main ingredient in DADs' daily nutrition. Whether this will change when vegan dog food becomes more widely advertised and available is an ethical question for the charity and clients to debate, bearing in mind their reliance on donation for many products aimed at the dogs' health and welfare. Certainly, the dogs' collars and leads are not made from tanned animal hide and instead are crafted from a lightweight synthetic material.

Morality and symbiotic ethics

David Goode (2007: 111) highlights differentiation between the companion 'pet' animal and the companion 'working' animal, recalling the words of Rod Michalko (1999: 74) who cites Aristotle's *Nichomachean Ethics* (Book Two, 15–25) to explain his guide dog's 'virtuous' work ethic:

> Moral virtue comes about as a result of habit . . . from this it is also plain that none of the moral virtues arise in us by nature; for nothing exists by nature can form a habit contrary to its nature . . . nor can anything else that by nature behaves in one way be trained to behave in another.

Michalko considers that his close companionship with working guide dog, Smokie, may be seen as an outcome of 'virtuous occupation' (1999: 74), since it is customary today to view work with blind persons as moral employment; indeed, Smokie can well be considered to be similarly engaged in 'virtuous occupation' as

Symbiotic practices of care 151

he guides the visually impaired sociologist according to the repetition and reward training he receives. By nature, states Michalko, dogs would not take on the role of virtuous guide work – 'this virtue is the result of habituation through training' (1999: 74) and is therefore not contrary to their nature. But an alternative view comes from Frans de Waal (2008: 292), who considers that empathy – being the basis of human altruism, which enables the ability to take the perspective of another – may also see such altruism inherent in the nature of other animals.

When reward is the result of requested goal achievement and tasks become habitual and are viewed as near natural, autonomous behaviours, all trained and qualified assistance dogs may then be considered to perform what Goode and Michalko refer to as 'virtuous occupations' when working with their human companions.

Perhaps this too is a 'virtuous occupation' for this human–canine minority group. Yet I am mentally diverted from the interspecies health behaviours to an image of cornetted heads bowed over pews, downcast eyes and folded hands, fingered rosaries and the whiteness of purity and cambric: connotations of goodness and spirituality also contained in 'virtuous occupation'.

But then the image changes again and the dictionary is called for to search for the roots leading away from the word 'virtue' and 'virginal' to 'virago', 'virility', and 'virulent' – this appears to be a tactic of procrastination, a moving away from the roles of virtuous occupation played by the assistance dogs and their diabetic companions in their communal activities, and by my thinly veiled preoccupation with writing about them. The mind is hauled back to contemplate 'virtuous' – 'possessing or showing moral rectitude' – and 'virtue' – 'moral excellence, uprightness, goodness' (Pearsall and Trumble, OERD, 1995: 1614). So virtuous occupation seems praiseworthy, potentially humble, but with a firm backbone of goodness ribbed by goal-directed endeavours.

Where Goode adds value is in his incisive perception of his own relationship with his canine companion, Katie, as being an emotional and affective bonding but one that is in contrast to the relationship between Michalko and Smokie; one that lacks the functional, purposeful, and determined effort to achieve a 'practical' goal and therefore fails to achieve the mutualistic coembodied identity of the two-in-one. Frans de Waal's (2006: 162) suggestion that 'morality helps people get along and accomplish joint endeavours', permits the comfortable 'do as you would be done by' ethic, and within such concept enables the decision to help, or not to help, an 'other'. There is moral behaviour in the companionship between animal companions and their caring guardians, but, as Goode remarks, it is not the morality gained from 'sharing some form of virtuous work together' (2007: 111).

The mutualism that binds together an assistance dog and a human weakened by ill health incorporates 'discovery and practice' (Goode, 2007: 111), as well as Coulter's 'respect and reciprocity' (2016b: 209), that lead to better management of the intricacies and complexities of chronic illness.

If virtuous shared work produces admirable morality, then the less-practical function of play between dog and human still succeeds in achieving routines of ethical reciprocity and interspecies interdependence. However, elements of trust

152 *Symbiotic practices of care*

that are expected in virtuous occupation may be exchanged for elements of deception in play, for example, when a toy is hidden completely or is brought into view and swiftly concealed several times. In this case, teasing can become overdone and result in a dog understandably snapping from frustration. Alternatively, positive lessons can be learned from a deceptive concealment: items of food can be placed out of sight – under upturned flowerpots, for example – the smell attracting the dog to the correct container and an instant reward.

Care is convoluted in meaning and in activation. Mol, Moser, and Pols (2010: 14) talk of the 20th-century definition of care as warm and emotional 'nourishing', in contrast to instrumental 'cold and rational' technology. There is always a motivation to care, to do better for the self or others, to perform 'maintenance and repair' work (De la Bellacasa, 2012: 198) that keeps individual and global existences spinning. Recalling Haraway's (2003: 5) 'dogs are here to live with', De la Bellacasa emphasises how 'laborious' living-with can be, contending that 'relations of "significant otherness" are more than about accommodating "difference", coexisting or tolerating' (2017: 83). She suggests (2017: 83) that

> thinking-with nonhumans should always be a living-with, aware of troubling relations and seeking a significant otherness that transforms those involved in the relation and the worlds we live in.

Natasha recalls Paul's complete lack of interest in leaving the house, unless she 'put him in the car and took him somewhere', which infers that he never enjoyed exercise or the appeal of scenic rural views and changing seasons observed while walking outdoors. She remembers:

> No, no, because obviously living where we are, he wouldn't go for a walk and I'd say: 'just go for a walk, there's loads of walks round here', but he'd say 'no, I can't'. But now, with the dog, there's a reason to go for a walk again; from a care perspective, that's one of the things they say with your health – anything that you can do, keep it going – whereas a lot of people won't, they'll sit there and just say I'm sorry for myself.

Free running, or being able to explore unleashed, is important for all dogs. Paul says he probably lets Nero run free for longer than he should, but 'you know it's got to be unkind for a dog if he's on a lead all the time; and anyway, it takes too much out of me so I let him off'. He seems to care not only for the dog as someone with personhood, but also shows concern for Nero's welfare and contentment.

Following Serpell et al. (2010) and MDD ethical guidelines for canine care, participants in this research maintain an unspoken but active adherence to ethics of care in relation to their companions' freedom to run, to play, to do what it might be expected that a 'pet' or nonworking companion dog would have opportunity to do. I have observed these assistant companion dogs interact

Symbiotic practices of care   153

unleashed with other members of canine society in city parks; seen them race across commonage and through wood and forest; chase dogs they know and don't know, and gambol muddily in puddles and ploughed fields. DADs have working occupations that can enrich their daily lives, have opportunity for 'time-out', are fully respected by those with whom they live and work, and are treated considerately by the charity which shares responsibility for their good welfare.

Separation anxiety is endured by many dogs every day when human families leave for school or work. But DADs are never left alone; like Apple, they may spend the working day among schoolchildren or, like Harley and Higgins, they share office space with their working companions.

Paul then remarks on the difficulties that occasionally arise from the very close relationship he has with Nero:

> I might say I'm going to send him back but I'd struggle not having him. There are times when I think I can't deal with him now and a couple of times when I've left him with my dad when I've gone shopping with my mother because I haven't had the strength – but dad walks the dog and he loves it.

Unsurprisingly, Paul lacks strength as well as poor vision and it requires intense concentration for him to focus on both dog and environment when walking with Nero.

Listening to Paul and Natasha describing the complexities and discomforts inherent in Paul's illness, I am struck by the invisibility of symptoms and observe aloud 'yet you look so well'. Paul laughs and says he had 'a really good walk' earlier in the day, but while agreeing that he does look well 'at the moment', Natasha wishes she could show me a picture of him before he went out.

Human care for a diabetes alert dog accepts and accommodates myriad differences between the two species, allows and tolerates unaccustomed behaviours until they become customary and reasonable, so that their relations, their ways of being are transformed to comfortable and progressing coexistences. However, Natasha worries what might happen if she's not at home and Paul has a bad day:

> How would he get on caring for the dog? There will be a time at some point potentially where there isn't somebody around; like when Nero kept licking and licking his paw and of course Paul couldn't see, in fact even his mum and dad looked and couldn't see anything wrong, but I did a proper thorough inspection; and it's things like that – yes, he cares for Nero very, very well but because he doesn't see very well . . . I don't know how blind people work with Guide Dogs.

But Paul says he would rely on the veterinarian if something seemed wrong with Nero. 'You'd notice and get the vet. If something occurs and reoccurs, then it's the vet – for example, if he keeps licking his paw, you're aware of it and you've washed his paws but he's still doing it'.

154 *Symbiotic practices of care*

Object and subject of care – collective identities

The highly perceptive canine sense of smell and prowess in olfactory detection enable a human-animal collaboration that advances medical exploration of Type 1 diabetes and improves lifestyle management and security for the members of this group, provided that the human collective can commit fully to the dog's health and welfare as well as to their own. Each person in a collective of humans and nonhumans is 'simultaneously an object and a subject of care', writes Myriam Winance (2010: 95), discussing disability and care, wheelchairs, and those hoping for rehabilitation: there is opportunity and need for 'care in shared work' dispersed among the multispecies group.

Chatjouli (2013: 88) encapsulates – through research in Greece with thalassaemics, people who inherit a form of anaemia – the way in which 'a biosocial approach to studying emerging biologies, normalities, and socialities in diverse contexts enables us to better understand the ways in which new biotechnologies interact with sociocultural forces'. In Type 1 diabetes, as in thalassaemic disease, research participants form and share a collective identity and their participation in local and national community congregations 'facilitates the exchange of knowledge and experience' which may lead to improved treatments and more considered research and support.

Exchanging 'insider' information – about pumps and pens, multispecies travel abroad, canine behaviour with young children and blood-testing, or how best to inform a knowledge-thirsty public keen to understand what the canine companion is doing for the human and, occasionally, vice versa – enables the continuous melding of the very different human and nonhuman individuals congregating under the banner of Type 1 diabetes, into a cooperative, collaborative, and caring progressive community – a group of multispecies members whose collective identity enables a welcomed sense of belonging.

The group members become an amoebic phenomenon, continually developing and reforming through trial and test of shared information, or increase or decrease in attendance numbers, in order to cope more easily with the intricacies of life with chronic illness. Newly advertised glucose tablets, most easily absorbed and quick-acting carbohydrates, blood glucose monitors, instructive courses and the like provide foundation for dialogue and communication among both the recently joined and more permanent members of the group.

Items and moments of irritation and frustration with health professionals are recalled:

> I get better reception when I talk to nurses than when seeing a doctor because the nurse is more understanding and inclined to steer you in the right direction, and then you go and see the doctor.
>
> But nurses are allowed to have a 15–20 minute appointment slot for you, and the GPs have a 5-minute slot and you can only go in with one issue – how can anybody know the emotional, psychological, you know . . . the doctors just look at the symptoms . . . (*fingers drum on the table*) . . . however, we can't complain about the treatment we have now.

Symbiotic practices of care 155

As with many who care for or are cared for by others, there is willingness to welcome new arrivals and I am frequently asked if I will be attending one or other gathering, if I would like to travel with others to a certain destination and what topic I would like to discuss with them.

There is a generosity of spirit that becomes visual, almost tactile, in this multispecies community; the dogs are amicable towards one another and towards the human complement, while the human contingent make obvious the pride and respect they hold for their canine companions – the prowess observed in rapid detection of rising or falling blood glucose levels, the condition and conformation of their other-than-human home-sharers, the attention paid so consistently to preventing hypoglycaemic episodes. There appears to be enjoyment in taking responsibility for the welfare of a multitalented partner, in displaying the beneficial and benevolent behaviours created and received, and perhaps in sharing status.

Paul responds to a question asking whether participants feel their dogs enhance life or assist in managing it:

> Enhance irrespective, because the dogs give you freedom to do stuff. As assistance dogs, they're there all the time and they keep a check on you; any problems they're there telling you, so it gives you more freedom, you're more relaxed, so it's got to be enhancement. The dog gives you freedom to be more adventurous, to actually go out into the world, rather than being shut in; basically, I was shut in.

He laughs: 'Oh god, I sound so sad'.

But inhabiting chronic illness allows for, and even expects, the playing of a xylophone of emotions, notes struck that are sometimes tuneful, sometimes discordant. That Paul can appreciate the difference in his life pre- and post-Nero's arrival so graphically, illustrates for me a little of what it must be like to be at least partially liberated from the grip of Type 1 diabetes.

Systems of cooperation and mutuality

Agustin Fuentes (2013: 57) draws attention to the 'widespread and complex patterns of cooperation (that) lie at the heart of human evolutionary success', and follows Nowak and Highfield's concept of humans as 'SuperCooperators' whose 'ability to cooperate goes hand in hand with succeeding in the struggle to survive' (2011: xviii), by suggesting that human societies are all based on extensive and exceedingly complex systems of cooperation and mutuality, rendering any consistently selfish behavioural strategy unsustainable.

'Humans are the selfish apes . . . the creatures who shun the needs of others . . . we are motivated by self-interest alone' (Nowak and Highfield, 2011: xiii). Yet, claim the authors, creatures of every persuasion and level of complexity cooperate to live, including the meerkats 'who risk their lives to guard a communal nest'. As Nowak and Highfield suggest, these complex systems appear to work equally

156 *Symbiotic practices of care*

for nonhuman animal societies and for the collaborative and unselfish interspecies communities of which the group under discussion is but one.

Cooperation and mutuality underlie the coexistences of the medical assistance dog and the health-impaired human. Compassion, even altruism, could not survive in their midst, were the practices of unselfish care not actively performed. Practices that include care for self, care for the assistant alert dog, mutual care based on an interspecies symbiotic coexistence, and the care practices occurring in social and institutional organisations, among health teams and hospital staff.

Communication and understanding

Dogs may not offer many vocal contributions to the researcher's learning but an ethnographer's field observation of the personalities of any canine character generally allows time and space at least to attempt to view and hear – and, occasionally, smell and touch – and to interpret canine efforts to hold interspecies conversation. Hurn (2012: 213) considers that there will always be 'a need for someone to "speak for" animal persons on a political or legal stage'. Donovan contends that 'we use much the same mental and emotional activities in reading an animal as we do in reading a human. Body language, eye movement, facial expression, tone of voice . . . helps us to know about the species' habits and culture' (Donovan, 2006: 321).

In the world of dogs, the gaze, the interval barks of the lonely, the repetitive monotone barks of the deaf, the pointing of direction, the wag of a tail or curl of a lip, and the posturing play-bow are among familiar communication signals to which we easily react, often physically as well as verbally. Vivid examples of canine communication appear in the writings of David Goode (2007: 30), who describes himself as 'an available playmate' in his dog, Katie's 'reckoning', but who also confesses to embarrassment at his 'babyish' verbal responses to her communications.

Coulter (2016a: 34) suggests that 'effective understanding and exchange is not automatic, but rather requires continuous reflection, control, augmentation, and adjustments to promote understanding'. Taking 'the dog' for a walk is mind-numbingly dull for both species if there is no communication, no recognition of previous enjoyable experience, no sharing of play strategies, no effort to instigate social interaction and conversation. Such lack of communication could also lead to the perpetuation of a sense of otherness, a perception of distance or a distancing method.

Highly attuned communication is essential between trainer and potential assistance dog. Because the former has learned over time to recognise varying signs and signals given and received by dogs in conversation, the knowledge gained from such experiences can be employed to augment training methods and produce significant dialogue that may be understood and responded to by both species.

Human actors in this chronically ill grouping recognise what some of them term 'the sulk', the refusal to alert because it seems that a voice has been raised too loudly or that signals performed in the previous alert have been ignored; they witness the enthusiastic nose-to-tail body language exhibited when all members

Symbiotic practices of care   157

of the multispecies family are shepherded together, or the firm nudge that means 'you need to check your blood sugar levels now'; the anxiety denoted by the angle of the ears or seen in the tightly-clamped tail curved under a lowered body, and the joy displayed out of doors when cavorting freely in the company of human or nonhuman others. In their recognition of the meaning embedded in their partners' attitude and behaviour, the human companions, as best they can, comprehend canine communication and become openly empathic and caring about the other's offered dialogue and way of well-being.

In Czerny's words, 'the flow of dog knowledge . . . informs the practices of humans' as exemplified between 'police dogs and their handlers, service dogs and their owners, and sniffer dogs and doctors' (2012: 13).

Travelling to visit a client with an MDD instructor and her in-training companion, Jessie, I learn the background that brought Gill to the charity. Her career started with Guide Dogs and what then was called Dogs for the Disabled (now Dogs for Good), first as a kennel staff member and then as a dog trainer. After 11 years, she continued working with dogs but this time in a prison with drug-scenting dogs.

> You have an active and a passive dog; the passive one searches people so that anybody coming into the prison including staff are searched; the pro-active dog searches cells, vehicles, workshops, everywhere else, and the one I had was trained on mobile phones as well so he could find mobile phones, SIM cards, chargers, any part of a mobile phone.
>
> (cf. Horowitz, 2016: 20)

The instructor worked with the drug-detecting dogs for several years but then her working environment became 'very violent' and demoralising. 'You're taught not to trust anyone, but I was lucky that I had my dogs and could trust them day-in, day-out – they were my pals.' Czerny's earlier examples as to how the 'flow of dog knowledge . . . informs the practices of humans' (2012: 13) is exemplified in this instructor's close social and working relationships with the dogs of her different vocations.

It is the image of 'flow' that is significant – the ongoing movement of information, the fluid circulation of intent and meaning, a stream of unspoken but graphic language pouring into the consciousness of an accepting other species.

Sara recalls Apple wanting to get on her unmade bed, but 'knowing' he could not until a throw was laid over the bedding:

> He's standing there and keeps looking as if to say 'are you going to make this then? You know I'm waiting here'; he stands (*she demonstrates Apple's head tilted upwards and to one side at the bed's edge*) as if to say: 'you know where I want to go'. It's almost like I can read him.

On another occasion, Mel actively describes the sports in which her child is now able to participate; we are sitting at the dining table on which lie the 'carbs and

158 *Symbiotic practices of care*

cals' book, our coffee mugs, and my recording equipment and notebooks. She explains how she tried to manage swimming lessons with all the necessities for a traveller with diabetes – the monitor, pen and test strips, the jelly babies, and extra food and drink – and the additional food, water, rewards, bowls, jacket and lead that accompany Gemma; and then the swimming towels and extra clothing for the children.

I enquire rather tentatively how the swimming lessons progressed and Mel starts to speak:

> I just . . . er Gemma, no, stop . . . (*Gemma has climbed onto the table and is sitting on the voice recorder*) . . . off, madam, go on the floor, you're a dog . . . (*Mel then speaks as Gemma*) 'I'm not, I'm one of the family . . .', (*Mel to Gemma*) I know you're beautiful, yes . . . (*Mel to me*) so she's erm very clever, (*then to Gemma*) 'aren't you'?

Fittingly relevant to Gemma's position in the family, Franklin suggests that 'animals are just as good as people for the expression of love and attachment and they are equally good at asserting their agency in human households', whether as medical assistants or as 'one of the family' (2006: 148).

Listening to Mel's 'dialogue' with Gemma, I realise that all the human participants addressed their canine companions as if they understood their words and, in turn, endeavoured to translate canine communication into English. They frequently attempted to take what they anthropomorphically considered to be the dog's perspective which helped them to understand why certain behaviours occur in their homes and in public. In addition to an emotional contiguity, they seem to take a commonsense approach often egomorphically (Milton, 2005) sharing a single identity to explain social occurrences, for example, using the plural 'we' as do mothers to their babies and nurses to their patients, exhibiting deep signs of attachment and attunement.

However, Cynthia Willett (2014: 38) maintains, as do many who live and work with animals, 'animals are not like our children; they are like us', a reflection of Milton's (2005: 261) inclusive egomorphism. Willett suggests animals 'are not vulnerable sites of protection and recipients of human sympathy, but kindred political agents in their own right, with interlocking histories, cultures, and technologies' (2014: 38).

Leslie Irvine (2012: s129) draws attention to our assignation of individual traits, preferences and personalities to dogs we know so that they become, in Sanders' words (2003: 410), 'much more than a breed or species representative'. Often the identity of the person walking with a dog in public takes on the identity of the dog in the eyes of the observer so that the man accompanying his medical alert dog gains a shared status. Together they may attract a united nomenclature reminiscent of Michalko's 'two in one in blindness', or become, for example, the 'sniffer-dog man we saw on the bus'; or of course Coetzee's Lurie who becomes a 'dog-man' in *Disgrace* (1999) and 'a guardian of animal souls' (Willett, 2014: 156).

Just as the dog is the likely topic of conversation with strangers or friends in the park, so he or she becomes the prominent and symbolic representative of both the chronic illness and of the human companion – and of the charity: weighty responsibilities for a creature caring for another, without verbal communication skills.

The medical alert assistance dogs learn through continuing education, through a sharing of emotion and experience, through their acute sensory perception, to know their human partners' bodies better than they do themselves. Through the close relationships narrated and described here, the dogs are perceived as becoming part of the human body and may therefore be considered to have reached a peak, if not the pinnacle, of Ingold and Palsson's (2013) 'biosocial becomings'. The trans-species partnership becomes greater than the sum of their parts as individual selves. Mol and Law's porosity of the body (2004) and Vaisman's (2013) embodied identities and differing perspectives share an image both of momentum and change.

Vaisman (2013) cites Viveiros de Castro's observations of Amazonian societies who perceive the world as inhabited by 'different sorts of subjects or persons, human and nonhuman, that apprehend reality from distinct points of view' (2012: 45). Vaisman (2013: 107) writes that 'animals see themselves as humans, they see their food as human food, they see their social system as organized in the same way as human culture, and they see humans as animals or prey'. By this means, 'animals *see* the same way we do *different* things because their bodies are different from ours' (Viveiros de Castro, 1998: 478 in Vaisman, 2013: 115). This notion of bodies refers to the 'affects, dispositions and capacities' (2013: 115), the skills and situations of life that make up Bourdieu's (1977) *habitus*; they are not just physical objects but 'assemblages' of experiences and emotions.

The assistance dog self and the human self have a single shared identity and two separate identities. Borrowing Vaisman's 'Magic Eye' illustration, for example, the question of seeing either one image or another in a drawing depends on your perspective, but once both are sighted, neither will become a fixed, static image. Perception is altered and it becomes impossible not to see one without the other. As Vaisman (2013: 122) suggests, alternative ways of perceiving are becoming more meaningful and require increased development for a better-enabled existence in our fast-changing technological and scientific world.

Welfare concerns

When I remarked on the welcoming attitudes shown me by all the human and nonhuman participants, Terry said they're all proud of their dogs and that the charity puts great care into the 'matching' process, beginning with a human-only interview before human training takes place over several days at varying intervals in the training centre. This is to ensure the client's commitment, to continue training and take full responsibility for the dog's welfare, is accepted and understood.

The charity is fast expanding, say the participants, but it hasn't lost the 'family feel', something the staff members appear keen to encourage and maintain. 'Everybody knows everybody and they're nice – it's not growing so fast that they lose

160 *Symbiotic practices of care*

touch [*with the interspecies partners the charity has brought together*]'. There are meetings at the training centre where administrative staff (I am informed that 'people love coming to work here'), human and canine clients, and trainers and volunteers get together to discuss improved ways of living with chronic illness, gain news of the charity's diverse health investigations sourced from canine olfactory capabilities, and learn from one another what works well or doesn't, as well as ways to keep the dog actively wanting to alert accurately and things to avoid in nutrition, when travelling, or when surrounded by interested strangers in the supermarket.

The following excerpts from narratives show human care and concern for non-human partner welfare. Janet takes on the work of monitoring her blood sugar levels when Alfie has 'free' time:

> Alfie's the first [*of the multispecies family*] to be fed because I always like to feed him two hours before we go out for a walk to make sure he's digested his meal properly. He does alert when we're out but I think this is his time – he's free then and because he sniffs everything, there are deer, pheasants, rabbits, he gets very caught up in the scents so I monitor myself then.

Janet explains how Alfie was enabled to cater for her lack of hypo-awareness and to continue his alerting practices when she spent time in hospital for the birth of her child:

> What was amazing was that they let Alfie stay with me. The nursing staff offered to find me a side room so that he could stay. He did find it incredibly boring and looked as if he was questioning 'why are we here?' but my mum took him out for walks and things, because the nursing staff obviously couldn't take responsibility for his care.

I ask Janet how Alfie has coped with the change in his position in the household hierarchy and she says that they have had to try and do things to boost him: 'Three times a week he and I go out together so that it's just our time'. We watch her baby's determined efforts to crawl; face on the carpet, bottom in the air, a lot of pushing and stretching but it doesn't come together, and he rolls onto his back:

> Alfie's hair gets everywhere . . . we're teaching the baby not to grab hair so much – Alfie would move away before, but I think he knows now that it's not being nasty; we keep all their interactions as being very positive . . . I praise Alfie for being good around the baby.

Paul keeps Nero close by during hospital consultations. Only when X-rays are being taken does he have to wait for Paul on the other side of the door because of radiation risk; Natasha recalls Nero not wanting to settle with her:

> Paul was out 10 minutes, maybe 15, and Nero's nose was going, his ears were going, he'd lay down, but he was alert the whole time.

Symbiotic practices of care   161

'He comes in when I have my eyes checked; wherever I go, he goes'. They walk together into medical consultations in the same way that they walk into shops but, Paul considers, 'probably more people stop you in the hospital than they do in the shops'.

Talking of pain or injury affecting dogs, Paul remarks the canine tolerance of human behaviours:

> That's the trouble with dogs; you never really know how bad they are because they cover it up with so much. The times I've had my hand halfway down his throat pulling bits of bread out or when he's stuffed down something he's found in the field, and he just stands there, not trying to shut his mouth, just looking at me as if to say 'please let me have it' . . . I could get into his dinner-bowl, take a bone off him, he's just brilliant.

The concern shown for Nero's welfare seems constant. Paul and Natasha worry that Nero may pick up and eat something with pesticide on, or drink from a puddle that might have 'antifreeze or some chemical in it' when he's free running in the fields, and they empty his mouth by hand if they can't tell whether he has ingested something toxic. Nero's teeth are brushed regularly, his coat groomed frequently, his pads checked for thorns or splinters, and his weight watched to maintain good health.

His human family feed him in three bowls at every meal, each amount weighed and set down only after he has eaten the first, sat and waited for the second bowl, and repeated the performance for the third. They hope this will help him to slow down his eating behaviour as he gulps the food at speed, and risks gastric torsion, a serious condition in which the stomach revolves closing the entrance and constricting blood circulation, thereby causing a gas build-up and extreme bloating – death can follow torsion. He is given carrot, interspersed with more special rewards for good alerting performances, and the weight – which he 'put on' over three months when the kitchen scales, thought to be accurately weighing his kibbles, proved erroneous and allowed him one-third extra pellets at every meal – is slowly disappearing.

> When we got him, he was 37.2 kilograms which is a lovely weight for him to be, and since then we've managed to keep him pretty much where he was . . . but he was losing a little bit of his waist so he went on the scales at the vet and it was 42.4kg [*because of the additional kibbles*]. He's now down to 41.2.

Nero's between-meals snacks involve carrot and cucumber:

> If you give him a chunk of cucumber, he just looks at it, but if you slice it, he chews it. But it's the opposite with carrot, if you give him a slice of carrot, he goes 'what's that, there's nothing there' – he likes the whole thing and crunches it. He likes apple too, but we've stopped giving it because it's so sugary.

162 *Symbiotic practices of care*

Tina's humour combines a sort of gallows glee and a genuine willingness to share moments of hilarity and warmth. Recalling a previous hypoglycaemic collapse, she assumes Harley alerted her as she remembers going into a supermarket to buy chocolate after a day at work and sitting on a bench at the bus-stop. 'I didn't know how to do my blood or even how to eat the chocolate, but one lady saw Harley was barking and licking my face and she stopped'.

Tina woke up on the hospital resuscitation table and the medical staff immediately asked her what time she generally fed Harley. Tina replied:

> Only at 6'clock, we'll be home by then; it's only 5pm now so we've got plenty of time. They said 'it's 8 o'clock' and I went 'ooh, don't worry, he'll be alright' but they ordered him two meat sandwiches . . . but they didn't feed me! I'm diabetic in coma but they didn't give me owt! (*she laughs at the memory*). But they were really taken with him and the ambulance man says 'I know you Harley, you're a good lad' and I said 'where do you know him from?' and he says he picked me up earlier on and repeats 'what a good dog, there were no way he were going to go with anyone else, just with you'.

No matter the degree of collaboration and friendship developed over time, the partnership will eventually draw to some form of conclusion, occasionally because the human's blood sugar levels become more balanced due to evolving medical technology, or because secondary illnesses take up prime medical positioning. However, most often the interspecies collaboration will end because signs emerge in the dog that exhibit diminishing good health and an increasing inability to recognise extreme blood sugar levels through their sense of smell.

7 Endings and 'ethical' decision-making

No longer useful?

Natasha responds to this question:

> If Paul's blood ends up being really, really stable and Nero doesn't have a job to do, it leads to the question of what happens to him because technically he then probably shouldn't be a fully-trained medical alert assistance dog out in public – but of course, he's never been left alone at home, he's always had someone with him 24/7.

Paul joins in:

> Obviously, I am still diabetic and there are going to be times when, providing he gets a bit stronger on the alert signals, I don't think there will be a problem. It's one of those things; every time there's a change, it knocks the dogs. So before, when I had all the problems with the other illness, it knocked him so he reacted differently, which meant he had to go back and be retrained.

Natasha:

> And that had another, different effect: Nero came back and the bonding was much better because he was like 'you're back, you really belong to me, and I really belong to you'. The connection between them has really strengthened since I was away and he's got very little respect for me now.
>
> He's not disrespectful in that he's naughty or anything but I really have to get his attention or tell him something three times before he takes any notice of me. Before I went away last year, I'd only got to look at him and lift a finger or say just one word – in fact he was much more obedient to me than he ever was to Paul – but because they had no choice but to be together all the time while I was away, the bond had completely shifted when I got back.

Paul is not a 'collapsing' diabetic so finds his 'biggest problem is that I think I can cope with this, I can manage, and I look around and see other people and think

164 *Endings and 'ethical' decision-making*

they're so much worse off than I am. . .' He is concerned that he could be taking Nero away from a partnership that really needs him, when 'in actual fact, I really need him'. Natasha confirms this, adding that without Nero, Paul would have 'no reason to get up in the morning because he gets up to feed him and take him for a walk round the village which he would not do on his own'.

Leslie Irvine (2013: 140) records a similar reasoning in her research on homeless people and their animal companions when Tommy speaks of his dog, Monty, helping him 'with' depression:

> He makes me come out and walk with other people. He gets me socializing with other people. . . . He gives me energy because he can make me get out and walk.

Nero and Monty may be identified as life-changers, as good companions, as social facilitators but, particularly, they are motivators who help channel idling thoughts or feelings into beneficial actions. Whether suffering from depression or from Type 1 diabetes, and the latter illness is likely to incorporate depression as a fluctuating symptom, the dogs provide animated encouragement to 'do' something positive, to move onwards to better things.

Recycling

Jan Shillum (2016: 23), writing in the charity's magazine, The Sniff, tells of a 'new' matching between a diabetes alert dog, who became 'redundant' when his MDD partner's circumstances changed, and an individual whose first canine partnership 'didn't work out'. A charity instructor worked with the 'redundant' dog to 'retrain' him to his new partner's 'hyper and hypo odour and range, which is below 5mmol and above 15mmol – slightly different to his previous partner'. This newly evolved partnership is developing successfully in terms of attachment and alerting, giving both more opportunity for a healthy symbiotic relationship and providing an 'example of recycling a . . . four-legged resource'.

The concept of recycling the dog was cause for deeper thought: recycling instantly produced mental images of waste disposal centres and artefacts contrived from melded others, leading on to further contemplation of a DAD as potentially faulty, disposable equipment. However, the 'proof of the pudding' was demonstrated in the renewed purpose provided for a trained and willing medical alert assistant whose new employment, albeit in accordance with Srinivasan's 'anthropogenic norms' (2013: 114), has reinvigorated the health and social life of his formerly reclusive, mobility-impaired partner. The latter has gained a personal companion whose attention is consistently directed towards him and who provides him with the best practices of care available to her. In this instance, 'recycling' has less of a cold and metallic feel, more of warm and re-entangled 'knotting' of lives (Haraway, 2008: vii).

The DAD may be a device, but not in the manner that glucometers or dialysis machines, for example, are cold, impersonal, and yet vitally assistive. The alerting

Endings and 'ethical' decision-making   165

dog is warm-blooded, a very personal partner, and vital in both senses of the word – vital in being regarded as essential and of high importance, but also vital in feeling alive and warm, physically, and emotionally sentient.

Jeannette Pols and Ingunn Moser (2009: 159), in an analysis comparing robotic companion animals viewed in a documentary with 'ethnographic material about a particular care technology', the Health Buddy, have drawn alternative meaning from 'cold technologies versus warm care', suggesting there is no opposition between them. The robot AIBO dog, who supplies entertainment for the inhabitants of a residential home, can refuse to do a requested action and instead is programmed to offer a different behaviour. It is said to offer 'affective appeal' (2009: 169) that cannot be matched by the speaking robot cat who provides certain services but is neither able to interact successfully nor warmly. However, the Health Buddy technology does provide an important communication system between a patient at home and a nurse in a hospital and, according to Pols and Moser, ensures a feeling of safety and being well looked after despite the distance between the independent patient and the offered care. They conclude that 'warm and cold, rational and affective, medical and social, technological and social, are not opposites' (2009: 176), but differently aligned in different practices.

However accurate their findings, which demonstrate the ability of cold or warm devices to suit a variety of contexts, the option of having a consistently warm and proximate companion, who can act and react in multiple situations and locations, may have more appeal to the chronically ill than a 'novelty item' that may be discarded under a chair once its repertoire becomes prosaic and its activities, limited.

Replacing

No one wants to think about replacing an affectionate, sentient companion, who has shared a home and a lifetime, with a new, 'other' dog, a necessarily alien usurper, but it happens. Whether through curtains of tears or a stoic determination, this event takes place in homes countrywide and is of prime importance to the human participants with whom I have conversed in this research. Daniel Miller's (2008: 105) chapter, '*Talk to the dog*', articulates one of the street's residents' regret that his dog Jeff would not 'be with him much longer' because of his advancing years. He records Harry's annoyance at a visiting fortune teller's 'presumption' in predicting his future meeting with 'a brown Labrador'; Miller gets the 'feeling that Harry no more wants to talk in terms of Jeff's replacement than one would of replacing a wife or a child whose demise looks imminent' (2008: 105).

It is this emotional 'replacement' concern that makes me hesitant to broach questions about DAD futures. However, Terry brings up the topic of Jim's working life:

> He's almost five so we're halfway through his working life and now I've got to start thinking along the lines of a replacement. I'm getting on and when he retires, I won't want a big dog, and not one that's too young either, as I will

166 *Endings and 'ethical' decision-making*

have to exercise a new dog myself. It will depend on whether the charity has anything physically available, possibly one of the smaller spaniel breeds.

The diabetes alert dogs' sense of smell is so good that they probably can go on working for longer but if they get arthritis or limp a bit, the charity would have to say they're sorry but you can't use the dog any more. The thing is that you can't put a jacket advertising the charity onto a dog and then go out shopping or whatever when the dog is obviously unwell, limping or seems to be in pain.

Serpell et al. (2010: 502) suggest the following in their recommendations for ethical decision-making regarding therapy animals:

Animals that, due to age or other reasons, become unduly stressed, should have their service scaled back or eliminated entirely. Attention should also be given to transition the animal as s/he begins to retire. This will help with the animal's sense of wellness.

Val explains the MDD policy regarding dogs who are no longer able to work as alerting dogs and I learn that

In the case of placing a successor dog with an existing client, if they are not in a position to home two dogs, we would discuss with the individual whether it is better to wait until the elderly dog has passed over, or if this is not viable, in the case of an MDD-owned dog, we would support the client by finding a foster home for the dog until the dog passes away.

In response to my question about change of owner, Val says that a fostered dog that is no longer working would remain in the ownership of MDD for the rest of his or her life.

Terry continues talking about the possibilities for Jim's future:

This is where your animate or inanimate become the same. When my wheelchair is starting to wear out, I will get rid of it; when our dog stops working or becomes unreliable with the blood sugars, I will have to replace him; and living here, I couldn't cope with two dogs, that would be my problem. So, in that way he is then being treated as a piece of equipment, even though he's a warm-blooded live creature.

I very tentatively pose the next question: 'in that case, if you couldn't cope with two dogs here, what would you do?' There is a moment of silence and Terry, looking forlorn already, hesitates before speaking:

I don't know – that's why it was such a shock this morning to think that he's five – the average age for a dog of this size is 10–12, not like the smaller ones who go on to live for 15 or 16 years.

Endings and 'ethical' decision-making 167

I realise that despite his earlier remarks about 'robots', he is thinking of Jim as his long-term, sentient companion and not of the length of time that he would continue to work as an animated piece of equipment.

They holiday together – 'the chair allows me to go out and he (Jim) makes me comfortable' – and to increase his fitness, Terry has been extending the length of time he is able to push himself in the wheelchair:

> I wouldn't have had the confidence to push myself for 49 miles without having him to check my sugar levels. I could have stopped and used the machine, but what draws people's attention? Me getting out the kit and stabbing myself, or stopping for a dog and putting my hand close to his nose? Nobody ever noticed it being done and I didn't bother testing because he was convinced.

There is pride in his voice as he states: 'I wouldn't have done it without him'.

> After my old dog, I said I'm never having another dog because it hurts and no dog will ever take his place. But he does (*he points to Jim*); he's just kicked the hole into a different shape, made it his shape instead of the previous dog's.

Some, like Mel, chose their assistance dogs as puppies for family companionship and only later discovered their sensitivity to odours of illness and their aptitude for medical alert assistance dog training; other participants selected their alert dogs from those who were fostered and socialised by volunteers before training by the charity.

In all cases, bonds of friendship developed throughout the entangled lives so that when it seemed likely that these could be broken in the not-too-distant future, anticipatory grief began to swirl and spiral like smoke from a November bonfire. Anticipatory grief can become a doom-laden cloud, evasive but ever-present. Susan Dawson (2010: 73) examines this form of grief which 'may begin when there is a threat of loss or of disruption of the bond' between the human and non-human companions. Emotion weighs heavy over the prospective death of a close relationship. Human voices whisper so dogs cannot hear conversation that might be disloyal, and human eyes avoid contact with those of the dogs for fear of emotional reflection or possible contagion.

Like Jim, Alfie is also more than five years old and on my second visit, I ask Janet if the charity has spoken to her about what might happen when his scenting ability slows and he has to stop working.

> Mmm, yeah . . . MDD say they would retire a dog who is achieving less than 50% of the alerts, so erm, yes, he would retire and be a pet, and then I would be given a choice either to have another dog to train alongside Alfie or to just wait and start afresh. (*She frowns and takes a deep breath.*) I'd probably wait and start afresh . . . mmm, I don't know.

168 *Endings and 'ethical' decision-making*

What next for human–canine biomedical collaboration?

What do the dogs gain from my interest in their work as medical assistants and in their lives as one-half of an interspecies coexistence, a close companion in a shared identity? So often multispecies ethnography portrays the human view of the nonhuman animal subject, understandably, but there is need for the canine perspective in order to bring balance to the research. Karen Emmerman (2014: 161) records her ecofeminist approach to 'inter-animal conflicts which is non-hierarchical, pluralist about moral significance and contextualized' in order to 'obtain as full a picture as possible of what is at stake for all parties'. Participant observation allows an experiencing of other lives instead of distant perception; it enables the physical reality of 'I wouldn't have believed it if I hadn't been there and seen it for myself'. But that is still a human experiencing of those lives. By examining what the dogs do in their everyday roles as medical assistants, by watching their communications with their own and other species, and by listening to polyvocal dialogues deciphering canine behaviours and human responses to those activities, I have attempted to 'bring in' diabetes alert dog perspectives and make more lucid their impact on multispecies families and on the possibilities of biotherapeutic and biomedical research.

Lynda Birke (2009: 2) questions whether we better the world for animals: she pleads for scholars to 'pause, to ask more overtly what the animals might think about what we do, about whether who they are, really informs our work?' It would be possible to reject research projects for ethical reasons if they were to risk the welfare of the animals in focus, she suggests, but to do research studies that result in animals becoming 'empowered' is less simple. It is to be hoped that, at least in some respects, the diabetes alert dogs have gained more tangible credibility and visible personhood through exposure of their work in these pages.

Hurn (2012: 211), like Birke, asks what animals gain from human research into their lives. What choice might an assistance dog make if given the opportunity to voice words in language understandable by humans? Whatever the answer and however phrased, the result is still derived from an anthropocentric imagining. A dog's rose-tinted image might endorse the release of their species' members from any form of cage, whether bars of a crate, walls of a house, or fences round farmland or prison; and the forbidding of any future milling or manufacturing of puppies for sale so that castration and spaying and culling to reduce numbers become historical applications and the hundreds of thousands of unwanted dogs are lessened in number and become persons who are cherished. Like humans who care and are cared for, dogs could be given the opportunity to demonstrate their capabilities more widely, as well as the possibilities they offer that enable them to be recognised and trusted presences in the world.

Alternatively, the human-admired and respected medical alert assistance dog might well feel that the mutual healthful gain of both species provides sufficient means of a comfortable and caring survival in which the loss of total freedom in terms of space, reproduction, or hunting, may be balanced by the provision of food, shelter, friendship, entertainment, and daily off-leash exploration of field

Endings and 'ethical' decision-making 169

and forest, with and without multispecies companionships. Franklin reminds that the companion animal, no longer an inferior 'pet' animal, 'ushers in the potential for greater mutual becomings' as both dogs and humans in this instance 'explore even more possibilities of co-presence' (2006: 137). Tolerance and trust seem prominent features of mutual coexistences, where care for each other's well-being includes empathy and 'touching comfort' (Haraway, 2008: 202–204).

What this shared identity, this mutualistic coexistence, brings to the fore is the concept of caring, the carer and the cared-for in a reciprocal relationship that they might never have known nor conceived of without the constant presence of chronic illness and its fluctuating individual odours. The interspecies partners are neither locked into nor entrapped by an illness such as Type 1 diabetes in the sense of an overpowering need to escape, but rather they make up an entanglement of bodies and minds that challenges and encourages, that evokes new learnings and new 'situated knowledges' so that life can go on with meaning, with purpose significant to both members of the dyad; life that is recognisable and acceptable to society.

Referring to the human exploitation or extinction of animals, Taylor (2017: 218) suggests that it is time to take responsibility for those with whom 'we have co-evolved':

> We could take seriously the ways domesticated animals contribute to our lives and world, in ways that don't involve slaughter. We could recognize our mutual dependence, our mutual vulnerability, and our mutual drive for life.

Although referencing multiple research studies to clarify and explain anthrozoological thinking and current sociological theories relating to health and illness, an objective throughout has been to evidence contemporary application of mutual care practices and to put forward examples of 'doing Type 1 diabetes'. The intention is that, through story-telling, others may learn of the highly complex routines and disturbances that affect the shared daily lives of those collaborating in, limited by, and embodying chronic illness; additionally, how unsettled lives are smoothed and shaped within an acceptable symbiotic ethic of care.

The collaboration between the dogs of olfactory biomedical detection ability and the humans, who train them in practices that advantage individuals with corporeal inabilities, combines to produce a mutualistic ethics of care and care practice that provides a living sensory resource of future use to the chronically ill of all populations. The interspecies cooperation performed between dog and human offers alternative means to benefit the multispecies unwell, without the contested need for invasive, often public, diagnostic procedures and subsequent treatments being conducted at medical and veterinary hospitals.

Imagining a diagnostic electronic nose and creating one that functions as effectively as that of a dog in multipurpose scent detection is the aim of biotechnologists and engineers who have researched canine nasal airflow patterns and produced printed examples (Craven, Paterson and Settles, 2010); but although these are

170 *Endings and 'ethical' decision-making*

valuable models and markers of progress in this field, the dogs as yet remain leaders, particularly so in the rapid and sensitive detection of illness symptoms.

In the introductory paragraphs, I stated that I would principally be discussing assistance dogs and their human partners because, apart from the staff members, they are the current 'components' of the MDD charity. However, recalling Singer's definition (1990: 6) that 'speciesism . . . is a prejudice or attitude of bias in favor of the interests of members of one's own species and against those of members of other species', and bearing in mind that dogs are the species incorporated in the charity's name, future research might encourage charities similar to MDD to consider the inherent speciesism of what they do and promote and to examine the 'use' of other species, not only dogs but perhaps the equally macrosmatic pigs, in the diagnosis of illness. As there is now widespread approval of APOPO's working rats, such species-collaborative charities might encourage change in public perception of other widely stigmatised and abused animals.

Although some breeds of rat become firm friends to their human guardians, and Giant African Pouched Rats are optimal sensors of Tb symptoms in sputum samples, the latter have personhood that has yet to sit comfortably in a domestic mutualistic relationship with a tuberculosis-infected human companion. The rats are sensitive and accurate in their diagnostic endeavours but lack the millennia of domestication procedures and interspecies familiarities that structure dog and human relating. Only now are they taking up a role in the compatible interspecies companionship that is currently enjoyed by dogs and humans across much of the world.

As discussed earlier, pigs are efficient olfactory sensors and expert truffle-detectives and they could become accurate sensors of VOCs for oncological purpose or for other medical diagnoses. They might take time in health assistance training to reach accreditation levels that qualify dogs, but companion pigs already share human homes, learn acceptable hygiene behaviours and offer good friendship. However, in the UK, the Department for Environment, Food, and Rural Affairs (DEFRA) currently considers pigs to be livestock so their employment, as home-based medical scent-detectives with family privileges, remains an ambitious objective. There seems sparse research into their ability to scent drugs or explosives, although an internet search revealed media stories of accolades to the pig's prowess in that regard.

The warm-hearted multispecies companions who have given time, space, histories, and anecdotes, to this research more than merit the impact of their narrations resonating beyond the ink of this text. It is hoped that coffee-shop conversation may now incorporate the responsive question: 'what type of diabetes does she have?' and perhaps lead to enquiry as to whether 'Jenny' may still be hypo-aware, or not. The imagined conversation might also include discussion of the possibilities for mutual care practices if one partner in the dyad embodying chronic illness, is a nonhuman animal and the other, a human one.

Neither the working assistance dogs nor their unwell partners should be marginalised or set aside as being different and 'other'. These canine–human cooperative practices may be complicated and not always fulfilling, but their collaboration in

Endings and 'ethical' decision-making 171

olfactory biomedical research to improve the lifestyles and better balance the bodies of those unsettled by chronic illness, is innovative and gaining rapid acceptance in the fields of health and society.

I: I've attended courses but unless you're close to someone who has diabetes, or you have it yourself, you can't really imagine . . .

TERRY: To see it [*canine medical alert assistance*] work gives you 100 times more than any lecture can give you. My specialist at the hospital would rather rely on him than the blood meter, to the point where he says: 'don't test unless the dog tells you to'. So instead of 20 or 30 tests a day, it's now two or three.

The diabetes alert dog becomes an ally, an affectionate and loyal friend, and an associate, in addition to acting as a highly efficient diagnostic device, saving minutes, hours, days and months, of human lifetime. In embodying the complexities of chronic illness, the assistance dog restructures the performance of that human life.

Adrian Franklin lists 'companionship, friendship, love and even community' as words that have been 'rescued for many through new relationships with companion animals' (2006: 138). Those four words of communal involvement may enlist, or be enlisted by, mutual concern and empathy, to demonstrate the warmth derived from close multispecies cooperation between trans-species partners, whether they work as independent dyads or among the collaborative 'relatings' (Haraway, 2003: 6–10, for example, and Franklin, 2006: 145) or groupings within the charity that has enabled these combinations.

Braidotti's intense 'rich new alliances' (2009: 529) are forged from disparate, but willingly congruent, 'living beings' (Hurn, 2012: 219), co-supporting attainment of bettered life within the elastic boundaries of chronic illness and demonstrating what they do in their bonded fellowship and shared identity to shape and achieve multispecies 'mattering'.

TINA: The dogs go out of their way to help. That's why when I meet people, I say to them tell the charity what you're having difficulties with, because it's amazing what the dogs can do – and they just love it. They just love to be there to care for you, you know.

References

Ache, B.W. and Young, J.M. (2005) Olfaction: diverse species, conserved principles, *Neuron*, 48, 417–430

Adams, C.J. and Gruen, L. (2014) *Ecofeminism: feminist intersections with other animals and the earth*, London: Bloomsbury

Adell-Bath, M., Krook, A., Sandqvist, G. and Skantze, K. (1979) *Do we need dogs? A study of dogs' social significance to man*, Gothenburg: University of Gothenburg Press

Agamben, G. (2004) *The open: man and animal*, trans. K. Attell, Stanford, CA: Stanford University Press

Alger, J.M. and Alger, S.F. (1999) Cat culture, human culture: an ethnographic study of a cat shelter, *Society & Animals*, 7(3), 199–218

Alger, J.M. and Alger, S.F. (2013) 'Canine soldiers, mascots and stray dogs in U.S. wars: ethical considerations', in R. Hediger (ed.) *Animals and war*, Leiden: Brill

Allon, F. and Barrett, L. (2015) That dog was marine! Human-dog assemblages in the Pacific war, *Animal Studies Journal*, 4(1), 126–147

American Psychiatric Association (2000) *Diagnostic and statistical manual of mental disorders* (4th ed.), Text Revision, Washington, DC: American Psychiatric Association

Aristotle (1962) *Nichomacheon ethics*, Indianapolis: Library of Liberal Arts

Arluke, A. and Sanders, C.R. (1996) *Regarding animals*, Philadelphia: Temple University Press

Armstrong Oma, K. (2010) Between trust and domination: social contracts between humans and animals, *World Archaeology*, 42(2), 175–187

Ascione, F.R. (2005) *Children and animals: exploring the roots of kindness and cruelty*, West Lafayette, IN: Purdue University Press

Assistance Dogs UK, accessed on the internet, 29 August 2015, www.assistancedogs.org.uk/

Baker, K. (2013) 'Chapter 3: home and heart, hand and eye: unseen links between pigmen and pigs in industrial farming', in E-J. Abbots and A. Lavis (eds.) *Why we eat and how we eat: contemporary encounters between foods and bodies* (*Critical Food Studies*), Farnham: Ashgate Publishing

Baur, G. (2008) *Farm sanctuary: changing hearts and minds about animals and food*, New York: Touchstone

BBC Technology (2016) Locusts to 'sniff out explosives', accessed on the internet, 4 July 2016, www.bbc.co.uk/news/technology-36702704

Bekoff, M. (2002) Awareness: animal reflections, *Nature*, 419(6904), 255–255

Bekoff, M. (2004) 'Foreword: to know them is to be them', in L. Irvine (ed.) *If you tame me: understanding our connection with animals*, Philadelphia: Temple University Press

References 173

Bekoff, M. (2011) Do wild animals suffer from PTSD and other psychological disorders? *Psychology Today*, 29.

Belk, R.W. (1988) Possessions and the extended self, *Journal of Consumer Research*, 15(2), 139–168

Belk, R.W. (1996) Metaphoric relationships with pets, *Society & Animals*, 4(2), 121–145

Bird-David, N. (2006) Animistic epistemology: why do some hunter-gatherers not depict animals? *Ethnos*, 71(1), 33–50

Birke, L. (2008) Talking about horses: control and freedom in the world of 'natural horsemanship', *Society & Animals*, 16, 107–126

Birke, L. (2009) Naming names – or what's in it for the animals? *Humanimalia: A Journal of Human/Animal Interface Studies*, 1(1)

Birke, L. and Hockenhull, J. (eds.) (2012) *Crossing boundaries: investigating human-animal relationships* (Human Animal Studies, Vol. 14), Leiden and Boston: Brill

Birke, L. and Hockenhull, J. (2015) Journeys together: horses and humans in partnership, *Society & Animals*, 23, 81–100

Birke, L. and Michael, M. (1998) The heart of the matter: animal bodies, ethics, and species boundaries, *Society & Animals*, 6(3), 245–261

Blaxter, M. (1990) *Health and lifestyles*, London: Routledge

Blue, G. and Rock, M. (2011) Trans-biopolitics: complexity in interspecies relations, *Health*, 15(4), 353–368

Bostrom, N. (2005) Transhumanist values, *Review of Contemporary Philosophy*, 4

Bourdieu, P. (1977) *Outline of a theory of practice*, trans. Richard Nice, New York: Cambridge University Press

Bowling, F.L., Salgami, E.V. and Boulton, A.J. (2007) Larval therapy: a novel treatment in eliminating methicillin-resistant Staphylococcus aureus from diabetic foot ulcers, *Diabetes Care*, 30(2), 370–371

Bradshaw, J. (2012) *In defence of dogs*, London: Penguin

Bradshaw, J. (2017) *The animals among us: the new science of anthrozoology*, London: Allen Lane

Braidotti, R. (2009) Animals, anomalies, and inorganic others: de-oedipalizing the animal other, *PMLA*, 124(2), 526–532

Brandt, K. (2004) A language of their own: an interactionist approach to human-horse communication, *Society & Animals*, 12(4), 299–316

Bryant, C. (1979) The zoological connection: animal-related human behaviour, *Social Forces*, 58(2), 399–421

Budiansky, S. (1997) *The covenant of the wild: why animals chose domestication*, London: Phoenix

Burrows, K., Adams, C. and Millman, S. (2008) Factors affecting behavior and welfare of service dogs for children with autism spectrum disorder, *Journal of Applied Animal Welfare Science*, 11(1), 42–62

Bury, M. (1991) The sociology of chronic illness: a survey of research and prospects, *Sociology of Health and Illness*, 13(4), 451–468

Bury, M. (2001) Illness narratives: fact or fiction? *Sociology of Health and Illness*, 23(3), 263–285

Callicott, J.B. (1989) *In defense of the land ethic: essays in environmental philosophy*, Albany, NY: State University of New York Press, *Ethnologist*, 37(2), 241–258

Carsten, J. (2013) '"Searching for the truth": tracing the moral properties of blood in Malaysian clinical pathology labs', in J. Carsten (ed.) *Blood will out: essays on liquid*

174 *References*

transfers and flows, Chichester, West Sussex, UK: Royal Anthropological Institute of Great Britain and Ireland: John Wiley and Sons

Carter, S., Green, J. and Thorogood, N. (2013) The domestication of an everyday health technology: a case study of electric toothbrushes, *Social Theory & Health*, 11, 344–367

Cassidy, R. (2002) *The sport of kings: kinship, class and thoroughbred breeding in Newmarket*, Cambridge: Cambridge University Press

Cassidy, R. and Mullin, M. (eds.) (2007) *Where the wild things are now*, Oxford: Berg

Cevetello, J. (2007) 'My elite glucometer', in S. Turkle (ed.) *Evocative objects: things we think with*, Cambridge, MA: The MIT Press

Chandler, C.K. (2005) *Animal assisted therapy in counseling*, Hove: Routledge

Charmaz, K. (1983) Loss of self: a fundamental form of suffering in the chronically ill, *Sociology of Health and Illness*, 5(2), 168–195

Charmaz, K. (1995) The body, identity and self: adapting to impairment, *The Sociological Quarterly*, 36(4), 657–680

Charmaz, K. (2006) Measuring pursuits, marking self: meaning construction in chronic illness, *International Journal of Qualitative Studies on Health and Well-Being*, 1, 27–37

Charmaz, K. and Rosenfeld, D. (2006) 'Reflections of the body, images of self: visibility and invisibility in chronic illness and disability', in D.D. Waskul and P. Vannini (eds.) *Body/embodiment: symbolic interaction and the sociology of the body*, London: Ashgate

Chatjouli, A. (2013) 'Thalassaemic lives as stories of becoming: mediated biologies and genetic (un)certainties', in T. Ingold and G. Palsson (eds.) *Biosocial becomings: integrating social and biological anthropology*, Cambridge: Cambridge University Press

Church, J.C.T. (1996) The traditional use of maggots in wound healing, and the use of larva therapy (biosurgery) in modern medicine, *Journal of Alternative and Complementary Medicine*, 2, 525–527

Church, J.C.T. (1999) Larva therapy in modern wound care: a review, *Primary Intention*, 7, 63–68

Church, J.C.T. (2013) 'Biotherapy – an introduction', in M. Grassberger, R.A. Sherman, O.S. Gileva, C.M.H. Kim and K.Y. Mumcuoglu (eds.) *Biotherapy – history, principles and practice: a practical guide to the diagnosis and treatment of disease using living organisms*, Dordrecht: Springer

Clifford, J. (1986) 'On ethnographic allegory', in J. Clifford and G.E. Marcus (eds.) *Writing culture: the poetics and politics of ethnography*, Berkeley, Los Angeles and London: University of California Press

Clifford, J. (2007) 'On ethnographic authority', in A.C.G.M. Robben and J.A. Sluka (eds.) *Ethnographic fieldwork: an anthropological reader*, Oxford: Blackwell Publishing

Clutton-Brock, J. (1995) 'Origins of the dog: domestication and early history', in J.A. Serpell (ed.) *The domestic dog: its evolution, behaviour and interactions with people*, Cambridge: Cambridge University Press

Coetzee, J.M. (1999) *Disgrace*, London: Vintage Books

Cohen, C. (1986) The case for the use of animals in biomedical research, *The New England Journal of Medicine*, 315, 865–870

Coles, J. (2015) The sniffer dog that detects secretive harvest mice, accessed from the internet, www.bbc.co.uk/earth/story/20150930-why-train-a-dog-to-smell-harvest-mice

Cooley, C.H. (1902) *Human nature and social order*, New York: Charles Scribner's Sons

Coppinger, R. and Coppinger, L. (2016) *What is a dog?* Chicago and London: University of Chicago Press

Coppinger, R., Coppinger, L. and Skillings, E. (1998) Observations on assistance dog training and use, *Journal of Applied Animal Welfare Science*, 1(2), 133–144

References 175

Coppinger, R. and Schneider, R. (1995) 'Evolution of working dogs', in J. Serpell (ed.) *The domestic dog: its evolution, behaviour and interactions with people*, Cambridge: Cambridge University Press, 21–47

Cornu, J-N., Cancel-Tassin, G., Ondet, V., Girardet, C. and Cussenot, O. (2011) Olfactory detection of prostate cancer by dogs sniffing urine: a step forward in early diagnosis, *European Urology*, 59, 197–201

Coulter, K. (2016a) *Animals, work, and the promise of interspecies solidarity*, Basingstoke: Palgrave Macmillan

Coulter, K. (2016b) Beyond human to humane: a multispecies analysis of care work, its repression, and its potential, *Studies in Social Justice*, 10(2), 199–219

Craven, B.A., Paterson, E.G. and Settles, G.S. (2010) The fluid dynamics of canine olfaction: unique nasal airflow patterns as an explanation of macrosmia, *Journal of the Royal Society Interface* 7, 933–943. doi:10.1098/rsif.2009.0490

Crețan, R. (2015) Mapping protests against dog culling in post-communist Romania, *Area*, 47(2), 155–165

Csányi, V. (2005) *If dogs could talk: exploring the canine mind*, New York: North Point Press

Curtin, D. (2014) 'Compassion and being human', in C.J. Adams and L. Gruen (eds.) *Ecofeminism: feminist intersections with other animals and the earth*, London: Bloomsbury

Czerny, S. (2012) 'Dogs don't speak': a consideration of the flow of knowledge between dogs, anthropologists and humans, *Narodna umjetnost-Hrvatski časopis za etnologiju i folkloristiku*, 49(1), 7–22

Dant, T. (2007) The 'pragmatics' of material interaction, *Journal of Consumer Culture*, 8(1), 11–33

Davies, G. (2013) Mobilizing experimental life: spaces of becoming with mutant mice, *Theory, Culture & Society*, 30(7–8), 129–153

Dawkins, M.S. (2006) Through animal eyes: what behaviour tells us, *Applied Animal Behaviour Science*, 100(1–2), 4–10

Dawson, S.E. (2010) 'Compassionate communication: working with grief', in C. Gray and J. Moffett (eds.) *Handbook of veterinary communication skills*, Oxford: Wiley-Blackwell

De la Bellacasa, M.P. (2012) 'Nothing comes without its world': thinking with care, *The Sociological Review*, 60(2), 197–216

De la Bellacasa, M.P. (2017) *Matters of care: speculative ethics in more than human worlds*, Posthumanities 41, London: University of Minnesota Press

De Nora, T. (2016) *Music Asylums: wellbeing through music in everyday life*, London and New York: Routledge

Department of Environment, Food and Rural Affairs (DEFRA) (2009) Code of practice for the welfare of dogs, *Animal Welfare Act 2006*, accessed on the internet, 2 January 2017, www.gov.uk/government/uploads/system/uploads/attachment_data/file/69390/pb13333-cop-dogs-091204.pdf

Despret, V. (2004) The body we care for: figures of anthropo-zoo-genesis, *Body & Society*, 10(2–3), 111–134

Despret, V. (2008) The becomings of subjectivity in animal worlds, *Subjectivity*, 23(1), 123–139

De Waal, F.B.M. (2001) *The ape and the Sushi master: cultural reflections by a primatologist*, New York: Basic Books

De Waal, F.B.M. (2006) *Primates and philosophers: how morality evolved*, Princeton, NJ: Princeton University Press

176 References

De Waal, F.B.M. (2008) Putting the altruism back into altruism: the evolution of empathy, *Annual Review of Psychology*, 59, 279–300

De Waal, F.B.M. (2010) *The age of empathy: nature's lessons for a kinder society*, London: Souvenir Press

Diabetes.co.uk (2014) Hypo alert dogs, accessed on the internet, 14 November 2014, www.diabetes.co.uk/hypo-alert-dogs.html

Diabetes.co.uk (2015) Closed loop artificial pancreas, accessed on the internet, 2 May 2017, www.diabetes.co.uk/artificial-pancreas.html

Diabetes.co.uk (2016) What is an autoimmune disease? accessed on the internet, 2 May 2017, www.diabetes.co.uk/autoimmune-diseases.html

Diabetes.co.uk (2017) Dead-in-bed (DIB) syndrome, accessed on the internet, 2 May 2017, www.diabetes.co.uk/diabetes-complications/dead-in-bed-syndrome.html

Diabetes UK (2010) Diabetes in the UK 2010: key statistics on diabetes, 1–21

Diabetes UK (2014) What is type 1 diabetes? accessed on the internet, 14 November 2014, www.diabetes.org.uk/diabetes-the-basics/what-is-type-1-diabetes

Diabetes UK (2016) Diabetic ketoacidosis DKA, accessed on the internet, December 2016, www.diabetes.org.uk/Guide-to-diabetes/Complications/Diabetic_Ketoacidosis/

Diabetes UK (2017) Diabetes prevalence 2017, accessed on the internet, November 2017, www.diabetes.org.uk/professionals/position-statements-reports/statistics/diabetes-prevalence-2017

Dodman, N. (2016) *Pets on the couch: neurotic dogs, compulsive cats, anxious birds, and the new science of animal psychiatry*, New York: Atria Books

Dogs Trust Stray Dogs Survey (2016) accessed on the internet, 2 May 2017, www.dogstrust.org.uk/newsevents/news/stray%20dogs%202016%20summary%20report%20-%20gfk%20social%20research.pdf

Doka, K.J. (ed.) (2002) *Disenfranchised grief: new directions, challenges, and strategies for practice*, Champaign, IL: Research Press

Dolphin, H. (2016) Fakes pose risk to assistance dogs, *Disability Now*, accessed on the internet, https://disabilitynow.org.uk/2016/01/04/fakes-pose-risk-to-assistance-dogs/

Donovan, J. (2006) Feminism and the treatment of animals: from care to dialogue, *Signs*, 31(2), 305–329

Douglas, M. (2002 [1966]) *Purity and danger*, Abingdon: Routledge and Kegan Paul

Eason, F. (2011) *Remembering 'best friends': the role of physical and virtual pet memorials in preventing socio-emotional isolation in grief*, unpublished thesis, University of Wales, Lampeter

Eisenberg, N. (2000) Emotion, regulation, and moral development, *Annual Review of Psychology*, 51, 665–697.

Elliker, K.R., Sommerville, B.A., Broom, D.A., Neal, D.E., Armstrong, S. and Williams, H.C. (2014) Key considerations for the experimental training and evaluation of cancer odour detection dogs: lessons learnt from a double-blind, controlled trial of prostate cancer detection, *BMC Urology*, 14(22)

Elliott, D.E., Pritchard, D.I. and Weinstock, J.V. (2013) 'Helminth therapy', in M. Grassberger, R.A. Sherman, O.S. Gileva, C.M.H. Kim and K.Y. Mumcuoglu (eds.) *Biotherapy – history, principles and practice*, Dordrecht: Springer

Elliott, D.E. and Weinstock, J.V. (2012) Where are we on worms? *Current Opinion in Gastroenterology*, 28(6), 551–556

Emerson, R.M., Fretz, R.I. and Shaw, L.L. (1995) *Writing ethnographic fieldnotes*, Chicago and London: The University of Chicago Press

References 177

Emery, N.J. and Clayton, N.S. (2001) Effects of experience and social context on prospective caching strategies by scrub-jays, *Nature*, 414, 443–446

Emmerman, K.S. (2014) 'Inter-animal moral conflicts and moral repair: a contextualized ecofeminist approach in action', in C.J. Adams and L. Gruen (eds.) *Ecofeminism: feminist intersections with other animals and the earth*, London: Bloomsbury

Endicott, K. (1979) *Batek Negrito religion*, Oxford: Clarendon Press

Ericsson, K.A. (2001) Expertise in interpreting: an expert performance perspective, *Interpreting*, 5, 187–220

Farthing, P. (2014) *Wylie, the brave street dog who never gave up*, London: Hodder and Stoughton

Fijn, N. (2011) *Living with herds: human-animal coexistence in Mongolia*, Cambridge: Cambridge University Press

Fine, A.H. (2010) *Handbook on animal-assisted therapy: theoretical foundations and guidelines for practice* (3rd ed.), London and San Diego, CA: Academic Press

Fine, A.H. and Beck, A. (2010) 'Understanding our kinship with animals: input for health care professionals interested in the human/animal bond', in A.H. Fine (ed.) *Handbook on animal-assisted therapy: theoretical foundations and guidelines for practice* (3rd ed.), London and San Diego, CA: Academic Press

Franklin, A. (2006) 'Be[a]ware of the dog': a post-humanist approach to housing, *Housing, Theory and Society*, 23(3), 137–156

Friedmann, E., Son, H. and Tsai, C-C. (2010) 'The animal/human bond: health and wellness', in A.H. Fine (ed.) *The handbook of animal-assisted therapy: theoretical foundations and guidelines for practice* (3rd ed.), San Diego, CA: Academic Press

Fuentes, A. (2010) Naturalcultural encounters in Bali: monkeys, temples, tourists, and ethnoprimatology, *Cultural Anthropology*, 25(4), 600–624

Fuentes, A. (2013) 'Life in the making: epigenesis, biocultural environments and human becomings', in T. Ingold and G. Palsson (eds.) *Biosocial becomings: integrating social and biological anthropology*, Cambridge: Cambridge University Press

Gadbois, S. and Reeve, C. (2014) 'Canine olfaction: scent, sign and situation', in A. Horowitz (ed.) *Domestic dog cognition and behaviour*, Berlin and Heidelberg: Springer

Gaita, R. (2004) *The philosopher's dog*, London: Routledge

Gileva, O.S. and Mumcuoglu, K.Y. (2013) 'Hirudotherapy', in M. Grassberger, R.A. Sherman, O.S. Gileva, C.M.H. Kim and K.Y. Mumcuoglu (eds.) *Biotherapy – history, principles and practice: a practical guide to the diagnosis and treatment of disease using living organisms*, Dordrecht: Springer

Goffman, E. (1959) *The presentation of self in everyday life*, London: Penguin Books

Goode, D. (2007) *Playing with my dog Katie, an ethnomethodological study of dog-human interaction*, West Lafayette, IN: Purdue University

Grassberger, M. and Sherman, R.A. (2013) 'Ichthyotherapy', in M. Grassberger, R.A. Sherman, C.M.H. Kim, O.S. Gileva and Mumcuoglu, K.Y. (eds.) *Biotherapy – history, principles and practice: a practical guide to the diagnosis and treatment of disease using living organisms*, Dordrecht: Springer

Grassberger, M., Sherman, R.A., Kim, C.M.H., Gileva, O.S. and Mumcuoglu, K.Y. (eds.) (2013) *Biotherapy – history, principles and practice: a practical guide to the diagnosis and treatment of disease using living organisms*, Dordrecht: Springer

Greene, A.N. (2008) *Horses at work: harnessing power in industrial America*, Cambridge, MA: Harvard University Press

Greenebaum, J. (2004) It's a dog's life: elevating status from pet to 'fur baby' at Yappy Hour, *Society & Animals*, 12(2), 117–135

178 *References*

Greenhough, B. and Roe, E. (2011) Ethics, space, and somatic sensibilities: comparing relationships between scientific researchers and their human and animal experimental subjects, *Environment and Planning D: Society and Space*, 29(1), 47–66

Gregory, S. (2005) Living with chronic illness in the family setting, *Sociology of Health & Illness*, 27(3), 372–392

Gruen, L. (2015) *Entangled empathy: an alternative ethic for our relationships with animals*, Brooklyn, NY: Lantern Books

Gruen, L. and Weil, K. (2012) Animal others – editors' introduction, *Hypatia*, 27(3), 477–487

Guest, C. (2013) 'Canine olfactory detection of human disease', in M. Grassberger, R.A. Sherman, O.S. Gileva, C.M.H. Kim and K.Y. Mumcuoglu (eds.) *Biotherapy – history, principles and practice: a practical guide to the diagnosis and treatment of disease using living organisms*, Dordrecht: Springer

Haddon, L. (2007) Roger Silverstone's legacies: domestication, *New Media & Society*, 9(1), 25–32

Haehner, A., Tosch, C., Wolz, M., Klingelhoefer, L., Fauser, M., Storch, A., Reichmann, H. and Hummel, T. (2013) Olfactory training in patients with Parkinson's disease, *PLoS One*, 8(4)

Hamilton, L. and Taylor, N. (2013) *Animals at work: identity, politics and culture in work with animals*, Leiden: Brill

Hamington, M. (2008) Learning ethics from our relationships with animals: moral imagination, *International Journal of Applied Philosophy*, 22(2), 177–188

Handlin, L., Hydbring-Sandberg, E., Nilsson, A., Ejdebäck, M., Jansson, A. and Uvnäs-Moberg, K. (2011) Short-term interaction between dogs and their owners: effects on oxytocin, cortisol, insulin and heart rate – an exploratory study, *Anthrozoös*, 24(3), 301–315

Hansen, A.K., Dahl, K. and Sørensen, D.B. (2002) Rearing and caring for a future xenograft donor pig, *Acta Veterinaria Scandinavica*, Suppl. 99, 45–50

Haraway, D.J. (1988) Situated knowledges: the science question in feminism and the privilege of partial perspective, *Feminist Studies*, 14(3), 575–599

Haraway, D.J. (1991) 'A cyborg manifesto: science, technology, and socialist-feminism in the late twentieth century', in *Simians, cyborgs and women: the reinvention of nature*, New York: Routledge, 149–181

Haraway, D.J. (1997) *Modest_witness@second_millenium.femaleman© _meets_oncomouse TM: feminism and technoscience*, London: Routledge

Haraway, D.J. (2003) *The companion species manifesto: dogs, people, and significant otherness*, Chicago, IL: Prickly Paradigm Press

Haraway, D.J. (2008) *When species meet*, Minneapolis: University of Minnesota Press

Haraway, D.J. (2016) *Staying with the trouble: making kin in the Chthulucene*, Durham and London: Duke University Press

Hare, B., Call, J., Agnetta, B. and Tomasello, M. (2000) Chimpanzees know what conspecifics do and do not see, *Animal Behaviour*, 59, 771–785

Hare, B., Call, J. and Tomasello, M. (2001) Do chimpanzees know what conspecifics know? *Animal Behaviour*, 61, 139–151

Hare, B., Call, J. and Tomasello, M. (2006) Chimpanzees deceive a human competitor by hiding, *Cognition*, 101, 495–514

Hart, L.A. (1995) 'Dogs as human companions: a review of the relationship', in J.A. Serpell (ed.) *The domestic dog: its evolution, behaviour and interactions with people*, Cambridge: Cambridge University Press

References 179

Hart, L.A. (2010) 'Positive effects of animals for psychosocially vulnerable people: a turning point for delivery', in A.H. Fine (ed.) *Handbook on animal-assisted therapy: theoretical foundations and guidelines for practice* (3rd ed.), London and San Diego, CA: Academic Press

Hartigan, J. (2014) *Aesop's anthropology: a multispecies approach*, Minneapolis: University of Minnesota Press

Hediger, R. (2013) Dogs of war: the biopolitics of loving and leaving the US nine forces in Vietnam, *Animal Studies Journal*, 2(1), 55–73

Helton, W.S. (2009) 'Canine ergonomics: introduction to the new science of working dogs', in W.S. Helton (ed.) *Canine ergonomics: the science of working dogs*, Boca Raton, FL: CRC Press

Higgin, M. (2012) 'Being guided by dogs', in L. Birke and J. Hockenhull (eds.) *Crossing boundaries: investigating human-animal relationships*, Leiden: Brill

Hobbes, T. (1962 [1651]) *Leviathan*. London: Collins

Hoffman, M.L. (1987) 'The contribution of empathy to justice and moral judgment', in N. Eisenberg and J. Strayer (eds.) *Empathy and its development*, New York: Cambridge University Press

Horowitz, A. (2009) *Inside of a dog: what dogs see, smell and know*, London: Simon & Schuster

Horowitz, A. (2016) *Being a dog: following the dog into a world of smell*, New York: Scribner International

Howes, D. and Classen, C. (2014) *Ways of sensing: understanding the senses in society*, London: Routledge

Hummel, T., Landis, B.N. and Huettenbrink, K-B. (2011) Smell and taste disorders, *GMS Current Topics of Otorhinolaryngology – Head and Neck Surgery*, 10

Hurn, S. (2008a) The 'Cardinauts' of the Western Coast of Wales: exchanging and exhibiting horses in the pursuit of fame, *Journal of Material Culture*, 13(3), 335–355

Hurn, S. (2008b) What's love got to do with it? The interplay of sex and gender in the commercial breeding of Welsh Cobs, *Society & Animals*, 16, 23–44

Hurn, S. (2010) What's in a name? Anthrozoology, human-animal studies, animal studies or. . .? (Respond to this article at www. therai. org. uk/at/debate). *Anthropology Today*, 26(3), 27–28

Hurn, S. (2011) Dressing down: clothing animals, disguising animality? *Civilisations*, 59(2), 109–124

Hurn, S. (2012) *Humans and other animals: cross-cultural perspectives on human-animal interactions*, London: Pluto Press

Huxley, R.R., Peters, S.A., Mishra, G.D. and Woodward, M. (2015). Risk of all-cause mortality and vascular events in women versus men with type 1 diabetes: a systematic review and meta-analysis, *The Lancet Diabetes & Endocrinology*, 3(3), 198–206

Ingold, T. (2000) 'From trust to domination: an alternative history of human-animal relations', in *The perception of the environment: essays in livelihood, dwelling and skill*, Abingdon: Routledge

Ingold, T. and Palsson, G. (eds.) (2013) *Biosocial becomings: integrating social and biological anthropology*, Cambridge: Cambridge University Press

Irvine, L. (2004) A model of animal selfhood: expanding interactionist possibilities, *Symbolic Interaction*, 27(1), 3–21

Irvine, L. (2007) The question of animal selves: implications for sociological knowledge and practice, *Qualitative Sociology Review*, III(1), 5–22

180 *References*

Irvine, L. (2009) *Filling the ark: animal welfare in disasters*, Philadelphia, PA: Temple University Press

Irvine, L. (2012) Sociology and anthrozoology: symbolic interactionist contributions, *Anthrozoös*, 25, S123–S137

Irvine, L. (2013) *My dog always eats first: homeless people and their animals*, London: Lynne Rienner Publishers

Juvenile Diabetes Research Foundation (JDRF), improving lives, curing type 1 diabetes (2013a) *Straight to the point: a guide for adults living with type 1 diabetes* (UK ed.), London

Juvenile Diabetes Research Foundation (JDRF), improving lives, curing type 1 diabetes (2013b) *Type 1 diabetes research roadmap*, London

Kellert, S.R. and Felthous, A.R. (1985) Childhood cruelty toward animals among criminals and noncriminals, *Human Relations*, 38(12), 1113–1129

Kirksey, S.E. and Helmreich, S. (2010) The emergence of multispecies ethnography, *Cultural Anthropology*, 25(4), 545–576

Knafl, K.A. and Gilliss, C.L. (2002) Families and chronic illness: a synthesis of current research, *Journal of Family Nursing*, 8, 178–198

Kopytoff, I. (1986) The cultural biography of things: commoditization as process, *The Social Life of Things: Commodities in Cultural Perspective*, 68, 70–73

Koski, M.A. (2011) Acupuncture for zoological companion animals, *Veterinary Clinics of North America: Exotic Animal Practice*, 14(1), 141–154

Krieger, S. (2005) *Things no longer there: a memoir of losing sight and finding vision*, London: The University of Wisconsin Press

Krieger, S. (2010) *Traveling blind: adventures in vision with a guide dog by my side*, West Lafayette, IN: Purdue University Press

Latimer, J. (2013) Being alongside: rethinking relations amongst different kinds, *Theory, Culture & Society*, 30(7–8), 77–104

Law, J. (2004) Matter-ing: or how might STS contribute? Centre for Science Studies, Lancaster University, accessed on the internet, 5 December 2016, 1–11, draft available at www.hetero geneities.net/publications/Law2009TheGreer-BushTest. pdf

Law, J. (2010) 'Care and killing: tensions in veterinary practice', in A. Mol, I. Moser and J. Pols (eds.) *Care in practice: on tinkering in clinics, homes and farms*, Bielefeld, Germany: Transcript Verlag

Leaf, M. (1955 [1936]) *The story of Ferdinand*, London: The Reprint Society

Leung, T.L.F. and Poulin, R. (2008) Parasitism, commensalism, and mutualism: exploring the many shades of symbioses, *Vie et Milieu – Life and Environment*, 58(2), 107–115

Levinson, B.M. (1969 [1997]) *Pet-oriented child psychotherapy* (2nd ed.), Springfield, IL: Charles C Thomas

Lewis, E. (2011) Cape Town's 230 000 stray dogs, *Western Cape News*, accessed on the internet, 12 December 2016, http://www.iol.co.za/news/south-africa/ . . . cape/cape-towns-230-000-stray-dogs-1093892

Linton, S. (1998) *Claiming disability: knowledge and identity*, New York: New York University Press

Lippi, G. and Cervellin, G. (2012) Canine olfactory detection of cancer versus laboratory testing: myth or opportunity? *Clinical Chemistry and Laboratory Medicine*, 50(3), 435–439

Lisney, T.J., Stecyk, K., Kolominsky, J., Graves, G.R., Wylie, D.R. and Iwaniuk, A.N. (2013) Comparison of eye morphology and retinal topography in two species of new world vultures (Aves: Cathartidae), *The Anatomical Record*, 296(12), 1954–1970

References   181

Low, K.E.Y. (2005) Ruminations on smell as a sociocultural phenomenon, *Current Sociology*, 53(3), 397–417

Madden, R. (2014) Animals and the limits of ethnography, *Anthrozoös*, 27(2), 279–293

Malamud, R. (2013) Service animals: serve us animals: serve us, animals, *Social Alternatives*, 32(4), 34–40

Mancini, C. (2016) Towards an animal-centred ethics for animal-computer interaction, *International Journal of Human-Computer Studies*, http://dx.doi.org/10.1016/j.ijhcs.2016.04.008

Maslow, A.H. (1943) A theory of human motivation. *Psychological Review*, 50(4), 370

Maurstad, A., Davis, D. and Cowles, S. (2013) Co-being and intra-action in horse-human relationships: a multi-species ethnography of be(com)ing human and be(com)ing horse, *Social Anthropology/Anthropologie Sociale*, 21(3), 322–335

McElligott, A.G., Maggini, I., Hunziker, L. and König, B. (2004) Interactions between red-billed oxpeckers and black rhinos in captivity, *Zoo Biology*, 23, 347–354

Mead, G.H. (1934) *Mind, self, and society: from the standpoint of a social behaviorist*, London: Chicago University Press

Michalko, R. (1999) *The two in one: walking with Smokie, walking with blindness*, Philadelphia, PA: Temple University Press

Midgley, M. (1983) *Animals and why they matter: a journey around the species barrier*, Harmondsworth: Penguin

Miklósi, A. (2009) *Dog behaviour, evolution and cognition*, Oxford: Oxford University Press

Miklósi, A. and Gacsi, M. (2012) On the utilization of social animals as a model for social robotics, *Frontiers in Psychology*, 3(75), 1–10

Miklósi, A. and Topál, J. (2013) What does it take to become 'best friends'? evolutionary changes in canine social competence, *Trends in Cognitive Science*, 1–8 (article in press)

Miller, A.K., Hensman, M.C., Hensman, S., Schultz, K., Reid, P., Shore, M., Brown, J., Furton, K.G. and Lee, S. (2015) African elephants (*Loxodonta africana*) can detect TNT using olfaction: implications for biosensor application, *Applied Animal Behavior Science*, 171, 177–183

Miller, D. (2008) *The comfort of things*, Cambridge: Polity Press

Miller, D. (2010) *Stuff*, Cambridge: Polity Press

Miller, S.C., Kennedy, C., DeVoe, D., Hickey, M., Nelson, T. and Kogan, L. (2009) An examination of changes in oxytocin levels in men and women before and after interaction with a bonded dog, *Anthrozoös*, 22(1), 31–42

Mills, D. and De Keuster, T. (2009) Dogs in society can prevent society going to the dogs, *The Veterinary Journal*, 179(3), 322–323

Milton, K. (2005) 'Anthropomorphism or egomorphism? The perception of non-human persons by human ones', in J. Knight (ed.) *Animals in person: cultural perspectives on human-animal intimacies*, New York: Berg

Mol, A. (2000) What diagnostic devices do: the case of blood sugar measurement, *Theoretical Medicine and Bioethics*, 21, 9–22

Mol, A. (2008) *The logic of care: health and the problem of patient choice*, Abingdon: Routledge

Mol, A. and Law, J. (2004) Embodied action, enacted bodies: the example of hypoglycaemia, *Body & Society*, 10(2–3), 43–62

Mol, A., Moser, I. and Pols, J. (eds.) (2010) *Care in practice: on tinkering in clinics, homes and farms*, Bielefeld, Germany: Transcript Verlag

182 References

Molan, P.C. and Betts, J.A. (2008) Using honey to heal diabetic foot ulcers, *Advances in Skin & Wound Care*, 21(7), 313–316

More, M. (1990) The extropian principles, *Extropy*, 5(5) (May)

More, M. (2013) 'The philosophy of transhumanism', in M. More and N. Vita-More (eds.) *The Transhumanist reader, classical and contemporary essays on the science, technology and philosophy of the human future*, Chichester: Wiley-Blackwell

Morrison, M. and Morgan, M. (1999) 'Models as mediating instruments', in M. Morgan and M. Morrison (eds.) *Models as mediators*, Cambridge: Cambridge University Press

Mullin, M. (2002) Animals and anthropology, *Society & Animals*, 10(4), 387–394

Mullin, M.H. (1999) Mirrors and windows: sociocultural studies of human-animal relationships, *Annual Review of Anthropology*, 28, 201–224

Nast, H.J. (2006) Loving . . . whatever: alienation, neoliberalism and pet-love in the twenty- first century, *ACME: An International E-Journal for Critical Geographies*, 5(2), 300–327

National Institute for Health and Care Excellence (NICE) (2014 [2004]) Type 1 diabetes: Diagnosis and management of type 1 diabetes in children, young people and adults, NICE clinical guideline 15, accessed on the internet, February 2015, www.nice.org.uk/guidance/cg15/resources/guidance- type-1-diabetes-pdf

Nettleton, S. (2013) *The sociology of health and illness* (3rd ed.), Cambridge: Polity Press

Newby, N.M. (1996) Chronic illness and the family life-cycle, *Journal of Advanced Nursing*, 23, 786–791

Nibert, D. (2002) *Animal rights/human rights: entanglements of oppression and liberation*, Plymouth: Rowman & Littlefield

Nobis, N. (2016) *Animals & ethics 101: thinking critically about animal rights*, Open Philosophy Press. ISBN: 0692471286

Nocella, A.J., Bentley, J.K.C. and Duncan, J.M. (eds.) (2012) *Earth, animal, and disability liberation: the rise of the eco-ability movement*, Oxford: Peter Lang

Nowak, M.A. and Highfield, R. (2011) *Supercooperators*, Edinburgh: Canongate

Nussbaum, M.C. (2009) 'Justice', in A. Taylor (ed.) *Examined life: excursions with contemporary thinkers*, New York: New Press

Odendaal, J.S.J. (2003) *What every dog owner should know: be aware of your dog's needs*, Pretoria: Ethology Consultancy

Odendaal, J.S.J. and Meintjes, R. (2003) Neurophysiological correlates of affiliative behavior between humans and dogs, *Veterinary Journal*, 165(3), 296–301

Palmer, C. (1997) The idea of the domestic animal contract, *Environmental Values*, 6, 411–425

Panksepp, J. (2005) Affective consciousness: core emotional feelings in animals and humans, *Consciousness and Cognition*, 14(1), 30–80

Panksepp, J. (2011) Cross-species affective neuroscience decoding of the primal affective experiences of humans and related animals, *PloS One*, 6(9), e21236

Panksepp, J. and Panksepp, J.B. (2013) Toward a cross-species understanding of empathy, *Trends in Neurosciences*, 36(8), 489–496

Pearsall, J. and Trumble, B. (eds.) (1995) *The Oxford English reference dictionary* (Thumb index ed.), Oxford: Oxford University Press

Pet Food Manufacturers Association (2018) Pet population report, accessed on the internet, 2 May 2017, www.pfma.org.uk/pet-population-2018

Pfungst, O. (1998) *Clever Hans (the horse of Mr Von Osten): a contribution to experimental animal and human psychology*, trans. C. Rahn, Bristol, Tokyo: Thoemmes Press and Maruzen Co. (first published 1911)

References 183

Phillips, M.T. (1994) Proper names and the social construction of biography: the negative case of laboratory animals, *Qualitative Sociology*, 17, 119–142

Pierson III, R.N., Dorling, A., Ayares, Rees, M.A., Seebach, J.D., Fishman, J.A., Hering, B.J. and Cooper, D.K.C. (2009) Current status of xenotransplantation and prospects for clinical application, *Xenotransplantation*, 16(5), 263–280

Pink, S. (2015) *Doing sensory ethnography* (2nd ed.), London: Sage

Poling, A., Weetjens, B., Cox, C., Beyene, N., Durgin, A. and Mahoney, A. (2011) Tuberculosis detection by giant African pouched rats, *The Behavior Analyst*, 34(1), 47

Poling, A., Weetjens, B.J., Cox, C., Beyene, N.W. and Sully, A. (2010) Using giant African pouched rats (Cricetomys gambianus) to detect landmines, *The Psychological Record*, 60(4), 715

Pols, J. (2010) Caring devices: about warmth, coldness and 'fit', *Medische Antropologie*, 2(1), 143–160

Pols, J. (2012) *Care at a distance: on the closeness of technology*, Amsterdam: Amsterdam University Press

Pols, J. and Moser, I. (2009) Cold technologies versus warm care? On affective and social relations with and through care technologies. *ALTER-European Journal of Disability Research/Revue Européenne de Recherche sur le Handicap*, 3(2), 159–178

Pongrácz, P., Miklósi, A., Timár-Geng, K. and Csányi, V. (2003) Preference for copying unambiguous demonstrations in dogs, *Journal of Comparative Psychology*, 117, 337–343

Porcher, J. (2014) The work of animals: a challenge for the social sciences, *Humanimalia: A Journal of Human-Animal Interface Studies*, 6(1), 1–9

Reid, P.J. (2009) Adapting to the human world: dogs' responsiveness to our social cues (Review), *Behavioural Processes*, 80, 325–333

Robinson, C., Mancini, C., van der Linden, J., Guest, C. and Harris, R. (2014) Empowering assistance dogs: an alarm interface for canine use, in *ISAWEL'14 Intelligent Systems for Animal Welfare*, 4 April 2014, London

Rock, M. and Babinec, P. (2008) Diabetes in people, cats and dogs: biomedicine and manifold ontologies, *Medical Anthropology: Cross-Cultural Studies in Health and Illness*, 27(4), 324–352

Rock, M. and Degeling, C. (2015) Public health ethics and more-than-human solidarity, *Social Science and Medicine*, 129, 61–67

Rolland, J.S. (1987) Chronic illness and the life cycle: a conceptual framework, *Family Process*, 26, 203–221

Rollin, B.E. (2011) Animal pain: what it is and why it matters, *The Journal of Ethics*, 15(4), 425–437

Rooney, N., Gaines, S. and Hiby, E. (2009) A practitioner's guide to working dog welfare, *Journal of Veterinary Behaviour*, 4, 127–134

Rooney, N., Morant, S. and Guest, C. (2013) Investigation into the value of trained glycaemia alert dogs to clients with type 1 diabetes, *PLoS One*, 8(8)

Roura, E. and Tedó, G. (2009) 'Feed appetance in pigs: an oronasal sensing perspective', in D. Torrallardona and E. Roura (eds.) *Voluntary feed intake in pigs*, Wageningen: Wageningen Academic Publishers, 105–140

Rowlands, M. (2008) *The philosopher and the wolf: lessons from the wild on love, death and happiness*, London: Granta

Rowlands, M. (2012) *Can animals be moral?* Oxford: Oxford University Press

Salvi, M. (2001) Transforming animal species: the case of 'OncoMouse', *Science and Engineering Ethics*, 7, 15–28

184 References

Sanders, C.R. (1990) The animal 'other': self-definition, social identity and companion animals, *Advances in Consumer Research*, 17, 662–668

Sanders, C.R. (2000) The impact of guide dogs on the identity of people with visual impairments, *Anthrozoös*, 13(3), 131–139

Sanders, C.R. (2003) Actions speak louder than words: close relations between humans and nonhuman animals, *Symbolic Interaction*, 26, 405–426

Sapolsky, R.M. (2006) Social cultures among nonhuman primates, *Cultural Anthropology*, 47(4), 641–656

Savalois, N., Lescureux, N. and Brunois, F. (2013) Teaching the dog and learning from the dog: interactivity in herding dog training and use, *Anthrozoös*, 26(1)

Schillmeier, M. (2014) *Eventful bodies: the cosmopolitics of illness*, Surrey: Ashgate Publishing

Serpell, J.A. (ed.) (1995) *The domestic dog: its evolution, behaviour and interactions with people*, Cambridge: Cambridge University Press

Serpell, J.A. (1996 [1986]) *In the company of animals: a study of human-animal relationships*, Cambridge: Cambridge University Press

Serpell, J.A. (2002) Anthropomorphism and anthropomorphic selection – beyond the 'cute response', *Society & Animals*, 10(4), 437–454

Serpell, J.A. (2010) 'Animal-assisted interventions in historical perspective', in A.H. Fine (ed.) *The handbook of animal-assisted therapy: theoretical foundations and guidelines for practice* (3rd ed.), San Diego, CA: Academic Press

Serpell, J.A., Coppinger, R., Fine, A.H. and Peralta, J.M. (2010) 'Welfare consideration in therapy and assistance animals', in A.H. Fine (ed.) *The handbook of animal-assisted therapy: theoretical foundations and guidelines for practice* (3rd ed.), San Diego, CA: Academic Press

Sewell, A. (2012 [1877]) *Black beauty*, Oxford: Oxford University Press

Shakespeare, T. (2014) *Disability rights and wrongs revisited* (2nd ed.), Abingdon: Routledge

Shell, M. (1986) The family pet, *Representations*, 15, 121–153

Sherman, R.A., Mumcuoglu, K.Y., Grassberger, M. and Tantawi, T.I. (2013) 'Maggot therapy', in M. Grassberger, R.A. Sherman, C.M.H. Kim, O.S. Gileva and K.Y. Mumcuoglu (eds.) *Biotherapy – history, principles and practice: a practical guide to the diagnosis and treatment of disease using living organisms*, Dordrecht: Springer

Shillum, J. (2016) Love is lovelier the second time around, *The Sniff*, 23

Shir-Vertesh, D. (2012) 'Flexible personhood': loving animals as family members in Israel, *American Anthropologist*, 114(3), 420–432

Silk, J.B. (2002) Using the 'F'-word in primatology, *Behaviour*, 139, 421–446

Silverstone, R. (1996) Future imperfect: information and communication technologies in everyday life, *Information and Communications Technologies: Visions and Realities*, 217–232

Silverstone, R., Hirsch, E. and Morley, D. (1992) 'Information and communication technologies and the moral economy of the household', in R. Silverstone and E. Hirsch (eds.) *Consuming technologies: media and information in domestic spaces*, London: Routledge

Singer, P. (1990 [1975]) *Animal liberation*, New York: Jonathan Cape

Slabbert, J.M. and Rasa, O.A.E. (1997) Observational learning of an acquired maternal behaviour pattern by working dog pups: an alternative training method, *Applied Animal Behaviour Science*, 53, 309–316

References   185

Sluka, J.A. and Robben, A.C.G.M. (2007) 'Fieldwork in cultural anthropology: an introduction', in A.C.G.M. Robben and J.A. Sluka (eds.) *Ethnographic fieldwork: an anthropological reader*, Oxford: Blackwell Publishing

Smith, T.D., Bhatnagar, K.P., Tuladhar, P. and Burrows, A.M. (2004) Distribution of olfactory epithelium in the primate nasal cavity: are microsmia and macrosmia valid morphological concepts? *The Anatomical Record Part A 218A*, 1173–1181

Smuts, B. (2001) Encounters with animal minds, *Journal of Consciousness Studies*, 8(5–7), 293–309

Smuts, B. (2006) Between species: science and subjectivity, *Configurations*, 14(1), 115–126

Sonoda, H., Kohnoe, S., Yamazato, T. et al. (2011) Colorectal cancer screening with odour material by canine scent detection, *Gut*, 60, 814–819

Soppelsa, P. (2015) Reviving animals as technology: Ann Norton Greene, horses at work (review), *Technology and Culture*, 56(1), 252–260

Spottiswoode, C.N., Begg, K.S. and Begg, C.M. (2016) Reciprocal signaling in honey-guide-human mutualism, *Science*, 353(6297), 387–389

Srinivasan, K. (2013) The biopolitics of animal being and welfare: dog control and care in the UK and India, *Transactions of the Institute of British Geographers*, 38, 1475–5661

Staymates, M.E., MacCrehan, W.A., Staymates, J.L., Kunz, R.R., Mendum, T., Ong, T-H., Geurtsen, G., Gillen, G.J. and Craven, B.A. (2016) Biomimetic sniffing improves the detection performance of a 3D printed nose of a dog and a commercial trace vapor detector, *Scientific Reports*, 6, 36876

Strauss, A. (ed.) (1964) *George Herbert Mead on social psychology*, Chicago: University of Chicago Press

Szot, G.L., Yadav, M., Lang, J., Kroon, E., Kerr, J., Kadoya, K., Brandon, E.P., Baetge, E.E., Bour-Jourdan, H. and Bluestone, J. (2015) Tolerance induction and reversal of diabetes in mice transplanted with human embryonic stem cell-derived pancreatic endoderm, *Cell Stem Cell*, 16(2), 148–157

Taylor, S. (2014) 'Interdependent animals: a feminist disability ethic-of-care', in C.J. Adams and L. Gruen (eds.) *Ecofeminism: feminist intersections with other animals and the earth*, London: Bloomsbury

Taylor, S. (2017) *Beasts of burden: animal and disability liberation*, London: The New Press

Tedeschi, P., Fine, A.H. and Helgeson, J.I. (2010) 'Assistance animals: their evolving role in psychiatric service application', in A.H. Fine (ed.) *The handbook of animal-assisted therapy: theoretical foundations and guidelines for practice* (3rd ed.), San Diego, CA: Academic Press

Teuscher, A. and Berger, W.G. (1987) Hypoglycaemia unawareness in diabetics transferred from beef/porcine insulin to human insulin, *The Lancet*, 330(8555), 382–385

Thurston, M.E. (1996) *The lost history of the canine race: our 15,000-year love affair with dogs*, New York: Avon

Toms, J. (2006) *Animal graves and memorials*, Princes Risborough: Shire

Tuan, Y-F. (2007) 'Animal pets: cruelty and affection', in L. Kalof and A. Fitzgerald (eds.) *The animals reader: the essential classic and contemporary writings*, Oxford: Berg

Turkle, S. (ed.) (2007) *Evocative objects: things we think with*, Cambridge, MA: The MIT Press

Turkle, S. (2011) *Alone together: why we expect more from technology and less from each other*, New York: Basic Books

186   References

Twine, R. (2015) *Animals as biotechnology: ethics, sustainability and critical animal studies*, London: Earthscan

Vaisman, N. (2013) 'Shedding our selves: perspectivism, the bounded subject and the nature-culture divide', in T. Ingold and G. Palsson (eds.) *Biosocial becomings: integrating social and biological anthropology*, Cambridge: Cambridge University Press

Van Dooren, T. (2010a) Pain of extinction: the death of a vulture, *Cultural Studies Review*, 16(2), 271–289

Van Dooren, T. (2010b) Vultures and their people in India: equity and entanglement in a time of extinctions, *Manoa*, 22(2), 130–146

Van Dooren, T. (2014) Care, *Environmental Humanities*, 5, 291–294

Vass, A., Thompson, C.V. and Wise, M. (2010) *New forensics tool: development of an advanced sensor for detecting clandestine graves*, Rockville, MD: National Criminal Justice Reference Service

Vegas, A.J., Veiseh, O., Gürtler, M., Millman, J.R., Pagliuca, F.W., Bader, A.R., Doloff, J.C. et al. (2016) Long term glycemic control using polymer encapsulated, human stem-cell derived β-cells in immune competent mice, *Nature Medicine*, 22(3), 306–311

Vila, C. Savolainen, P., Maldonado, J.E., Amorim, I.R., Rice, J.E., Honeycutt, R.L., Crandall, K.A., Lundenberg, J. and Wayne, R.K. (1997) Multiple and ancient origins of the domestic dog, *Science*, 276, 1687–1689

Viveiros de Castro, E. (1998) Cosmological deixis and Amerindian perspectivism, *Journal of the Royal Anthropological Institute*, 4, 469–488

Viveiros de Castro, E. (2012) Cosmological perspectivism in Amazonia and elsewhere, *HAU Masterclass Lectures*, 1, 45–168

Von Uexküll, J. (2010 [1934]) *A foray into the worlds of animals and humans, with a theory of meaning*, trans. Joseph D. O'Neil, London: University of Minnesota Press

Walker, J.C., Hall, S.B., Walker, D.B., Kendal-Reed, M.S., Hood, A.F. and Niu, X.F. (2003) Human odor detectability: new methodology used to determine threshold and variation, *Chemical Senses*, 28(9), 817–826

Walker, D.B., Walker, J.C., Cavnar, P.J., Taylor, J.L., Pickel, D.H., Hall, S.B. and Suarez, J.C. (2006) Naturalistic quantification of canine olfactory sensitivity, *Applied Animal Behaviour Science*, 97(2–4), 241–254

Weil, K. (2012) *Thinking animals: why animal studies now?* New York: Columbia University Press

Wells, D.L. and Hopper, P.G. (2000) The discrimination of dog odours by humans, *Perception*, 29, 111–115

Wells, D.L., Lawson, S.W. and Siriwardena, A.N. (2008) Canine responses to hypoglycaemia in patients with type 1 diabetes, *The Journal of Alternative and Complementary Medicine*, 14(10), 1235–1241

Whittemore, R. and Dixon, J. (2008) Chronic illness: the process of integration, *Journal of Clinical Nursing*, 17(7b), 177–187

Willis, C.M., Church, S.M., Guest, C.M., Cook, W.A., McCarthy, N., Bransbury, A.J., Church, M.R.T. and Church, J.C.T. (2004) Olfactory detection of human bladder cancer by dogs: proof of principle study, *British Medical Journal*, 329–712

Willett, C. (2014) *Interspecies ethics*, New York: Columbia University Press

Wilson, C.C. and Turner, D.C. (eds.) (1998) *Companion animals in human health*, London: Sage

Winance, M. (2010) 'Care and disability: practices of experimenting, tinkering with, and arranging people and technical aids', in A. Mol, I. Moser and J. Pols (eds.) *Care in practice: on tinkering in clinics, homes and farms*, Bielefeld, Germany: Transcript Verlag

References   187

Wolbring, G. (2006) Emerging technologies (nano, bio, info, cogno) and the changing concepts of health and disability/impairment: a new challenge for health policy, research and care, *Commentary*, 2(1–2), 19–37

Yamaguchi, T., Sato, H., Kato-Itoh, M., Goto, T., Hara, H., Sanbo, M., Ota, Y., et al. (2017) Interspecies organogenesis generates autologous functional islets, *Nature*, 542(7640), 191–196

Zamir, T. (2006) The moral basis of animal-assisted therapy, *Society & Animals*, 14(2), 179–199

Zelano, C. and Sobel, N. (2005) Humans as an animal model for systems-level organization of olfaction, *Neuron*, 48, 431–454

Zinsstag, J. and Weiss, M.G. (2001) Livestock diseases and human health, *Science*, 294, 477–478

Index

Acarine tick (*Rhipicephalus* or
    Amblyomma) 32
Ache, B.W. 65
Adams, Carol J. 9, 22, 115, 144–145,
    148
Adell-Bath, M. 8
ADI Minimum Standards and Ethics
    Document 44
Aesop's Anthropology (Hartigan) 39
affective appeal 165
African elephant (*Loxodonta africana*) 68
Agamben, G. 6
AIBO robot dog 50, 165
AIDS 118–119
Alger, J.M. 108
Alger, S.F. 108
Allon, F. 108
alternative medicine 56
'Anifesto' 114
animal-assisted activities/therapy (AAA/T)
    108, 140
animal-assisted therapy (AAT) 56, 108,
    138–140
animal-computer interaction 111–112
animal-human social contracts 38–39
animal 'mattering' 3, 171
'animal mirror' 62
animal models for human treatment
    118–121
Animal Welfare Act (2006) 47, 105
animate equipment 104–106; *see
    also* biomedical resources/health
    technologies
anthropocentrism 3–5, 22, 93, 108,
    116–117, 145, 168
anthropogenic norms 98, 164
'anthropological machine' 6
anthropomorphism 2, 14, 42, 137, 141

anthrozoological/sociological perspectives
    28–62
anthrozoology 3–4
anxiety 110–113, 153
APOPO (anti-personnel landmines
    removal) 108
Aristotle 150
Armstrong Oma, K. 38
Ascione, F.R. 16
Assistance Dogs Europe (ADEU) 44
Assistance Dogs International (ADI) 44
Assistance Dogs UK (ADUK) 44, 110
assistive inanimate aids 9–10, 99–101
autoimmune disorders 19, 21, 25, 119, 176

Babinec, P. 30, 93
baboons, Forest Troop anubis (*Papio
    anubis*) 44
Baker, Kim 107
Baranidharan Raman 68
Barrett, L. 108
Batek (Peninsular Malaysia) 65
Baur, G. 149
Beck, A. 7
bees (*Apis mellifera*) 21, 33
Begg, C.M. 33
Begg, K.S. 33
behaviour modification 41–42
Bekoff, M. 123
Belk, R.W. 31, 103
Bentley, J.K.C. 29
Berger, W.G. 92–93
Betts, J.A. 21
biomedical resources/health technologies:
    animal models for human treatment and
    118–121; animals as health technologies
    and 125–127; animate instruments
    concept 104–106; anxiety/fear of

Index 189

failure and 110–113; canine emergency alert system 112; canine sense of smell and 64; coercion tools and 131–134; continuous glucose monitor 100–101, 103; disabling identity and 124–125; domestication of dogs and, contemporary 127–129; domestication theory and 129–132; exploitation and 106–108; interactive devices 111–112; transhumanism and 101–103; use versus exploitation and 108–110, 138; xenotransplantation and 118–121
biotherapy 21
Bird-David, N. 93
Birke, Lynda 7, 61, 110, 113, 127, 168
Blaxter, M. 60
blood glucose levels: awareness of, losing 1, 18, 90; blood glucose monitor/meter and 74–76; blood testing and 20–21; care in balancing 71, 74–75; complications of fluctuations in, extreme 58; continuous glucose monitor and 100–101; glucose tablets for controlling 154; high, danger of maintaining 93–94; hyperglycaemia and 18, 69, 95, 116; hypoglycaemia and 12, 19, 69, 92; insulin pump and 103; nocturnal hypoglycemia and 92; nutrition and 83; PSC-derived islets and 118; test strips and 80; vision and 86
blood glucose monitor/meter 74–76
blood management and Type 1 diabetes 76–77
blood testing 20–21
Blue, G. 106
Boran (Kenya) 33
Bostrom, N. 100–101
Bourdieu, P. 159
Bowling, F.L. 21
Bradshaw, John 3, 48–49, 64, 70
Braidotti, Rosa 5, 171
Brandt, Keri 15
Brunois, F. 46, 51–52, 97
Bryant, C. 30
Budiansky, S. 33, 98, 126, 133, 146
buffalo (*Syncerus caffer*) 32–33
Burrows, K. 115
Bury, M. 55, 58, 60

Callicott, J.B. 146
cancer odour, canine detection of 14, 38
canine alert communication 68–69, 75

canine emergency alert system 112
canine sense of smell/olfactory acuity: alert communication and 68–69, 75; biomedical resources/health technologies and, dogs as 64; cancer odour and 14, 38; contribution to human health and 64; human sense of smell versus 68; human uses for 66; multisensory integration and 64; narcotic detection 43; nasal structure of dogs 67–70; scenting as a dog, fieldwork on 64–65; Semtex and 15; Type 1 diabetes and 18, 66
care, meanings of 135–136; *see also* ethics of care; multispecies care
Carsten, Janet 76–77
Carter, S. 128
Cassidy, Rebecca 37, 39, 113, 121–122, 136
Cell Stem Cell study 118
cemeteries for dogs 37
Cevellin, G. 129
Cevetello, Joseph 99–100, 103
Chandler, C.K. 21
Charmaz, Kathy 11, 55, 57, 59–61, 74
Chatjouli, A. 154
chimpanzees (*Pan troglodytes*) 35
chronic illness 1–4, 20, 28, 53–57, 59; *see also* Type 1 diabetes
Church, John 17, 21
Classen, C. 56, 63, 65
Clean Neighbourhoods and Environment Act (2005) 40
Clever Hans 6
Clifford, James 13, 70, 72
Clutton-Brock, J. 36–37, 126
Code of Practice for Dogs in the Animal Welfare Act (2006) 47
Code of Practice for the Welfare of Dogs (DEFRA) 51, 105
co-domestication 39
coercion, tools of 7, 131–134
Coetzee, J.M. 104–105, 158
Cohen, C. 119
Coles, J. 68
commensalism 3, 32–35
communication, trans-species 6, 156–159
continuous glucose monitor (CGM) 100–101, 103
control, improving 92–93
conversion 131
Cooley, C.H. 60
cooperation, multispecies 9–12, 156

190 *Index*

cooperative enterprise 107
Coppinger, L. 31–36, 43, 110–111, 114, 139, 146
Coppinger, R. 31–36, 43, 110–111, 114, 139, 146
Cornu, J-N. 13
Coulter, Kendra 5, 9, 20, 23, 45, 97, 108, 114, 126, 135–137, 151, 156
Cowles, S. 4, 35, 97
Craven, B.A. 68
Creţan, R. 38
Csányi, V. 36
Curtin, Deane 141, 145
cyborgean 53, 100
'cyborgean relationship' 100
Czerny, S. 157

Daisy 17
Dant, Tim 128
Davies, Gail 119
Davis, D. 4, 35, 97
Dawkins, M.S. 38
Dawson, Susan 167
'dead in bed (DIB) syndrome' 92
Degeling, C. 114
De Keuster, T. 134
de la Bellacasa, M.P. 135, 152
De Nora, T. 56
Department for Environment, Food, and Rural Affairs (DEFRA) 170
Descartes, R. 31
Despret, V. 6, 52, 128
De Waal, Frans B.M 22, 123, 140, 142–143, 151
Diabetes UK 19, 72, 80, 93, 101
diabetic ketoacidosis (DKA) 14, 72
diet and Type 1 diabetes 81–84, 99
disability concept 10–11, 28, 53
Disability Rights and Wrongs Revisited (Shakespeare) 55
Disgrace (Coetzee) 104, 158
Dixon, J. 56, 58
Dodman, N. 108
dogs (*Canis familiaris*): behaviour modification of 41–42; as best friend of humans 117; biotherapy and 21; breeding of, selective 37; breeds 45; cemeteries for 37; communication with 156–159; death of domestic 16; diabetes alert 59, 75, 115, 122, 124–126, 130–131, 150, 153, 164–165, 171; domestication of 35–39, 127–129; ergonomics, canine 40–47; free running

and 152; greyhounds, racing 106; guide 8, 44, 28–129; life enrichment and 112–113; microchipping of, compulsory 40; nasal structure of 67–70; as pets 30–32, 103; post-traumatic stress disorder in 108; puppy-milling 106; stray 38–40; in UK 39–40; village 34, 38–40, 139
Dogs for the Disabled (now Dogs for Good) 157
Dogs for Good 44, 157
Dogs Trust Stray Dog Survey (2016) 39–40
Doka, Kenneth 55
Dolphin, Helen 122
domestication of dogs 35–39, 127–129
domestication theory 129–134
Donovan, Josephine 22, 72, 148
Dose Adjustment for Normal Eating (DAFNE) 78
Douglas, Mary 20, 77
driving and Type 1 diabetes 87–88
Duncan, J.M. 29

ecofeminist theory of care 2, 22
egomorphism 42, 137
Eisenberg, N. 142
Elliker, K.R. 14
Elliott, D.E. 20–21
Emerson, R.M. 72
Emery, N.J. 35
Emmerman, Karen 168
empathy 22–23, 27, 30, 142–144
Endicott, K. 65
endings: questioning need 163–164; replacing 165–167; retraining 164–165
entangled empathy 143
Environmental Protection (Stray Dogs) Regulations 40
ergonomics, canine 40–47
Ericsson, K.A. 41
ethics of care: feminist 145; moral basis of animal-assisted therapy and 138–140; symbiotic practices of care and 2, 144–147; theory 2–3
Eventful Bodies (Schillmeier) 11
Evocative Objects 99
exploitation and PTSD 106–108

Farthing, Pen 107
fear of failure 110–113
feel 6
feminist animal care theory 22

Index 191

feminist ethics of care 145
feminist objectivity 64
Fijn, N. 39
Fine, A.H. 7, 29, 115, 140
foot-and-mouth epidemic in UK 22
Franklin, Adrian 2, 19, 171
Friedmann, E. 29
Fuentes, Agustin 32, 155

Gadbois, S. 45
Gaines, S. 43, 49, 115
gas sensor arrays 67
genetics and Type 1 diabetes 60
Giant Pouched Rat (*Crietomys ansorgei*)
    68, 108, 170
glucometer 99–100, 103
Goffman, Erving 62, 126
Goode, David 52–53, 150–151, 156
Grassberger, M. 21
green bottle fly (*Lucilia sericata*) 21
Greene, Ann Norton 126
Greenebaum, J. 37
Greenhough, B. 99
Gregory, S. 59
Gruen, Lori 9, 22–23, 140, 142–144, 148
Guest, Claire 13–14, 17, 45
guide dog 8, 44, 128–129
Guide Dogs for the Blind 44

Haddon, L. 126, 129
Haehner, A. 65
Hamilton, L. 9
Hamington, Maurice 22, 141, 145
Handbook of Animal-Assisted Therapy
    (Fine) 140
Handlin, L. 109–110
Hansen, A. 118
Haraway, Donna J. 7, 9, 31, 52, 62, 100,
    103, 118–119, 128, 135
Hart, Lynette 8
Hare, B. 35
Harley 25–26, 56, 59, 62, 69, 87,
    111–112, 153, 162
Hartigan, John 39
Health Buddy 165
Hediger, Ryan 107
Helgeson, J.I. 115
Helmreich, S. 12
Helton, W.S. 40–41, 67
hESC-derived therapy 118
Hiby, E. 43, 49, 115
hierarchy of needs 9
Higgin, Marc 9, 47

Highfield, R. 9, 155
Hirsch, E. 126, 129–131
Hobbes, T. 39
Hockenhull, Jo 61, 110
Hoffman, M.L. 142
honey badger (*Mellivora capensis*) 33
honeyguide (*Indicator indicator*) 33
Hopper, P.G. 63
Horowitz, Alexandra 63–64
horse-human miscommunication 110
horse (*Equus caballus*) 6, 21, 110, 113,
    116, 127; *see also* Clever Hans
Howes, D. 56, 63, 65
Huettenbrink, K-B. 65
human-animal social contracts 38–39
human immune deficiency 118–119
Hummel, T. 65
hummingbird (*Trochilidae*) 33
Hurn, S. 4, 7, 32, 42, 52, 72, 98, 105, 106,
    114, 117, 124, 136, 140, 156, 168
Huxley, R.R. 93
Hyde Park cemetery 37
hygiene 20–21
hyperglycaemia 18, 69, 95, 116
hypo-awareness, losing 76, 88–90, 98
hypoglycemia 12, 19, 69, 92

ichthyotherapy 21
identities in human-animal relationships,
    collective 154–155
inanimate technologies 9–10, 99–101
incorporation 130–131
In Defence of Dogs (Bradshaw) 70
Ingold, Tim 5–6, 7, 38, 119, 127, 159
insulin (bovine, porcine, synthetic) 92–93
insulin injection 77–78
insulin pump 78–81, 128
Intelligent Systems for Animal Welfare
    (ISAWEL) 112
interspecies reciprocity 113
interspecies solidarity 23, 137
intersubjectivity 5, 42, 98, 136, 140
Irvine, Leslie 2, 8, 13, 15, 37, 41, 44, 64,
    158, 164

Juvenile Diabetes Research Foundation
    (JDRF) 23, 119

Kellert, S.R. 16
Kennel Club 45
ketoacidosis 14, 72
ketones 72
Kirksey, S.E. 12

192 *Index*

Knafl, K.A. 59
Kopytoff, Igor 105
Koski, M.A. 56
Krieger, S. 29

LABRADOR (light-weight analyser for decomposition odour recognition) 67
Landis, B.N. 65
landmine removal 108
Latimer, J. 4
Law, John 12, 19, 22, 54, 72, 106–107, 159
Lawson, S.W. 18, 40
Leaf, M. 16
leash, dog 131–132
leeches (*Hirudo medicinalis*) 21
legal rights of working dog 29, 40
Lescureux, N. 35, 46, 51–52, 97
Leung, T.L.F. 33–35, 114
Levinson, B.M. 29–30
Lewis, E. 38
liberationist perspective 138–140
Linton, S. 10
Lippi, G. 129
Lisney, T.J. 68
locusts (*Acridae*) 68
looking-glass self concept 60
Low, Kelvin 63–64

macrosmia 15, 68, 101
Madden, Raymond 4
Malamud, Randy 21, 113
Mancini, Clara 111
Maslow, A.H. 9
mathematical balance 22
Maurstad, A. 4, 35, 97
McElligott, A.G. 32–33
Mead, George Herbert 41
medical alert assistance dog (MAAD): alerting behaviour of 66–67; as animate aid 104–106; anxiety and 110–113; criteria for 44, 46; empathy and 142–144; ethics of care and 144–147; legal rights of 29, 40; welfare of 20, 159–162
Meintjes, R. 7, 109
Mel 26–27, 51–52, 68–69, 83–84, 122, 157–158, 167
memory training and sense of smell 65
Michael, M. 118
Michalko, Rod 6, 10, 29, 34, 44, 53, 62, 122, 126, 150–151, 158
microchipping of dogs, compulsory 40
Midgley, Mary 38

Miklósi, Adam 34–36, 64, 117, 123, 126
military working dog 107–108
Miller, A.K. 68
Miller, Daniel 128, 165
Miller, S.C. 109
Millman, S. 115
Mills, D. 134
Milton, K. 137, 141
'mirrors and windows' 62
Mol, Annemarie 6, 12, 19–20, 27, 54, 72, 74–76, 100, 149, 152, 159
Molan, P.C. 21
mood swings 90–92
'moral imagination' 22
Morant, S. 45
More, Max 101–102
Morgan, M. 119, 126
Morley, D. 126, 129–131
Morrison, M. 119, 126
mortality 92–93
Moser, Ingunn 149, 152, 165
Mullin, Molly 37, 39, 53, 60, 62
multisensory integration 64
multispecies care: anthrozoological/ sociological perspective and 3–4, 21; biotherapy and 21; blood testing and 20–21; chronic illness and 1–4, 20; commodification and 21–23; cooperation and 9–12; ethics of care and 2–3, 21–23; hygiene and 20–21; practices 19–20
mutualism/mutuality 3, 32–35, 39, 155–156

narcotic detection 43
nasal structure of dogs 67–70
Nast, Heidi 31–32
National Institute for Health and Care Excellence (NICE) 94
Nettleton, S. 1, 54–55
Newby, N.M. 59
Nibert, David 28–29
Nichomachean Ethics 150
Nobis, N. 31
Nocella, A.J. 29
nocturnal hypoglycaemia 92
Nowak, M.A. 9, 155
Nowzad Dogs 107
Nussbaum, Martha 147
nutrition and Type 1 diabetes 81–84, 99

objectification 130
objectivity, feminist 64
Odendaal, J.S.J. 7, 45, 109

one-self, becoming 3, 6, 19
'othering' 4–5
oxpecker (*Buphagus erythrorhynchus*)
32–33
oxytocin 7, 110

Palmer, Clare 5, 39
Palsson, G. 159
Panksepp, J. 123
Panksepp, J.B. 143
parasitism 3, 32–35, 113–114
'Paro' (robotic seal) 49–50
Paterson, E.G. 68
Pauling, Linus 43
Pavlov, I. 48
People's Trust for Endangered Species 68
pet, concept of 31–32, 103
Pet Food Manufacturers Association
(PFMA) 40
Pfungst, O. 6
Phillips, Mary 15
Pierson, R.N. III 118
Pink, Sarah 63
pluripotent stem cells (PSCs) 118
Pols, Jeannette 128, 132–135, 149, 152, 165
Pongrácz, P. 34
Porcher, Jocelyne 48
porcine whipworm (*T. suis*) 21
post-traumatic stress disorder (PTSD)
107–108
Poulin, R. 33–35, 114
pregnancy and Type 1 diabetes 94–95
Pritchard, D.I. 21
probiotics and antibiotics 21
psychiatric service dog (PSD) 115

Rasa, O.A.E. 43
rat (*Rattus norvegicus*) 34
Reeve, C. 45
Reid, P.J. 35
Robben, A.C.G.M. 64
Robinson, C. 43, 112
Rock, M. 30, 93, 106, 114
Rolland, J.S. 59
Rollin, B.E. 3
Rooney, N. 43, 45, 49, 115
Rosenfeld, D. 60–61
Roura, E. 67
Rowlands, Mark 103

Salvi, M. 119
Sanders, Clinton R. 7–8, 15, 30, 41, 124, 158
Sapolsky, R.M. 44

Savalois, N. 46, 51–52, 97
Schillmeier, M. 11, 18
Schneider, R. 43
school and Type 1 diabetes 88
self-care practices for Type 1 diabetes 26–27
separation anxiety 153
Serpell, J.A. 36, 64, 108–109, 117,
140–141, 152, 166
Settles, G.S. 68
Sewell, A. 16
Shakespeare, Tom 10, 53, 55, 121
Shell, Marc 31
Shillum, Jan 164
Shir-Vertesh, D. 93, 113, 125
Silk, J.B. 117
Silverstone, R. 126, 128–131
Singer, P. 170
Siriwardena, A.N. 18, 40
Skillings, E. 43, 110–111
Slabbert, J.M. 43
Sluka, J.A. 64
smell, sense of: Batek and classification
of 65; historical perspective of 63;
importance of 65–67; lived experience
and 63; memory training and 65;
multisensory integration and 64;
recognition and 63; social interaction
and 63; vision and 65
Smith, J P 38
Smith, T.D. 18
Smuts, B. 140, 143
Sobel, N. 63
social contract theory 39
Son, H. 29
Sonoda, H. 13–14
Soppelsa, Peter 126–127
speciesism 28–29
Spottiswoode, C.N. 33
Srinivasan, K. 98–99, 146, 164
Staymates, M.E. 66
Strauss, A. 41
Stray Dog Euthanasia Law (2013) 38
symbiosis 3, 34, 114
symbiotic ethics 150–153
symbiotic interactionism 2, 23
symbiotic practices of care:
communication 156–159; compassion
140–141; cooperation 155–156;
empathy 142–144; ethics in animal-
assisted therapy and 138–140; ethics of
care and 9, 144–147
symbiotic relationships: Acarine tick and
buffalo 32; commensalism and 32–35;

194   *Index*

dependencies in 33; divisions in 33–34; multispecies care and 2–3; mutualism and, 32–35; oxpecker and buffalo 32–33; parasitism and 32–35; reciprocity in 33; species involved in 32–34
sympathy 141–142
synthetic insulin 92–93
Szot, G.L. 118

Taylor, N. 9
Taylor, Sunaura 9, 22, 145–148, 150, 169
Tedeschi, P. 115
Tedó, G. 67
test strips 80
Teuscher, A. 92–93
Thurston, M.E. 37
Tomasello, M. 35
Toms, J. 37
Topál, J. 34–35, 123
touch 7
'touching comfort' 7
touch therapy 56
transgenic animals 118–119
transhumanism 101–103
transport and Type 1 diabetes 87–88
trans-species coexistence 5–6
trans-species communication 6, 156–159
trans-species interactions 27
Tsai, C-C. 29
Tuan, Y-F. 5
turkey vultures (*Cathartes aura*) 68
Turkle, Sherry 103
Turner, D.C. 29
Twine, Richard 118
Type 1 diabetes: animal models for researching 119; assistive inanimate technologies and 9–10; biomedical research on 93; blood management and 76–77; canine alert communication 68–69, 75; canine detection of cancer and 18; complications arising from 84; control of, keeping and improving 92–94; dead in bed syndrome and 92; defining 72–73; hypo-awareness and, losing 88–90; inanimate devices and 99–101; insulin injection and 77–78; insulin pump and 78–81; nutrition and 81–84, 99; pregnancy and 94–95; presentation of self and 60–62; prevalence of 53; transport and 87–88; vision difficulties 85–87; volatile organic compounds 17, 66, 170
Type 2 diabetes 54

use versus exploitation 108–110, 138

Vaisman, N. 159
van Dooren, Thom 135
Vass, A. 67
Vegas, A.J. 66
Vila, C. 36
village dogs 34, 38–40, 139
vision: smell and, sense of 65; Type 1 diabetes and difficulties with 85–87
Viveiros de Castro, E.B. 159
volatile organic compounds (VOCs) 17, 66, 170
voluntary work category 136
Von Uexküll, J. 123

Walker, D.B. 68
Walker, J.C. 68
Weil, K. 123, 148
Weinstock, J.V. 20–21
Weiss, M.G. 22
Wells, D.L. 18, 40, 63
Whittemore, R. 56, 58
Willett, Cynthia 141, 158
Willis, C.M. 13
Wilson, C.C. 29
Winance, Myriam 154
Wolbring, Gregor 100, 102–103
wolf (*Canis lupus*) 36
working dog: ADUK recognition of 44; breeds of 45; canine ergonomics, science of 40–47; categories of work 136; criteria 46–47; domestication of 35–40; empowering and enriching life of 111–113; 'foster home' for 43; historical perspective of 35–37; legal rights of 40; medical detection dogs in training 49–51; medical detection dogs in work 51–53; military 107–108; psychiatric service dog (PSD) 115; stray dogs and 38–40; tasks performed by 37; training 41, 43; village dogs and 38–40; 'works-in-progress' 9, 47–49

xenotransplantation 118–121

Yamaguchi, T. 118
Young, J.M. 65–66

Zamir, Taschi 9, 108, 138–140, 146
Zelano, C. 63
Zinsstag, J. 22

Printed in the United States
by Baker & Taylor Publisher Services